Connected and Respected

Lessons from the Resolving Conflict Creatively Program

Grades K – 2

Connected and Respected

Lessons from the Resolving Conflict Creatively Program

Grades K – 2

Ken Breeding, PhD and Jane Harrison

ESR is deeply grateful to the following donors, foundations, and corporations for their support of the Resolving Conflict Creatively Program and the development and production of this curriculum: Joan S. Dodd, The Geraldine R. Dodge Foundation, John C. and Chara C. Haas, The William and Flora Hewlett Foundation, Houghton Mifflin Company, Charles Evans Hughes Memorial Foundation, Inc., The Prudential Foundation, Sidney Stern Memorial Trust, Surdna Foundation, Inc., and Third Millennium Foundation. In addition, we greatly appreciate the support of the JAMS Foundation for the dissemination of this curriculum and the program. ESR also thanks ESR Metropolitan Area for their generous permission to incorporate material from *Resolving Conflict Creatively: A Teachers Guide for Grades Kindergarten Through Six* into *Connected and Respected*.

esr

EDUCATORS FOR SOCIAL RESPONSIBILITY

Connected and Respected: Lessons from the Resolving Conflict Creatively Program
Grades K–2 by Ken Breeding, PhD and Jane Harrison
© 2007 Educators for Social Responsibility

esr

Educators for Social Responsibility
23 Garden St.
Cambridge, MA 02138
www.esrnational.org

Cover and book design by Schwadesign

10 9 8 7 6 5 4 3 2 1
Printed in the United States of America

ISBN 10: 0-942349-21-0
ISBN 13: 978-0-942349-21-4

Table of Contents

Grade K

Grade 1

Grade 2

Appendices

Foreword

At a time when standards, testing and accountability dominate the education landscape, we can lose sight of the fact that students perform best when they are accepted, included, and cared about by the adults and other students in the school, when they feel competent both socially and academically, and when they believe that they can stand up for themselves and others and make a difference. These social and emotional skills are the grounding upon which students develop character, competence and confidence. These skills are essential in times of great change and uncertainty. We live in a time where global conflict is the norm and many of our children are exposed to it on the daily news. We also see a rise in bullying and bias among children and youth. It is critical that our children learn to respect themselves and those who are different.

When ESR launched its conflict resolution efforts in the early 1980s, it was one of only a few organizations pioneering the integration of social and emotional learning into classroom instruction and school culture. Not only did ESR develop exemplary conflict resolution materials for teachers to use, but they also launched a systemic effort to deeply integrate social skills, intergroup relations, and conflict resolution throughout whole schools and districts. It became apparent that helping students become more socially competent required more than the efforts of individual dedicated teachers; it required a consistent approach to social skills instruction that fostered skill development over time and helped teachers model those skills within the classroom and the school.

The RCCP approach has been shown to have a significant impact on both social and academic development. An intensive study of RCCP involving hundreds of teachers and thousands of students in fifteen New York City elementary schools by the National Center for Children in Poverty at Columbia University found that children receiving substantial RCCP instruction showed more positive social and academic development. They perceived their world in a less hostile way, saw violence as an unacceptable option, and chose non-violent ways to resolve conflict. They also performed significantly better on standardized academic achievement tests than other children. (See Appendix A)

The RCCP study results are consistent with other national studies of the impact of social and emotional learning programs in general. Providing children with opportunities to learn skills that improve their knowledge of themselves and their understanding of others is the foundation for building a strong democracy. Improved academic achievement has been an important added benefit. A meta-analysis of more than 700 positive youth development, social-emotional learning, character education, and prevention interventions conducted by Roger Weissberg and Joseph Durlak (presented at the Annual Meeting of the American Psychological Association, 2005) found that programs in social and emotional learning "tended to yield multiple benefits for their youthful participants that included gains in personal and social skills, and reductions in problem behaviors." Not surprisingly, helping young people develop social competence also resulted in improved academic performance.

They concluded that, "our findings suggest that social-emotional development programs can make an important contribution toward enhancing young people's development in multiple ways, including their school performance." Clearly, the investment of time and energy in helping young people develop the skills to get along with each other and helping school staff members create a caring school community provides the right conditions for young people to be successful socially and academically.

Building on twenty years of experience in developing and refining conflict resolution curricula and in working with schools and districts on program implementation, *Connected and Respected* offers teachers and administrators an up-to-date and comprehensive set of tools designed in a highly accessible format. Using a spiraling approach to teaching conflict resolution skills, students deepen their understanding of core conflict resolution concepts and skills each year. The recommendations within each lesson for extensions, infusion of ideas, and connections to literature allow teachers to integrate these lessons into other areas of the curriculum and into the basics of classroom management and school culture.

However, *Connected and Respected* is more than a collection of lessons for classroom use. As with any high quality curriculum, it supports the professional development of teachers so that they improve their ability to manage classroom behavior and to create a caring and supportive environment for students. They learn how to better resolve differences and deal with challenging students in a constructive way. And they learn how they can deal with prejudice and bullying to promote a more just climate in their classroom.

In addition, *Connected and Respected* creates the opportunity for administrators and teachers to approach social development in a consistent and comprehensive way. It provides a common language for students and adults to use in conflict situations as well as consistent responses to behavior and conflict issues. It provides the scaffolding that allows students and adults to model the skills they are learning in an accepting environment. This consistency helps students understand social expectations, feel safe within the school environment, and be more productive academically.

Although any teacher can draw upon the lessons in *Connected and Respected* to teach important social skills and create a peaceable classroom community, we would encourage schools and school districts to take a more systemic approach. As a core element of the RCCP program, Connected and Respected can serve as a guide to create a positive school climate. In fact, RCCP has become widely regarded as one of the most promising prevention and social and emotional learning programs among education and public health experts. The US Department of Education, the Carnegie Council on Adolescent Development, and the Harvard School of Public Health have cited RCCP as one of the most successful school models. The Collaborative for Academic, Social and Emotional Learning (CASEL) cites RCCP as one of 22 "Select" programs nationwide, and the Substance Abuse and Mental Health Services Administration (SAMHSA) has designated RCCP as an "Effective" research based program.

This is not an easy time for educators. We are facing the ever-increasing strain of improving test scores with limited resources. The pressures of accountability and financial limitations can narrow our vision and our focus. It is at times likes these that make our focus on the social development of students and the social climate of the school even more critical. *Connected and Respected* provides the path back to that larger and inclusive vision.

Sheldon Berman
Superintendent Hudson Public Schools

Janice Jackson
Assistant Professor, Boston College School of Education

Acknowledgements

Connected and Respected: Lessons from the Resolving Conflict Creatively Program
is the product of many hours on the part of many individuals. Its lessons and
design are rooted in the Resolving Conflict Creatively Program (RCCP) developed in the 1980s by the New York City Board of Education and Educators
for Social Responsibility Metropolitan Area (New York). Linda Lantieri and
Tom Roderick conceived this program and with the help of New York City
classroom teachers and principals brought it to the children of New York City.
Their early partnership is the cornerstone of this work. RCCP continues to be
one of the most successful, longest running programs in social and emotional
learning, character education, conflict resolution, and intergroup relations.

In these volumes we've drawn upon the work Tom and Linda began. The
experience and support of past and present RCCP and ESR staff, classroom
teachers and administrators from across the country and experts and researchers in the fields of conflict resolution education, social and emotional
learning, youth development and student success in school have guided the
development of *Connected and Respected*.

ESR wishes to thank the following foundations and corporations for their
support of our work to refine the Resolving Conflict Creatively Program
model and create this curriculum: The Geraldine R. Dodge Foundation, The
William and Flora Hewlett Foundation, Houghton Mifflin Company, Charles
Evans Hughes Memorial Foundation, Inc., The Lippincott Foundation of the
Peace Development Fund, Sidney Stern Memorial Trust, Third Millennium
Foundation, Tides Foundation, and Working Assets.

Resolving Conflict Creatively Program staff, past and present, has not only
contributed their expertise but also their creative talents. The late Sheila Alson,
and Zephryn Conte made significant contributions to the early development
of the guide. Ken Breeding and Jane Harrison have served as principal writers.
Carol Spiegel wrote the Connecting to Literature section and Maureen Carroll
and Laurel Blaine contributed activities to the Extension and Infusion section.
Material written by Peggy Ray, Sheila Alson, Linda Lantieri and Tom Roderick
for the previous guide has also been incorporated in this curriculum. Cassandra
Bond, Gayle Burnett, Kim Jones and Lisia Morales were key reviewers. Former
RCCP program director Jinnie Spiegler coordinated extensive planning meetings that laid the foundation for the project in its early days and benefited
from contributions from Sherrie Gammage, Sandy Whitall, Bill Kreidler, Betsy
Sason and Mariana Gaston. Former RCCP program director Jennifer Selfridge
led the team that made important decisions about the framework for the
cirriculum and moved it toward completion. Linda Lantieri, founding director
of RCCP provided counsel and guidance throughout the process.

RCCP site coordinators and classroom teachers provided guidance in the
development process and helped "test" new activities and formats in
classrooms in Alaska, New Hampshire, California and New Jersey. Thank
you to Ken Breeding (Vista, CA), Wendy Constantine (Anchorage, AK) and
Terri Granato (West Orange, NJ) for their help in identifying great teachers
to test the waters. And thanks to Jennifer Colantuoni, 4th grade teacher in
Londonderry, NH, for lending her fresh eye to the new volumes.

Many ESR staff and consultants influenced the content, strategies, and approaches of these new volumes. The work of the late William Kreidler, Carol Miller Lieber, Sara Pirtle, and Sandy Whitall has been incorporated and integrated into *Connected and Respected*. We thank them for providing their wisdom, guidance, and suggestions.

We give a special thank you and accolades to our publications team, headed by Denise Wolk. Former publications director Jeff Perkins' leadership, organization and perseverance kept us all on track as we reached the final stages of the process. Thanks also to Audra Longert for her critical work shepherding the final stages of editing, design, preparation and publication. We would also like to thank former ESR publications staff members Lisa Archibald and Laura Parker Roerden for their work on the early stages of this curriculum.

And thanks to all of you who bring your hearts, minds and talents to school every day to nurture, inspire and educate all of our children to make a better world.

Larry Dieringer
ESR Executive Director
Cambridge, Massachusetts 2007

We welcome you to this curriculum! We hope that it will help you to create a caring, productive, respectful learning environment in your classroom. Both of us have spent over thirty years in classrooms, as a teacher and a counselor, and have seen the power of these lessons to help students become more skillful in managing their conflicts and respecting one another.

Research suggests that our students today are actually *less* socially skilled than students in previous generations. This presents us with many challenges in managing a classroom. The pressure of high-stakes testing has led many schools to lose sight of the importance of these concepts. The link to academic performance, however, is clear; students perform better when they feel connected to the classroom and respected for who they are.

Enjoy these explorations with your students. You may find, as we did, that you are learning and growing with them, and becoming more skilled in your interactions with others, just as you hope your students will. You will certainly find your classroom becoming friendlier and more productive.

Ken Breeding, PhD
Jane Harrison

Introduction

Designed as an efficient and easy-to-use guide, *Connected and Respected: Lessons from the Resolving Conflict Creatively Program* provides a sequenced, developmentally appropriate set of skill building lessons and activities that help students develop social and emotional literacy that not only is important to their academic success, but also to their success in building and maintaining relationships over the course of their lifetime. In addition, the guide helps teachers create a welcoming classroom environment built on a sense of community that provides students an opportunity to connect with their peers and their teachers and to feel that they are an important part of their school.

According to recent research, spending time developing social and emotional skills and competencies facilitates students' academic gains. Evidence suggests that feeling connected to the classroom and becoming socially competent increases academic motivation.[1] Social and emotional learning programs, like RCCP, can have a positive influence on academic outcomes including: successfully mastering subject matter, sustaining motivation to continue learning, improving student attitudes toward school, reducing suspensions, expulsions and grade retentions, improving attendance, and building peer leadership skills.[2] Studies also show that when social and emotional skills are infused into curricular areas, in addition to academic learning, students gain sensitivity to other's feelings, better understand the consequences of their behavior, have higher self-esteem, and exhibit more prosocial behavior.[3] As our knowledge of human biology and psychology continues to advance, there is more evidence we have that emotions and cognitive functioning are intricately connected. And the more successes in business and government are analyzed, the more we see that character and social competence are essential to effective results. If ever there was an example of a win-win outcome, it is consciously addressing social and emotional learning and raising academic success at the same time.

The RCCP Program: Background

This curriculum grew out of, and is based on, the pioneering and nationally recognized Resolving Conflict Creatively Program (RCCP). It is the culmination of nearly 20 years of RCCP experience and research in schools across the country from New York to California, and Alaska to New Orleans. Its goal is to distill what has been learned about the core practices and key skills that contribute to academic excellence and the development of ethical and contributing community members.[4]

---

[1]   Barbara L. McCombs. "The Learner Centered Psychological Principles: A Framework for Balancing Academic and Social Emotional Learning," CEIC Review 10, no. 6 (2001): 8-9.

[2]   Joseph E. Zins, Herbert J. Walberg and Roger P. Weissberg. " Recommendations and Conclusions: Implications for Practice, Training, Research and Policy," in Building Academic Success on Social and Emotional Learning (New York: Teachers College Press, 2004).

[3]   Maurice J. Elias. "Strategies to Infuse Social and Emotional Learning into Academics," in Building Academic Success on Social and Emotional Learning (New York: Teachers College Press, 2004).

[4]   See Appendix A for information on RCCP research.

Developed in 1984 as an initiative between the New York City Board of Education and Educators for Social Responsibility Metropolitan Area (ESR Metro), RCCP has served over 400 schools in urban, suburban, and rural districts across the country and is one of the nation's largest and longest running, research-based school programs in intergroup relations and conflict resolution.

The RCCP model depends not only on the curriculum based instruction that helps students learn how to get along, appreciate each other's individuality, solve problems, express emotions appropriately, and manage their own behavior, but also includes a comprehensive, multiyear strategy for creating caring and peaceable communities of learning.[5]

Over the years, RCCP has been widely recognized in the fields of both social and emotional learning and violence prevention. The program was featured at the October 1998, White House Conference on School Safety and it was cited as a successful school model in the US Department of Education's *Safeguarding our Children: An Action Guide.*[6] The US General Accounting Office also praised RCCP in its report, *School Safety: Promising Initiatives for Addressing School Violence,* saying it is "widely regarded as one of the most promising violence-prevention programs among public health experts."[7]

More recently, the Collaborative for Academic, Social, and Emotional Learning (CASEL) chose RCCP from among more than 250 programs as one of 22 "Select" programs that meet the highest standards of effectiveness in its study *Safe and Sound: An Educational Leader's Guide to Evidence-Based Social and Emotional Learning Programs,*[8] and the federal Substance Abuse and Mental Health Services Administration (SAMHSA) designated RCCP as an "exemplary research-based program."

In addition, RCCP has been featured in the National Institute of Justice's *Program Focus,* the Millbrook Memorial Fund report, *Toward Safer Schools and Healthier Communities* (1999), the Mott Foundation report, *A Fine Line: Losing American Youth to Violence* (1994), and the journal *Reclaiming Children and Youth* (2001).

---

[5] See Appendix B for a full model description and Appendix C for the theoretical background.

[6] K. Dwyer, and D. Osher. *Safeguarding Our Children: An Action Guide.* (Washington, D.C: U.S. Departments of Education and Justice, American Institutes for Research, 2000).

[7] United States General Accounting Office. *School Safety: Promising Initiatives for Addressing School Violence,* 1995.

[8] Collaborative for Academic, Social and Emotional Learning. *Safe and Sound: An Educational Leader's Guide to Evidence-Based Social and Emotional Learning (SEL) Programs.* (Chicago, IL: Author, 2003).

Using This Book

Connected and Respected is divided into three grade levels: Kindergarten, Grade 1, and Grade 2. Each grade level includes 16 core lessons designed to build on one another sequentially throughout the year. Each lesson takes about 20 to 45 minutes. Extension and infusion activities are provided at the end of each core lesson, along with examples of relevant children's literature, brief summaries, and questions. Although the material for each grade level builds on the foundation of the previous year, it can also stand independently. Notes direct teachers to previous lessons when background information is needed or review is recommended. Feel free to experiment with lessons from other grade levels that may cover certain content or that you feel may more appropriately address the developmental needs of your students.

Lesson Format

The Workshop Approach

The workshop structure is designed to build community in the classroom and, once students are familiar with it, helps them be engaged with lesson content in a personal and affective way. This format, successfully implemented in RCCP classrooms, encourages a facilitative style of teaching and creates a sense of community structure or ritual whose positive effects extend beyond the scope of the lesson.

Visual Guide to Lesson Format

GRADE 2, LESSON 11

Escalation

Conflict Management and Decision Making — ESR Theme

CASEL SEL COMPETENCIES — CASEL

SA Self-Awareness

SM Self-Management

Collaborative for Academic, Social and Emotional Learning Competencies

1.

Gathering: When I Get Upset

When you get upset about something, what pushes your anger up to a higher level? As our gathering today, I am going to ask you to complete this sentence, "When I get upset, one thing that makes it worse is...." Explain that students may say what they do to that makes things worse, or what someone else may say or do that makes things worse. Model by completing the sentence yourself. Repeat the prompt and have students complete the sentence in a go-round or popcorn style.

2.

Agenda Check

One of the things we need to do in order to resolve problems and create win-win solutions is to stay calm enough to be able to think clearly. When conflict gets worse, we say it "escalates." What does an escalator do? (Briefly discuss what an escalator is. The important point is that escalators go up, or down, one step at a time.) Conflict usually begins with something very small. It might start when someone says or does something that upsets you. Then you might say something mean. That upsets the other person get even more so they may say or do something mean back. Now you're both more upset. At this point your own anger thermometer could be close to the top which is not a good position to be in to think of a peaceful solution.

In our gathering, we talked about things that can make a conflict worse. Today we're going to do a role-play to see how escalation works. (Conflict Skit) Then we'll make a chart of the different steps up the escalator and the feelings that go with them (Conflict Escalators). At the end, we will talk about what we learned (Summary) and do a closing (Closing).

3.

Activity: Conflict Skit

1. Choose two students and give them copies of the Backpack Conflict script ahead of time (page XX). Have students choose names that are unrelated to anyone in the class. If time permits, you may want to coach them before their performance.

2. Have the two student volunteers act out the Backpack Conflict. Ask the audience to see if the conflict gets "hotter" and to notice the things that push the conflict up toward the top of the escalator.

3. At the end of the role-play, ask students if the conflict seemed to go right to the top all at once or if it seemed to go up step–by–step.

Workshop Agenda — Workshop Agenda

- Gathering: When I Get Upset
- Agenda Check
- Activity: Conflict Skit
- Activity: Conflict Escalators
- Summary
- Closing: What Helps You Cool Off

overview of lesson

Materials — Materials

- Workshop agenda, written on chart paper and posted
- Copies of Backpack Conflict for each group of 2–3 students (See page X)
- Copies of Escalator worksheet for each group of 2-3 students (See page X)
- Talking Object

Materials needed for lesson

Learning Outcomes — Learning Outcomes

- Students will be able to identify factors that escalate conflict.
- Students will be able to analyze conflict and label the behaviors that contribute to conflict escalation.
- Students will be able to name the feelings associated with the behaviors that escalate conflict.

Student capabilities by end of lesson

Connections to Standards — Connections to Standards

Language Arts

Reading

- Identifies setting, main characters, events, sequence, and problems in stories

Working with Others

- Determines the causes of conflicts

Lesson correlation to the Mid-continent Research for Education and Learning (McREL) standard

235

The workshop structure includes:

1. **Gathering** – An experiential activity or sharing that relates to the main purpose of the lesson and helps children focus on the learning to come. Gatherings are intended to be positive, community-building experiences.

2. **Agenda Check** – A brief review of what will happen during the lesson that lets children know what to expect. The Workshop Agenda section in the sidebar of each lesson provides agenda wording that can be written on the board or on chart paper.

3. **Main activities** – The heart of the whole-class or group activities that provide structured situations that focus on the lesson's subject.

4.

Summary

A conflict can feel like taking a ride on an escalator – once it starts, you're on your way to the top. Fortunately, understanding things that make conflict escalate can help you control where the conflict is going. You noticed that we put the feelings the characters were having underneath the steps of the escalator. Feelings are like the motor underneath an escalator, they drive the escalator. The higher one goes, the harder it is to come down because our feelings have intensified. Sometimes our feelings carry us away from clear thinking. Then we do things we are sorry for later. This is why it's helpful to recognize escalation, so we can choose to stop and stay cool. This allows us to work toward strong, win-win solutions to conflicts.

5.

Closing

We started the lesson today sharing things that push our anger up the escalator. For the closing, I am going to ask you to think about what kinds of things help you de-escalate, or come down the escalator when you are starting to get mad. Have students form a circle either standing or sitting. Begin by sharing one thing that helps you calm down. Then pass the Talking Object to the next student. Students can either share things they like others to do or things they can do themselves. Examples of things they'd like from others might be, "when people apologize to me, " or "when they really listen to what I am saying." Examples of things they can do themselves might be, "saying to myself that I am not going to get hot" or "walking away and thinking of a favorite song."

6.

Extensions and Infusion Ideas

Identifying Conflict Escalation

When students experience conflicts with each other, unless they are already at the top of the escalator, you could ask them to plot the events that happened and the feelings involved. As an exercise in self-reflection, this can further the calming required for problem solving. It can also help students begin to take responsibility for their choices and the consequences of their choices. If a student is too upset about something that just occurred, however, he may need other things to cool him down before this can be attempted successfully.

7.

Connecting to Literature

Children's literature is full of books in which a conflict escalates to a climactic point and then is resolved in some fashion. Have students identify conflicts in stories and then use the conflict escalator handout to plot the step-by-step development of the action and the corresponding feelings that the characters experience.

Little Bear and the Big Fight, by Jutta Langreuter and Vera Sobat (Brookfield, CT: The Millbrook Press,1998) Gr. P-2

236

4. **Summary** – A recap that helps children review and internalize what has occurred. This can simply be asking questions such as "How did it feel to.....?", "What was one thing you learned today about...?", "Why is it important to...?" or it may include an art expression, writing exercise, or small-group sharing and reporting out. The Summary in the kindergarten lessons is integrated into the activity or the closing.

5. **Closing** – A song, quote, or exercise to provide closure to the lesson.

6. **Extension and Infusion Ideas** – Classroom activities to reinforce and expand the lesson such as additional sharing, art and writing, games, and role-plays. The ideas encourage you to recognize times when children incorporate lesson skills throughout the day and to integrate skill practice and community building into the core academic curriculum.

7. **Connecting to Literature** – A sampling of age and level- appropriate books with brief summaries and guided questions that connect the lesson theme and targeted skills.

Scripting

Most of the directions in each lesson are scripted in bold-faced type to give you a feel for how the lesson might sound if it were delivered by a teacher familiar with that lesson. The language is based on what we have learned in presenting these lessons in hundreds of classrooms across the nation. It is not intended, however, to be prescriptive. You may want to put directions and explanations in your own words.

Talking Object

A Talking Object is an object that is passed to the person whose turn it is to speak, providing a visible, concrete sign that focuses everyone on a single speaker. It could be a stuffed animal, beanbag, or glitter wand etc. Young children often have a hard time taking turns talking and sharing; it is difficult for anyone to listen actively in group situations, even professional adults. For this reason, a "talking object" is strongly suggested for group work.

Using Puppets

Several of the lessons use puppets as a vehicle for presenting key concepts. Using puppets can be a very effective way to engage students in important learning activities and they can be fun for you as well as your students. Many elementary teachers use puppets extensively. If you are not one of them and feel that you would be uncomfortable using puppets, we encourage you to give them a try anyway. Students don't care about your performance abilities; they will focus directly on the puppets and you'll be amazed at their concentration and attention!

Correlations

Each lesson lists outcomes and has been correlated to the Mid-Continent Research for Education and Learning (McREL) standards, the Collaborative for Academic, Social, and Emotional Learning's Social and Emotional Learning Competencies (CASEL SEL Competencies), and Educators for Social Responsibility (ESR) Themes.

McREL Standards

The Mid-Continent Research for Education and Learning is a nationally recognized organization of educators and researchers who provide field-tested, research based approaches to educational challenges. Although a national list of standards does not exist, the McREL compendium of standards and benchmarks provides nationally recognized standards in most content areas, including Behavorial Studies, Health, and Life Skills. All lessons in this book will help students meet multiple McREL benchmarks in one or more content areas. For more information go to http://www.mcrel.org

CASEL SEL Competencies

The Collaborative for Academic, Social, and Emotional Learning is an organization whose mission is to enhance children's success in school and life by promoting coordinated, evidence-based social, emotional, and academic learning as an essential part of education from preschool through high school. Housed at the University of Illinois at Chicago, CASEL synthesizes the latest empirical findings and theoretical developments and provides scientific leadership to foster progress in SEL research and practice. CASEL has identified five central competencies to achieve social and emotional literacy. Each lesson has been correlated to the CASEL competencies it addresses. The following chart describes the SEL skill clusters and composite skills CASEL views as essential.

SEL Competencies
Self-Awareness
• **Identifying emotions:** Identifying and labeling one's feelings • **Recognizing strengths:** Identifying and cultivating one's strengths and positive qualities
Social Awareness
• **Perspective-taking:** Identifying and understanding the thoughts and feelings of others • **Appreciating diversity:** Understanding that individual and group differences complement each other and make the world more interesting
Self-Management
• **Managing emotions:** Monitoring and regulating feelings so they aid rather than impede the handling of situations • **Goal setting:** Establishing and working toward the achievement of short- and long-term pro-social goals
Responsible Decision Making
• **Analyzing situations:** Accurately perceiving situations in which a decision is to be made and assessing factors that might influence one's response • **Assuming personal responsibility:** Recognizing and understanding one's obligation to engage in ethical, safe, and legal behaviors • **Respecting others:** Believing that others deserve to be treated with kindness and compassion and feeling motivated to contribute to the common good • **Problem solving:** Generating, implementing, and evaluating positive and informed solutions to problems
Relationship Skills
• **Communication:** Using verbal and nonverbal skills to express oneself and promote positive and effective exchanges with others • **Building relationships:** Establishing and maintaining healthy and rewarding connections with individuals and groups • **Negotiation:** Achieving mutually satisfactory resolutions to conflict by addressing the needs of all concerned • **Refusal:** Effectively conveying and following through with one's decision not to engage in unwanted, unsafe, unethical, or unlawful conduct

Implementing *Connected and Respected* in Your Classroom

Themes

Whether you are working independently to develop your own classroom values and environment, or implementing this curriculum as part of your school's Resolving Conflict Creatively Program, the RCCP model views the classroom as a caring and respectful community. Five themes are emphasized:

 ### Making Connections

Learning is most likely to take place when students have developed respectful and caring relationships with one another. The lessons within this theme set the stage for developing these relationships, and introduce interactive and affective teaching strategies that are used throughout this curriculum. By helping students make connections with each other in the beginning of the year and providing opportunities for cooperation throughout the year, these lessons build a foundation that enables students to work together. This not only helps students feel more connected to their classmates and their school, but also helps them develop critical social and emotional skills.

 ### Emotional Literacy

When working together in a classroom, students need to be able to recognize their own feelings and tell others about them. They also need to be able to acknowledge and respect the feelings of others. The goals of these lessons are to improve students' ability to name and describe feelings, to develop empathy for others, and to find productive ways of working with anger.

 ### Caring and Effective Communication

Good communication is at the heart of a classroom community dedicated to working together. Caring and effective communication encourages children to engage in dialogue, to understand and observe the process of sending and receiving messages, and to acknowledge that each person has a unique perspective. In these lessons students will learn active listening skills as well as how to give assertive and clear messages.

 ### Cultural Competence and Social Responsibility

These lessons give students opportunities to explore individual and cultural diversity in ways that preserve the integrity of each person, and that encourage them to be more accepting of one another's strengths, needs, and idiosyncrasies. By understanding and accepting differences, students learn to work together more effectively in the classroom and develop a sense of responsibility to one another: they learn how to make a positive difference.

Conflict Management and Decision Making

These lessons introduce students to a variety of cooperative and collaborative problem-solving techniques that help them to develop a "toolbox" of strategies and skills for resolving conflicts positively, constructively, and nonviolently. This "toolbox" includes understanding the concepts of escalating and deescalating conflict, group problem solving, and working out win-win solutions.

These themes influence every activity in this curriculum and are identified in the sidebar of each lesson. There is deliberate emphasis on cooperatively structured activities, and most of the activities encourage students to learn through sharing with each other and with you, the teacher. Students are also encouraged to relate skills and concepts to their own lives and to talk about feelings in a non-intrusive and comfortable way. Similarly, the activities model appreciation for diversity and are focused on helping children learn to deal with peers and others and to understand and handle conflict more effectively.

Our experience has shown us that it is not enough to teach children social and emotional skills. Schools and classrooms where the adults model positive conflict management skills, openly (and appropriately) express feelings, and communicate respectfully to each other and to students are those in which students thrive and succeed.

Addressing Specific Issues

Social and Emotional Competencies

We strongly believe that the most effective approach for helping children succeed is a comprehensive one that combines social and emotional and academic skill development in a consistent and sustained way. We also recognize that there are circumstances in which you may need to choose to "do the best you can" and opt to select a limited number of lessons to address specific skill sets. If you are implementing the curriculum independently you may choose to use one of the implementation suggestions on page xxxiii, or selectively implement core lessons to address specific skills that will benefit your students.

We've identified core lessons you may want to consider for addressing the major topics in this curriculum.

Topic	Kindergarten	Grade 1	Grade 2
Making Connections	1,2,3,4	1,2	1
Emotional Literacy	6,7	5,6,7,10,12	2,3,4
Caring and Effective Communication	5,8,9,10,11,12,15	8	5,7,8,9,15
Cultural Competence and Social Responsibility		3,4,13,14,15	13,14
Conflict Management and Decision Making	13,14	9,11	6,10,11,12

Countering Bullying

Bullying and harassment are not new issues in schools. In the past, bullying was often seen as a normal part of growing up or as a childhood rite of passage. Today, attitudes about and responses to bullying have changed, so much so that in 2001, the director of the National Institute of Child Health and Human Development called bullying "a public health problem that merits attention."[9] At least once a week, 1.6 million children are bullied and 1.7 million more children are bullying others. The reality of this situation doesn't just affect the victims and perpetrators. The emotional well-being and academic achievement of all students are affected.

The *Connected and Respected* curriculum addresses bullying in two essential ways: by fostering a classroom community in which every person (adult and child) is respected, valued, appreciated, and nurtured, and by providing specific skills to help students not only deal with bullying themselves but also support those who may be targets of bullying.

From the very first day, *Connected and Respected* provides teachers with activities and strategies that help children get to know one another. At each grade level, early lessons provide a foundation for establishing a caring community of learners. Students have the opportunity to create connections with classmates by learning their names, working together to create guidelines for behavior, working together on common projects, and interacting with different classmates in different situations.

According to the National Association for the Education of Young Children, children need effective communication skills in order to stand up assertively for themselves in the face of teasing or bullying. The *Connected and Respected* curriculum provides teachers with skill lessons to help children develop, practice, and apply effective communication skills that enable them to stand up assertively for themselves, or others, in a bullying situation. Specific lessons address active listening, assertive communication, and the difference between "mean and strong" words. Other lessons address recognizing emotions and expressing them appropriately and building empathy. When students are able to feel empathy for others who may be targets of teasing or bullying, they can become the critical mass in a school or classroom that says and demonstrates that "being mean to each other is not OK here."

See Appendix D for lesson correlations to this issue.

---

[9] Steineger, Melissa. (2001). Preventing and Countering School-Based Harassment: A Resource Guide for K-12 educators. Portland: Northwest Regional Educational Laboratory Equity Center, 2.

Building Character through Social Skills Development

Character education is a learning process that enables students and adults in a school to understand, care about, and act on core ethical values such as respect, justice, civic virtue and citizenship, and responsibility for self and others. It teaches the habits of thought and deed that help people live and work together as families, friends, neighbors, communities and nations. Identifying and internalizing the core values of character is just one instructional component of a comprehensive character education plan.

The *Connected and Respected* curriculum provides teachers with activities, lessons, and strategies that help children develop character skills that will serve them in all aspects of their lives and enable them to become socially responsible people. These qualities and skills include empathy, cultural competence, self-management skills, a sense of fairness and social justice, respect for themselves and others, and relationship skills. For some very young children, school is their first encounter with the larger world. The skills and habits they develop in elementary school will influence and positively impact the way they navigate adolescence and adulthood.

As children participate in making decisions and establishing guidelines for their own classroom environment, they learn they can make a difference, and that their contributions have meaning. They understand that their actions affect not only themselves, but all members of the classroom community. This awareness leads to accepting responsibility to act for the common good, to promoting fairness and justice, and to respecting themselves and others – the early stages of being socially responsible.

See Appendix F for lesson correlations to this issue.

Preventing Risk-Taking Behavior

Connected and Respected, when implemented consistently and effectively, provides activities and strategies that can help reduce risk factors associated with anti-social behavior and that can enhance and build protective factors that help students develop socially, emotionally, and academically.

Among the risk factors commonly associated with substance abuse and violence in adolescence are poor impulse control, an inability to manage anger and other strong feelings, inadequate problem-solving skills, and a lack of connectedness to school. By implementing *Connected and Respected* lessons and strategies, teachers help students develop the skills to counter these risk factors. As they internalize and practice these skills throughout elementary school, they will become better prepared to enter the turbulence of adolescence, face life decisions, and develop meaningful relationships.

Community-building exercises, such as those that begin each grade level, help students create connections with each other, the teacher and the school. Strategies such as working together as a class to establish behavioral guidelines and creating a Peace Place (See page xxxii.) develop self-management skills by involving students in behavior expectations and providing a place for them to manage their emotions. Lessons and extensions that foster emotional literacy help students manage anger by helping them recognize its triggers and providing productive, nonviolent strategies for dealing with their feelings. Conflict management skills, including understanding how conflicts escalate and ways to de-escalate them, provide a foundation of useful problem-solving techniques. Together, the skills and strategies in *Connected and Respected* provide students with the skills and strategies to prepare them to meet academic challenges, as well as the challenges of growing up and living in a healthy and productive way.

See Appendix G for lesson correlations to this issue.

Teaching Tools

Strategies for Grouping and Sharing

Group Sharing in Gatherings and Closings

Gatherings and Closings are activities that set the stage for the lesson and bring closure to it. Often, they require individual responses to a sentence completion or a specific question. Two common structures for these activities are **go-rounds** and **popcorn-style sharing**. In a go-round, each student has the opportunity to respond briefly, and the order of sharing follows the format in which students are sitting (i.e circle, horseshoe, etc.) All students should have the right to pass. In popcorn-style sharing, you call on a few students to respond in no particular order. It takes less time but does not allow all students to respond. With both styles of sharing, students should always have the option to pass.

Using Random Methods to Call On and Pair Students

Research tells us that no matter how hard we try to be fair, we can't help making biased choices. Using a random method of calling on students eliminates gender biases or preferences for more verbal students that we may not even be aware that we have. Over time, by using random methods of pairing students, we create opportunities for students to get to know and to work with all of their classmates. Lastly, using random strategies takes you off the hook of being the one responsible for "making" a particular student work with someone not of his choosing.

There are several strategies that can be used. Having cards with a different student's name on each one, shuffling, and then taking whichever card is on top is one way. Another way is to use pairs of cards (postcards, etc.) that are shuffled and distributed. Students find the person with the matching card to form a pair. Probably the most common method is using wooden name sticks. With a felt marker, put each student's name on a wooden tongue depressor and keep them handy in a can, pencil holder, or old coffee mug. Randomly pick one each time to call on students. When forming pairs, randomly take two at a time to form partners.

Forming Small Groups

Small, cooperative, working groups can be ideal for helping foster social and emotional skill building. Here are a few ways to form these groups randomly. There are many ways to make this task both fun and effective.

- Have students count off. To make nine groups of three in a class of twenty-seven, have students count off from one to nine three times. Then have all the one's, two's, three's, four's (and so on) come together as a group.

- Cut up pictures or create puzzle pieces on index cards. Students can then mill around the room looking for others who complete their puzzle.

- Playing cards are useful for making groups of four. For example, if you had 24 students, you would separate the suits and six cards with the same face value. You would then have all students with cards of the same face value come together. For groups of six you would have students holding hearts, spades, diamonds, or clubs come together.

Other options for grouping may connect to a topic you're studying in your academic curriculum. For example, creating index cards using "healthy snacks" or foods within a food group can reinforce a health or science lesson on nutrition and healthy eating. Have students gather by food group or by creating a "balanced daily diet." Use your imagination and have some fun.

For young children, you may want to start with pair sharing rather than with larger groups. As children become accustomed to actively listening to one another and can manage their behavior, you may want to try groups of three or four.

Supporting New Skills

Imagine spending only 16 lessons each year to have students attain literacy or math goals! To be successful in helping students attain the social and emotional literacy goals addressed in this curriculum, it is important to reinforce the learning that occurs in the lessons. Supporting the development of new skills is crucial. The following concepts can help you do that.

Feedback

As students are learning new skills, they need lots of feedback about how well they are doing. Take opportunities to state verbally the positive things you notice. "As I was talking, I could look around the group and see everyone's eyes looking at me. I also noticed that most of you were very still, with your bodies sitting up and facing me." Or, "I notice Jamie's group is working very quietly together with everyone participating." It's important to focus on positive things. It is almost always best to ignore behavior that is not positive.

Shaping Behavior

Like any skill, social and emotional competencies are realized by degrees. Students will be at different skill levels. An important behavioral principle is that to "shape behavior" we have to start by establishing the first steps toward eventual goals. For example, for a student struggling with active listening, the first goal may simply be not interrupting. Tailoring positive feedback to the student's skill level is particularly helpful in getting them to move forward.

Teachable Moments

Teachable moments surface in the classroom every day. They can bring the lessons presented here into real life application. Keep your eyes open for these moments and try to predict when they might come up. For example, certain activities lend themselves to modeling problem-solving skills and cooperation, others to students practicing put-ups and appreciation. Conflicts, both big and small, arise regularly. Be prepared to help students identify the problem and brainstorm solutions.

The more you can help students identify everyday moments that allow them to use their new skills, the more natural and easily integrated the skills will become to them. Students will truly absorb these lessons when they can apply their new learning as they discuss and examine their real-life issues. Use examples from particular issues that occur in your classroom during these lessons. We have peppered Teachable Moments throughout the book and hope that you will find many ways to make the themes and content of these lessons part of the daily fabric of your classroom.

Connecting to Literature

Children's literature is a powerful medium for teaching the concepts and skills presented in this curriculum. Engaging in literature is an emotional experience that can hold students' interest while broadening their perspective and exploring their feelings and the feelings of others. We hope that the books suggested for each lesson, along with their follow-up questions for discussion, will give you ideas for incorporating other children's books you may be aware of and help you infuse social and emotional skill building into literature of all kinds.

The Classroom Environment

Setting Up Your Classroom

The *ideal* classroom setup for building classroom community and developing social and emotional skills is to have space that enables students to engage in activities during which they move around and where you and your students can sit in a circle or horseshoe either on the floor or in chairs for other activities. The circle or horseshoe formation enables children to have an unobstructed view of each other, you, and a blackboard, whiteboard, or easel and chart paper. A second space could have tables or desks grouped together so that children can work together in small groups. You should be able to move easily from group to group during small group work.

Unfortunately, most of us have to make do with the space and setup we have. Fortunately, we teachers are a resourceful lot and are able to adapt where space is limited. Here are the principles that guide our recommendations in an ideal classroom.

- Students can see each other, you, and your visuals and other props.

- Students have an opportunity to engage in active community-building activities (look for alternative, unoccupied spaces where noise is not a problem; collaborate with the physical education teacher to incorporate group cooperative games during regular physical education; move outside when weather permits).

- Students can work in small groups to generate lists on chart paper, draw collaboratively, share and record observations and ideas, and you can support and monitor their work.

Establishing a Peace Place

A Peace Place is a space in your classroom set aside for students to use when they need to calm down, reflect on their feelings and behavior, and/or solve a conflict. Establishing a Peace Place is an effective way to help students implement the skills they learn in this curriculum. A space that can fit a table and has wall space for posting charts is ideal, but any space will work. When a conflict arises, encourage students to go to the Peace Place to work it out. Establish a time limit for them to try to resolve the issue before asking a teacher for help (for example, seven minutes). Provide a timer in the space and post charts that will help students remember the conflict resolution skills they have learned. If you need to be involved in solving a conflict, go with the children to the Peace Place to work it out.

Class Jobs and Responsibilities

Having students actively involved as much as possible in the ongoing running of the class is important for several reasons. By having students participate and be responsible for the daily tasks required in running the classroom (cleaning, attendance, collecting and distributing supplies, etc.) they feel ownership and belonging. When all students participate, there is a sense of equality and connectedness. The encouragement that comes from feeling that they make important contributions to the class community increases each student's likelihood of academic success as well as her self-esteem. Another benefit is that you have less menial work to do and can focus even more on "teaching."

Behavior Management and Discipline

A meta-study of research on different factors that influence student outcomes came up with an important finding. Of all the factors studied, including teacher preparation and experience, time-on-task, funding, parent support, size of classrooms and schools, etc., classroom management and discipline had the most impact. Unfortunately, none of us get enough training and support in this all-pervasive and important area.

Discipline and management are where "the rubber meets the road" – where we are challenged the most directly to continue our own social and emotional growth. How we handle our own emotions and our behavior while we manage group dynamics and deal with conflicts with students teaches volumes to all students. Our social and emotional skills are not perfect; they don't need to be. What students need to see is our commitment to integrity, to practicing what we preach. If we expect students to learn to listen openly and intently, acknowledge diverse points of view, and assert themselves respectfully, then we need to demonstrate a commitment to do the same.

The following are a few guiding principles you may find useful.

- **Mutual Respect** Respect for each student and respect for ourselves (or the learning community) are equally important.

- **Equal but Different** We are all equal in terms of worth and dignity, but we have different rights and responsibilities. Fairness does not mean equality.

- **Intention – What's the Goal?** The intent of most discipline is to teach/instruct. What is it you really want students to learn? As educators, what is the most effective way to facilitate that learning?

- **Perspective** Behavior is purposeful. Misbehavior is often the student's best available solution to a problem. When in a conflict, consider the other's point of view. What need is the student trying to meet by his choice of behavior?

- **More about Being than Saying** Discipline and learning is all about relationship. Who we are and what we do teaches students more than anything else. It's about modeling. We have to start with ourselves.

Developmental Considerations

There are developmental considerations to keep in mind as you use this book with elementary-grade children. Here are some general guidelines:

- Think in terms of readiness, as well as mastery. Concepts such as conflict resolution, problem solving, and point of view are difficult for young children. This means that children may not yet be at an age where they can master the skill or concept. However, they may at least become familiar with it and be able to work with it, which will prepare them to master the skill when they are older.

- Be as concrete as you can. It's easy to start talking about a concept in abstract terms, but this goes over the head of young children. Discuss a concept first in terms of specific actions and situations, then move to abstract ideas, such as motivations or positions and interests.

- Primary-grade children need help understanding the relationship between cause and effect. When discussing either actual or hypothetical situations, help them to see the whole problem and how specific actions and behaviors contribute to it.

- Strive to expand children's choices. Young children tend to have a limited array of approaches to a problem or situation. Gently help them see that there are other options. For example, during a discussion a child will sometimes insist that violence is the only solution to a conflict ("I'd kick his head.") Rather than arguing with the child, help the child to understand the consequences of that action ("What might happen if you kick his head?" Or, "If you kick his head that will hurt him and you might get into trouble.") Then generate or present some alternatives.

Implementation Suggestions

Research suggests that exposure to significant numbers of teacher-led RCCP lessons per year for multiple years yields the most significant positive results. This book's 16 core lessons for each grade are critical; it is highly recommended that you complete all 16 lessons over a sustained period of time. Using extensions and integrating the skills and practices, either by using the suggestions in this book or developing your own lessons, provides more practice and reinforcement for your students.

Every classroom is different – what works to implement these lessons in one, may not work in another. Integrate the lessons into your schedule during a time period that is consistent, and at intervals that work for you. The following are only two suggestions from a myriad of possibilities.

Suggestion 1

Begin with teaching one core lesson each day for the first week and once a week after that. Reinforce skills and concepts by using extensions and infusion at least twice per week for the remainder of the school year.

Advantages: Students are introduced to a variety of skills early in the year, giving you more opportunities to reinforce all of the skills and concepts sooner.

Suggestion 2

Teach at least one core lesson every other week. Reinforce the skills and concepts with extension and infusion lessons at least twice during the two-week period.

Advantages: This model provides sustained exposure to the curriculum skills and concepts, one at a time, throughout the school year. It allows students time to integrate their new skills and master concepts over time.

Making Connections

Gathering: "Come Join in the Circle"

The song "Come Join in the Circle" will be used in the first five lessons. It can be found in the book *Linking Up!*, by Sarah Pirtle, and on the *Linking Up!* CD, Track 4. It will be helpful to familiarize yourself with the words and the music before using it for the first time. You could also use another song of your choice that emphasizes inclusion. Just be sure to use it consistently through the next four lessons.

Have the students sit in a circle. Tell them you are going to sing a song, and ask them to clap with you at the appropriate time and to wave and look at each other when they hear the words, "Wave around the circle." Sing the song, "Come Join in the Circle." (Music and song lyrics can be found at the end of the lesson.)

Agenda Check

Go over the agenda and explain that the class will be doing some lessons that will help them learn about themselves and each other. Say something like: **In these lessons we will learn about each other, learn about dealing with our feelings, and learn about solving problems.** Have the students look at and say the word *agenda*. Explain that an agenda is a plan for the lesson. **A lot of things have a beginning, a middle, and an end. For the beginning today, we heard the song, "Come Join in the Circle." The lessons at the beginning are called the *Gathering*** (Gathering). **We "gathered" together to listen to the song. For the middle, we are going to play a name game** (point out Name Game on the agenda). **One of the most important ways to start to get to know each other is to know everyone's name. Then we will do something to end our lesson. We call this a *Closing*.** Have students look at and say the word *closing*. Ask if they can think of another word for "closing," i.e., "end."

Activity: Name Game

1. Show students the Talking Object. Explain that whoever is holding the object is the only person allowed to talk and everyone else should listen quietly. Briefly review that good listening means sitting up, looking at the person who is speaking, listening to what he is saying, keeping one's body still, and thinking about what that person is saying. Explain that when each person receives the object, he should hold it quietly in his lap.

Workshop Agenda
- Gathering: "Come Join in the Circle"
- Agenda Check
- Activity: Name Game
- Closing: Group Handshake

Materials
- Workshop agenda, written on chart paper and posted
- Talking Object

Learning Outcome
- Students will know each other's names and will be able to greet each other by name.

2. Introduce the activity by saying: **For this game, when you are holding the Talking Object in your lap, I would like you to say your name (first name) in a nice, loud voice that everyone can hear. Then raise the Talking Object above your head with both arms. When you raise the Talking Object, the rest of us are going to say your name together. After we have said your name, bring the Talking Object back down and then pass it to the person on your right.**

3. Model the activity by holding the Talking Object in your lap, saying your name, holding up the Talking Object, and prompting the class to repeat your name.

4. Pass the Talking Object to your right. Remind and prompt students when needed. If there are pauses, you may want to comment on specific focused listening behavior you observe.

5. Depending on the group, you may want to go around several times.

6. If the object can be rolled or tossed, roll or toss it to random individuals and challenge the group by having them say out loud that student's name.

Closing: Group Handshake

Ask: **Why is it important to know someone's name?** Elicit responses and make the point that each person is special and that their name is one of the special things about them. **It feels good when people know us and we know the other people in our group.** Have students stand in a circle, holding hands. Ask: **Have you ever seen adults shake hands when they meet someone? Well, we are going to do a group handshake for our Closing today. When I say to start, we will continue holding hands with the people on both sides and all together move our hands up and down three times.**

Extensions and Infusion Ideas

Once Upon a Time

For this activity you will need a card for each student with his name written large enough so that other students can read it when they are seated in a circle. You will also need some information about each child's name. Beforehand, send home a note to each child's parent or guardian asking them to provide information about what makes their child's name unique. For example,

Does their child's name have a special meaning?
Is their child named after someone special?
What do they like about their child's name?

Have the students sit in a circle. Give each child his Name Card. Instruct the children to put their Name Card face down on the floor in front of them. Ask them not to touch their card until it is their turn. When it is their turn, they should hold up their Name Card for everyone to see. Begin the game by saying: **Once upon a time a very special child was born and that child's name was...** (name one child).

The child who was named then holds up his Name Card. Now ask all the students to look at the person's Name Card and repeat his name. Continue until every child has been called.

Go around the circle again, this time saying one thing that is special about each child's name. For example: **Once upon a time a very special child was born and that child's name was Rose. Rose was named after her grandmother. Once upon a time a very special child was born and that child's name was Larry. Larry's name means lion.**

This game can be as long as you would like and/or it can be played at different times with different additions. Here are some other lines to add:

- **Once upon a time a very special child was born. Her name was Rose. Rose was named after her grandmother. One day, Rose was feeling...** (e.g., **happy**) **because she...** Each child says how she is feeling that day and why.

- **One day she came to school and...** (e.g., **passed out snacks**). Each child says something he did that day at school.

- **One day she came to school and said...** (e.g., **I'm hungry**). Each child says a word or sentence. If a child cannot think of anything to say, that is fine. You can end the sentence by saying, **One day she came to school and was quiet,** and go on to the next child. You might want to come back to the quiet child later and see if she has thought of something to say.

- **One day she came to school and made a sound. It went like this...** Each child makes a sound such as a cow mooing, teeth clicking, wind blowing, etc.

- **One day she came to school and made a movement. It went like this...** Each child makes a movement such as waving, opening and closing his hands, patting his head, squinting his eyes, shaking his head, etc.

Right, Left, and Me

This is a good activity to do once students are somewhat familiar with each other's names. Coach and prompt students when needed. This activity also reinforces concepts of right and left.

Have everyone gather in a circle, including you. Tell students that this game will help everyone to know each other's names better. Start the game by holding the Talking Object (or a small, soft ball) and explain: **When you get the Talking Object, say the name of the person to your right.** Review the meaning of right and left. Begin by modeling. Pass the object to your right. Continue until everyone has had a turn. Then, explain: **Now, when you get the Talking Object, say the name of the person to your left.** Model and pass the object to your left. Again, continue around the circle. Finally, explain: **This time, when you get the Talking Object you will need to say three names: first the name of the person to your right, then the name of the person to your left, and then your own name.** Model and pass the object to the right. Continue passing and naming until everyone has had a turn.

A fun variation once children have the knack of the game is to try timing it. What world speed record can the group achieve? Encourage the group to beat their own score. Spend a few moments marveling at the speed at which the class was able to go around the circle.

Chrysanthemum

Chrysanthemum, by Kevin Henkes (New York: HarperTrophy, 1996), is a great book that builds respect for people's names and helps students to identify the way it feels to have someone make fun of your name. In this book, a little girl loves her name until she goes to school and the children make fun of it. Mrs. Twinkle, the music teacher, helps the children see that Chrysanthemum's name is really beautiful.

Read *Chrysanthemum* up to the end of the first day of school, when Victoria says, "If I had a name like yours, I'd change it," and Chrysanthemum, feeling miserable, wishes she could.

Lead a discussion using the following questions:

- What happened on Chrysanthemum's first day of school?

- How is Chrysanthemum feeling?

- What is the problem here?

- What could Chrysanthemum do about this problem?

- What do you think will happen in this story?

Read the rest of the story, and then lead a discussion using the following questions:

- Was the problem solved?

- Do you like the way the problem was solved?

- How does Chrysanthemum feel now?

- Have you ever heard anybody make fun of your name?

- How did you feel?

- Have you ever heard anybody make fun of someone else's name?

- How did you feel?

Connecting to Literature

ABC I Like Me!, by Nancy Carlson
(New York: Viking, 1997) Gr. P-3

Summary: For each letter of the alphabet, a character tells something about himself, including his limitations.

1. Say: There are lots of things that are true about each of us. Probably some of the parts of this story are true about you. Choose several pages. After reading each, ask students: Thumbs up if this is true for you, thumbs down if it is not.

2. Use the Talking Object and ask students to tell something about themselves. Tell them that if they feel comfortable, they can mention something they think is one of their limitations.

The Crayon Box that Talked, by Shane De Rolf
(New York: Random House, 1997) Gr. K-3

Summary: Crayons don't get along until the artist takes them home and they see each other in a picture.

1. What helped the crayons begin to like each other? What did they mean when they said, "Each one of us is unique"?

2. Why is no one color better than any other?

3. The crayons said, "When we get together ... the picture is complete." What would happen if one of the crayons were missing? What happens in our classroom when one of us is missing?

Come Join in the Circle

Come join in the cir - cle.___ Moon, moon, the moon and sun.

Come join in the cir - cle.___ There's room for eve - ry - one.

(clap)

I'm so glad you're here. I'm so glad you're here.

Come join in the cir - cle.___ There's room for eve - ry - one.

Come Join in the Circle

Come join in the circle,

Moon, Moon, the moon and sun.

Come join in the circle,

There's room for everyone.

I'm so glad you're here. *(clap, clap)*

I'm so glad you're here. *(clap, clap)*

Come join in the circle,

There's room for everyone.

Wave around the circle,

Moon, Moon, the moon and sun.

Wave around the circle,

Wave to everyone.

Wave the way you like,

Wave the way you like,

Wave around the circle,

Wave to everyone.

GRADE K, LESSON 2
Alike and Different

Gathering: "Come Join in the Circle"

Have students sit in a circle. Play and sing the song, "Come Join in the Circle."
See page 6 for the music and song lyrics.

Agenda Check

Today we are going to do some more things to get to know each other better. We just finished our song for the gathering (Gathering). **Some puppets will help us start to look at ways we are alike and ways we are different** (Alike and Different). **Then we will play a game called Stand Up If** (Stand Up If). **We will close our lesson by talking about some of the things we learned** (Closing).

Activity: Alike and Different

1. Introduce the puppets to the students, saying something like: **Here are two friends who are going to help us learn about things that people have in common – things that are alike, or the same about us – and things that are different.** Have the puppets introduce themselves. (Puppets' names should not be those of people in the class.)

2. Through the mouths of the puppets, engage students in noticing differences and similarities by saying something like:

    PUPPET ONE: Look at us. We are friends; we are *just like* each other.

    PUPPET TWO: No, we're not. My mom says *everybody* is different.

    PUPPET ONE: Well, I think we are more alike than different. Maybe these students can help me out. What ways can you see that we are alike or the same?

3. After some discussion, Puppet Two could ask: **There are lots of ways that we are alike, but there are also many ways that we are different. I bet these smart students could think of lots of things that are different about us. How are we different?**

4. Listen actively as the students notice differences in skin color, hair, eyes, facial characteristics, gender, and clothing.

5. Depending on your class, you may or may not want to go to a more abstract level. For example, after they have identified differences that can be seen, you could ask them about other things that could be the same or different about them, things that cannot be seen.

Workshop Agenda

*   Gathering: "Come Join in the Circle"
*   Agenda Check
*   Activity: Alike and Different
*   Activity: Stand Up If
*   Closing: Summary

Materials

*   Workshop agenda, written on chart paper and posted
*   Two different puppets

Learning Outcome

*   Students will be able to identify how they are similar to and different from one another.

Through a discussion, you could come up with such things as: kinds of families, numbers of brothers and sisters, hobbies and interests, favorite color, favorite food, etc. Point out that we can't know these things about others until we get to know them.

6. Have two volunteers stand in front of the group. Ask the class to identify ways the students are different. Next, ask them ways the two students are alike. You can repeat this several times so that eventually everyone who would like to participate has had a turn. This makes a good, quick activity when you are transitioning from one activity to another and have a little time.

Activity: Stand Up If

1. Introduce the activity by saying: **We are going to play a game that will let us get to know some of the ways in which we are the same and some of the ways in which we are different from each other. This is a special game with NO TALKING. Sometimes we can say things without using words.** Bring up examples, like waving hello or smiling at someone. **The game is called Stand Up If. The way we will show that we are the same or different is by standing up or staying seated. We will be able to "listen" by looking to see who is standing and who is sitting. How could we say *yes* or *no* without talking?** Elicit that *yes* will be thumbs up, and that they can answer *no* by thumbs down.

2. For the first statement, say something that will get everyone to stand, such as: **Stand up if you have two ears.**

3. After they are all standing, ask if this is a way that we are alike and elicit a thumbs up.

4. Continue with a variety of topics that will be of interest and will show similarities and differences between different students. Possible topics include: number of siblings, if they are the youngest or oldest child, number and types of pets, likes and dislikes in areas such as food, games, etc. Encourage students to observe who is standing and who is sitting, who is the same as they are and who is different from them. Occasionally ask them to nod *yes* or *no* to questions like: **Is this a way that we are different from some people in our class? Are we all alike in this way?**

Closing: Summary

Today we have learned that there are ways that we are different from each other and that there are also ways that we are alike. Being different can be fun. Can you image what it would be like if we were all *exactly* the same? It is also very nice to know that in many ways, underneath our differences, we are all alike. What is something new you learned today about somebody else in our class?

Extensions and Infusion Ideas

Concentration

This activity requires a photo of each student. For each photo, cut a piece of cardboard to the same size. Laminate or glue each photo onto the cardboard pieces, making a set of cards.

These cards can be used for several variations of the game Concentration. Lay out all the cards face up. Have the children take turns at finding cards with certain similarities. Examples include finding all the cards with certain hair color, curly hair or straight, short or long, etc. Children's observations can allow for discussion about who has dark skin, light skin, who likes to wear certain clothing, etc.

For larger classes, these activities could be done in small groups with groups of cards, if desired.

You could also try the more traditional version of Concentration in which the cards are placed face down and children try to match cards with certain characteristics from memory.

Stellaluna

Stellaluna, by Janell Cannon (San Diego: Harcourt Children's Books, 1993), is a classic story that shows that friends can be both different and very much alike at the same time. Through the story of a baby bat that tries to act like his adoptive family of baby birds, the book explores the pitfalls of not being who we really are.

Class Graphs

Graphs allow students to see similarities and differences in a concrete, obvious way. There are many ways and countless topics that can be graphed. Some examples of topics include:

·   Favorite color

·   Favorite food

·   Favorite game

·   Pets

·   Number in family

The following is an example of a graph from Diane Levin's book, *Teaching Young Children in Violent Times* (Cambridge, MA: Educators for Social Responsibility, 2004). The teacher who used this graph took Polaroid pictures of each student, laminated them and attached a piece of Velcro to the back. If you didn't use pictures, you could make name cards for each student that could be attached to the graph instead.

OUR CLASS GRAPH

The Question
of the Day:

How do you get to school?

	Car	Walk	Bus	Subway – T
8	☐	☐	☐	☐
7	☐	☐	☐	☐
6	☐	☐	☐	☐
5	☐	☐	☐	☐
4	☐	☐	☐	☐
3	☐	☐	☐	☐
2	☐	☐	☐	☐
1	☐	☐	☐	☐

Connecting to Literature

Whoever You Are, by Mem Fox
(New York: Harcourt Brace and Company, 1997) Gr. P-3

Summary: Several drawings of children around the world show their superficial differences, and several drawings show the ways in which they are the same in their feelings and needs.

1. What are some of the ways you are different from some of the children in the story?

2. What are some of the ways you are like the children all over the world?

Best Friends, by Marcia Leonard
(Brookfield, CT: Millbrook Press, 1999) Gr. P-2

Summary: Best friends don't always have to agree.

1. Name some of the ways these two friends are different; name some ways they are the same.

2. Tell a way you are different from one of your friends. Does that mean one of you is better or worse than the other? Tell a way you and one of your friends are the same.

3. How do you and your friends settle disagreements?

All Kinds of Children, by Norma Simon
(Morton Grove, IL: Albert Whitman & Company, 1999) Gr. P-2

Summary: Children around the world have things in common.

1. All children wear clothes. How are your clothes different from or like some of the other children's clothes?

2. What do you like to hold when you are tired or sad?

3. What are the different ways you go for a ride or get from one place to another?

4. What are some of the things all children need?

GRADE K, LESSON 3
Groups We Belong To

Gathering: "Come Join in the Circle"

Have students sit in a circle. Play and sing the song, "Come Join in the Circle." See page 6 for the music and song lyrics.

Agenda Check

We have been learning about ways that we are alike and ways that we are different. The groups we belong to can make us alike or different. Today we are going to play a game to discover some more things we have in common with each other and some things that make us different from each other (Groups).

One thing that is true for all of us is that we all have families. Do we all have the same kind of family? Even though we all have families, families can be very different. (You may want to use this as an opportunity to highlight differences in families that are appropriate to your class.) After we play our game, we are going to make a picture that shows our families (Family Pictures), and then we'll close our lesson by sharing our pictures and something we like to do with our families (Closing).

Activity: Groups

1. Introduce the activity by saying: **We belong to many different groups. Some groups are large and some groups are small. One of the things that makes life interesting is that there are different people in the different groups we belong to. If the people in our groups were always the same, it would get pretty boring.**

   In this game we are going to make different groups. As in the game Stand Up If (page 8), you will be able to see who is in the same group you are in and who is not just by looking. First, we are going to make a group of boys and a group of girls. How many groups will we have altogether?

2. Have the girls stand in a group on one side of the space and the boys on the other side. Ask students to notice who is in their group, how many people are in the group, and how it feels to be in that group.

3. The next group will be based on birth order. (You may or may not want students to return to their seated position in the circle.) Explain that some people in the class may be the only child or the oldest child in their family. Ask those who do not have older brothers or sisters to form a group standing in one part of the space.

Workshop Agenda
- Gathering: "Come Join in the Circle"
- Agenda Check
- Activity: Groups
- Activity: Family Pictures
- Closing: Sharing Family Pictures

Materials
- Written agenda, written on chart paper and posted
- Compression sponge paper cut into people shapes
- Paint
- Felt–tip markers
- Large sheets of paper

Learning Outcomes
- Students will identify different groups to which they belong.
- Students will be able to identify their place in their family.

Ask students who are the youngest to form a different group, standing in another part of the space. Lastly, ask the students who have at least one younger and one older sibling, those in the middle, to form a third group. Ask them again to notice who is in their group, how many people there are, and how it feels to be in that group.

4. The last groupings relate to family size. Explain: **Every family size has good things about it. Some children live with just one adult, so their family consists of two people.** Ask children who live with just one adult to form a group. Continue: **Some families have three members. There may be two adults, with you being the only child, or there may be two children living with one adult.** Ask these students to form a second group. Continue: **Other families have four people in them.** Explain that this can be any combination of adults and children. They may live with a single parent and grandparents or there could be two or three children. Have them form a third group. Continue: **The last group we are going to make is for children who live in a family where there are five or more people who live together.** Ask them again to notice who's in their group, how many there are, and how it feels to be in that group.

5. Have students come back to a circle and process the experience by asking such questions as:

   - Were the other people in your groups always the same people?

   - Were the sizes of your groups the same or different?

   - How did you feel about being in different groups?

Activity: Family Pictures

(Note: *In this activity it is very important to create a safe climate in which students can describe their own families. Give consideration to particular issues that may come up with individual students. Many students, and most of the students in some classrooms, do not live in traditional families. There are many family structures, including same-sex and single-parent families. Be sensitive to those students who may be in foster placements, who live with extended family members, or have one or more important people missing in their lives because of legal or medical reasons.*)

1. To prepare for the activity, cut the compression sponge paper into the shapes of adults and children. Put the shapes in water to expand them into thick sponges. (You may need to practice this process with one shape to learn how to cut the sponge paper so that the shapes are recognizable when the sponges have expanded.) Make several sets of these people shapes. As an alternative to the sponges, you could use people shapes of various sizes and shapes cut out of colored paper that students then simply glue to a paper.

2. Invite students to a place suitable for this activity.

3. Distribute large paper to each child. Have the children dip the appropriate sponges in paint and use them to stamp images on their own paper to represent the members of their families. Allow the paint to dry.

4. Alternatively, distribute die-cut figures and paper and have students glue figures on their papers to represent their families.

5. Identify family members and help students to write names under each figure.

Closing: Sharing Family Pictures

Ask students to come back to the circle and bring their family picture. To minimize distractions, have students put their pictures face down on the floor or carpet in front of them. Tell students you are going to go around the circle and give everyone who would like to, the opportunity to share his or her picture with the class and to tell one thing they like doing with their families. Ask them to think about what they are going to share so that they will be ready when their turn comes. Remind them of the importance of good listening while others are sharing. Review the things that you, and the student sharing, can expect from the others in the group – body sitting up straight with minimal movement, no touching of their pictures while someone else is sharing, eyes looking at the speaker, and minds thinking about what the person is saying. Prompt when necessary and allow students to pass if they would rather not share.

The closing is rather lengthy. You could choose one of the following options, or schedule it for a separate time.

1. Paired sharing: Have the students partner. Tell them that each person in their pair will have a turn showing the picture to his partner and telling something he likes to do with his family.

2. Get a few volunteers to share their pictures with the whole class. Make sure you get a representative sample of the different kinds of family constellations. Post all of the pictures on the bulletin board.

3. Make time during the day for every child to share his picture and what he likes to do with his family.

Extensions and Infusion Ideas

Barnyard

Children form groups organized by different animal sounds. (Note: *It may be helpful to gather animal pictures as visual prompts for your students ahead of time.*)

Make a list for yourself of common farm animals. Put as many animals on your list as the number of groups you want to form. Include animals that make sounds children can identify and repeat easily, like a dog, cat, duck, cow, sheep, or pig.

Have the children form a circle. Explain that you are going to whisper an animal name into their ear. They should try very hard to remember that animal and should think about the sound that animal makes. Tell them that when you give the signal, they will then make their animal's noise and try to find the other children making that noise.

They should make the noise several times, until students making the same noise have found each other and formed a group.

Go around the circle and give each child an animal name. Then give the signal to start.

After a few minutes all the children will be in groups. You can then give instructions for a small-group activity, or just play this game again.

Family Photos

Send a note home to parents asking them to send photographs of immediate family members to school, either group or individual photos. In the note explain, "It is up to you and the students to define who is in your family in any way you choose. Therefore, send photos of those who you consider your child's family to be." Have children share the photos and display them prominently in the class.

Family Trees

Talk about what a family tree is. Use photos or drawings to create family trees for each child. Include the child's parents or guardians. Include the adults in grandparent roles as well. The family tree should represent relationships to care-givers as well to biological ancestors.

Some children may be in foster placement and not able to identify stable family members. Be sensitive and accepting of the following:

- Some children's parents are biological parents.
- Some children's guardian or primary caregiver is not their biological parent.
- A biological parent may be quite involved with the child, but not be his primary caregiver.
- Some children may live with two moms or two dads.

Create the trees by having students draw a tree with branches, or by providing a "tree" shape to color. Make copies of each child's family photos to paste on the tree. Children may need help in deciding where to place pictures on the tree.

Family Words

Focus on key words: *father, mother, brother, sister, aunt, uncle, grandmother, grandfather, cousin, friend*. Elicit any other word that the children might use to describe their family members. Use these words as labels for pictures, stories, or family trees.

Draw attention to any words children may use from other languages. Have children learn these words from each other.

Family Roles and Responsibilities and Family Fun

Point out that sometimes families work together around the house and outside the house. Each person helps in some way. Elicit and chart a list of what family members do to help each other. Draw pictures or write stories of family members helping each other.

The same activity could also focus on what families enjoy doing together for fun.

Connecting to Literature

Barn Raising, by Craig Brown
(New York: Greenwillow Books, 2002) Gr. P-2

Summary: After a fire, Amish neighbors help raise the barn of Jacob's father.

1. Show the title page and the double-page picture that follows. Jacob is a young boy, and this is the barn on his farm. What do you think just happened?

2. After reading the book, say: One group that Jacob belongs to is his family. Name one way Jacob helped his family before they got their new barn.

3. Another group Jacob and his family belong to is their group of Amish neighbors. How did Jacob and his family help this group when they came to build the new barn?

4. Name some groups you are a part of. Do you help each other in these groups? How?

There's Only One of Me!, by Pat Hutchins
(New York: Greenwillow Books, 2003) Gr. P-2

Summary: A birthday girl identifies all the relationships she has to the members of her family.

1. On the final page listing relationships, read the beginning of each sentence and let students end it: "I'm my great-grandmother's _____."

2. After reading the book, say: When you have the Talking Object, tell one of the ways you are related to someone. For example, "I'm my sister's brother." or "I'm my uncle's niece."

GRADE K, LESSON 4
Our Class

Gathering: "Come Join in the Circle"

Have students sit in a circle. Sing the song, "Come Join in the Circle." See page 6 for the music and song lyrics.

Agenda Check

We have been learning about ways that we are alike and different from each other. In the last lesson, we talked about groups we belong to. A very special group that we all belong to is our class. Today we are going to do an art project (Our Class) **to show everyone that even though we may be different as individuals, we are all important members of our class. After we have created our** (tree, garden, rainbow, etc.) **we will spend a little time talking about how we want to treat each other in our class. As a group, we will decide on some agreements we can all promise each other that will make our class the kind of place we all want it to be** (Group Agreements). **We'll end by making a promise to keep our agreements** (Closing).

Activity: Our Class

1. Decide ahead of time which project you will be doing (suggestions below) and prepare the appropriate art materials and bulletin board or poster. You might consider doing this workshop over several time periods.

2. The goal of this activity is to create a focus point in the classroom – for example, a bulletin board or large poster that represents the importance of the classroom as a community. This focus point could take any number of forms, as long as it represents all the unique individuals in the classroom community connected together as one important group. Each individual will create something that becomes part of the whole, for example, a drawing, a self-portrait, or a photograph of the person.

   Suggestions:

   - A class tree (either drawn or cut out of brown construction paper), where individuals add their own leaves or blossoms

   - A class garden, where each individual is represented by a flower that is "planted" in a strip of brown to represent the earth

   - An aquarium, where individuals are represented by fish

   - A zoo, where individuals are represented by different animals

   - A rainbow of different-colored hands labeled with individual's names and/or pictures

Workshop Agenda

- Gathering: "Come Join in the Circle"
- Agenda Check
- Activity: Our Class
- Activity: Group Agreements
- Closing: Y-E-S

Materials

- Workshop agenda, written on chart paper and posted
- Appropriate art materials
- Bulletin board or large poster
- Chart paper and markers

Learning Outcomes

- Students will recognize they are a valued part of the classroom community.
- Students will generate a list of Class Agreements.

3. After individuals have created their contribution, have them add their pieces to the class project and then re-form in a circle. Students' names should be on their contribution. Acknowledge the group's accomplishment.

Activity: Group Agreements

1. Explain: **Before we talk about making some promises to each other about how we want our class to be, I would like you to think about someone you really like to be with. This could be a grandparent, someone else in your family, a special friend, or someone else who takes care of you. Think about the ways they treat you that make you feel safe and good when you are with them. For example, you might like spending time with your grandpa because he always asks for a hug but you might not like it when he pinches your cheeks. Then think about some places and groups you like to be in. How do people treat you that makes you like being in these groups? For example, maybe you like going to day care because everyone says, "Hi!" and smiles when you arrive. Or maybe you don't have to wait long to play with your favorite toy because everyone takes turns.**

2. Tell students you are going to pair them with a partner and have them talk about how they like to be treated. Divide students into pairs. If you feel your class would not be able to do this successfully, you might adapt the activity for the whole group. (See Teaching Tools for ideas about pairing.) Establish a quiet signal so students know when they are to stop talking. Ask them to tell their partner about someone they like to be with and what that person does and does not do that makes them like being with them. Give them a short amount of time to talk and then tell them to switch partners. Depending on your class, you may want to provide more structure by preassigning who will speak first, stopping them and having the second person speak.

3. Next, ask them to share with their partner a group or a place where they like to be. Have them say how they are treated and what people do and don't do that makes them feel safe and welcomed in that group.

4. Have the class gather in a circle again. Ask for volunteers to describe behaviors that other people do that they like, and things that they do that they don't like. Make a list of these things on a chart with simple words and symbolic pictures, if you would like.

5. Review the lists, grouping things and pointing out similarities.

6. Briefly discuss what promises and agreements are. Promises are not always kept, but the intent of a promise is that it is a thoughtful commitment to something important. You will want to use vocabulary that will invite this level of commitment to generating class agreements but that still leaves room for "mistakes."

7. Ask: **Can you think of some things that would make our class the kind of place where we would all feel great? Some things we could promise each other that we could all agree to do?**

8. Make a chart of "Class Agreements." Help students clarify with prompting questions, if necessary. Keep agreements simple, avoiding "don'ts" and keeping the focus on expected behavior. The classroom agreements may include things like:

   - We will listen to each other and let one person at a time talk.

   - We will use kind words with each other.

   - We will take turns.

   - We will help each other.

   - We will treat each other with care.

   The chart might have the stem "We will" and then a list of simple words and phrases like *listen, say kind words, take turns, help,* etc., along with illustrations. Be sure children understand what the behavior looks like and be specific. Ask questions such as: How do we treat each other with care? What are we promising to do and not to do?

   Be careful not to go beyond the point of interest and involvement. When it seems appropriate, review the agreements and make sure everyone can promise to do the things on the list. Have students give examples of each behavior and talk about things that might be hard to do. Let students know that more agreements can be added in the future.

Closing: Y-E-S

Acknowldege: **We have just done a lot of hard work. We are going to end our lesson today with a fun way of promising each other to be the kind of group that we all want to be a part of.**

Ask students to stand in a circle and join hands. Explain that when you make the signal, everyone will bend over so that their hands almost touch the floor. The class will then begin saying *yes* together softly, drawing the word out, getting louder and louder as everyone slowly raises their hands into the air. The class will end with their hands as high above them as possible, completing the word energetically. Tell them that saying *yes* together represents a commitment to keep all of the promises they just made to make the class the kind of place where everyone feels good about being together as a group.

Extensions and Infusion Ideas

Revisiting Class Agreements

Post the finished list of agreements in a prominent place in the classroom. Every once in a while, review the list and ask students how they think the class is doing with their agreements. Ask students to add promises as issues come up that could be helped by an additional agreement.

Consequences

Revisit the Class Agreements and ask how students think things have been going. Keep the conversation centered on general behaviors rather than discussing specific students. Brainstorm with students: **What can we do when we, or someone else, forget to keep one of our agreements?** (List the children's ideas and add any of the following: make the person an apology picture, do something else nice for that person, apologize and tell that person something you like about her, etc.) Help students see the difference between consequences that are just punitive and those that might help people learn to do better next time. Remind them that everyone, including you, makes mistakes from time to time. **The important thing is for us to have some ideas about how to make things right again. Things that can help us are respectful to everyone involved.**

Our Colors Mural

Introduce the mural by saying something like: **We will make a beautiful mural that celebrates all the different colors of our body. First, we will color paper that matches the colors of our body. Then, we'll take all the paper squares and paste /tape them onto this big sheet of paper, making something very pretty to hang in the class.**

Creating color squares Distribute one paper square and crayons that match different eye colors to each child. Ask students to color the square the same color as the big circle in their eye. Tell them to color the whole square. If a student does not know her eye color, help her look in the mirror to see it. After the squares are colored, collect them.

Then give out another square and crayons that match skin tones. Since no one is really white, black, red, or yellow, these colors should not be choices here. Point out that there are a lot of different browns, a lot of different beiges, etc. Tell them to use the crayon that matches the skin on their arm the best. Not all children will be able to match the colors closely. In matching skin tones, the goal is to make children aware of the many different shades of people's skin and celebrate them all. Awareness more than accuracy is important here.

After you have collected the skin tone squares, do squares for hair color.

Creating the Mural The mural can be created in several ways:

- After collecting one set of squares, help small groups of children take turns pasting or taping the squares on the mural paper while the rest of the class is working on the next set of squares.

- After a student has finished coloring a square, she can come up to the mural with her own square and paste it on.

- Create the mural over a few days, using "pasting squares" so that students who are interested can take turns pasting or taping the squares to the big paper and arranging the colors in the way they think is beautiful.

Discussing the Mural Once the mural is created, discuss the following ideas with the children during "circle time," if you have one, or incorporate them into any other classroom discussion.

- What do you see in this mural?

- How do you feel about this mural?

- Which colors on you change from day to day? Which colors on you stay the same?

During the discussion, acknowledge everything that emerges, using active listening techniques. Paraphrasing students' contributions is effective here.

Other Group Art Projects

As the year progresses, choose other art projects that emphasize each individual as an important member of the group. These projects can be related to seasons or to literature. For example, if you were reading a story about a beehive, you could have students color and cut out bees that represent themselves and have them attach their creation to a class hive on a bulletin board. This activity can be especially useful after one or more new students have joined the class.

Connecting to Literature

Big Al, by Andrew Clements
(Framingham, MA: Picture Book Studio, 1988) Gr. K-3

Summary: Big Al is a big, scary fish that wants to be a friend. He tries to be like other fish and only succeeds when he uses his own gifts.

1. What helped the small fish learn to love Big Al? Why do they like to be with Big Al?

2. Tell about a time when you were afraid of someone at first and then something happened that changed your feelings about that person.

New Kid, by Susan Hood
(Brookfield, CT: The Millbrook Press, 1998) Gr. P-1

Summary: Sid acts up until he feels accepted. Then the whole class is glad.

1. Tell why the other kids did not enjoy being with Sid when he first came to their class.

2. The boy who tells the story figures out how to help Sid. Why do you think Sid was acting like that? How did the class help Sid?

3. How can you help each other enjoy being together as a class?

The Colors of Us, by Karen Katz
(New York: Henry Holt, 1999) Gr. P-1

Summary: Lena learns that people have many different shades of skin color. She mixes her paint just right to paint herself and everyone else she sees.

1. What are the different shades of brown that Lena discovered?

2. What color paints did Lena use to mix the brown that she used?

3. After reading the book, ask: What does your own skin shade remind you of?

GRADE K, LESSON 5
Being Together

Gathering: "Come Join in the Circle"

Have students sit in a circle. Play and sing the song, "Come Join in the Circle." See page 6 for the music and song lyrics.

Agenda Check

In the last lesson we talked about the importance of our group and we made some promises about how we want to treat each other. Today we are going to have some fun learning more about how to work together as a group. The first thing that we will do is talk a little about the word, *cooperation* (Cooperation). **Then we will get to practice working together in an activity, trying to get everyone across the river** (Chocolate River). **For our closing, we'll share what we experienced in the lesson and then cooperate to make a snail** (Closing).

Activity: Cooperation

1. Ask students what it means to cooperate with another person. You may want to remind students of times when you have asked them to work together on something, such as the projects in the last lesson. Attempt to come up with a simple definition of the word.

2. Lead a brief discussion by asking questions such as the following:

   - Why is it important to cooperate when working with others?

   - What are some ways that you cooperate with others at home?

   - Have you ever been in a group where someone was bossy or didn't participate? How did that feel?

   - What can you do if you are in a group where someone is not very cooperative?

Activity: Chocolate River

1. Use masking tape to make two parallel lines approximately 12 feet apart.

2. Explain that these are the banks of a chocolate river. The goal of this game is to get everyone across the river without anyone falling in.

3. Have the group gather on one side of the river.

4. Show students the squares and explain that they are the marshmallows. The students will use them to get across the river.

Workshop Agenda

- Gathering: "Come Join in the Circle"
- Agenda Check
- Activity: Cooperation
- Activity: Chocolate River
- Closing: Snail

Materials

- Workshop agenda, written on chart paper and posted
- Square paper marshmallows, made from 8" x 12" pieces of white gripliner or heavy construction paper
- Masking tape

Learning Outcomes

- Students will be able to define cooperation in their own words.
- Students will be able to cooperate with each other to reach a common goal.

5. Put one marshmallow into the river area and hold on to the others. Stand on the marshmallow and ask: **Now what do we do? How can we use the marshmallows to get across the river?** The children will suggest continuing to place marshmallows in the river and using them as stepping-stones to get across.

6. Remind them that the goal is to get everyone across the river and encourage them to follow you, but to do it carefully so that no one steps in or falls into the river. Continue crossing the river until everyone has made it across without stepping off the marshmallows.

7. Ask: **During Chocolate River, what were some of the ways you helped each other? What worked best when you were crossing? What might you try the next time we play this game?**

Closing: Snail

Have the students stand in a circle and hold hands. Form a line by breaking the circle at some point and have the line move around the play space. Encourage students not to let go if they can help it, but also not to hold hands too tightly.

Once students are able to move in a line without letting go of hands, join the line yourself at the end. Explain that the group is going to make a snail by wrapping the line around you. Have the leader walk slowly around the play space, wrapping the line around you in a spiral. When no one is left moving, the snail is complete.

Extensions and Infusion Ideas

Follow Me Freeze

You will need a CD or cassette with music.

Explain the activity to students by saying something like: **This game is just like Follow the Leader, but instead of just following what the leader does, you'll copy the leader's movement until I stop the music. Then everyone freezes.** Designate one child as the leader. The leader will make body movements that the rest of the class will follow. Play music while the other children follow the leader. Stop the music. Have the leader pick another child to be the next leader and start the music again. Repeat, being sure to rotate leaders so that everyone who wants to lead has a turn.

Pass the Ball (or Bag)

You will need small, soft balls or beanbags for each student. Balls could be made by crumpling recycled paper.

Have students sit in a circle and have them place their ball in front of them on the ground. Explain that they will be passing the balls around the circle to the beat of a chant. The goal is to get the balls all the way around the circle so that each person gets the ball they started with. Teach the chant: "We pass the ball from me to you. We pass like this and we never, never miss."

Demonstrate the first part of the game, saying the words very slowly and giving students plenty of time to practice.

We (*Put your hand on the ball in front of you.*)

pass (*Pass the ball to your right.*)

the (*Put your hand on the new ball in front of you.*)

ball (*Pass the ball to your right.*)

from (*Put your hand on the ball in front of you.*)

me (*Pass the ball to your right.*)

to (*Put your hand on the ball in front of you.*)

you (*Pass the ball to your right.*)

Demonstrate the second part of the game (the passing pattern gets a little tricky).

We (*Put your hand on the ball in front of you.*)

pass (*Pass the ball to your right.*)

like (*Put your hand on the ball in front of you.*)

this (*Pass the ball to your right.*)

and we (*Put your hand on the ball in front of you.*)

never (*Pass the ball to your right, but don't let go.*)

never (*Bring the ball back in front of you.*)

miss (*Pass the ball to the person on your right and let go!*)

This game takes practice. Gradually you can increase the pace of the game. You always know when the group has made a mistake because someone will have a pile of balls in front of him. When a mistake is made, have everyone claim a ball, then start over.

Connecting to Literature

Messy Lot, by Larry Dane Brimner
(New York: Children's Press, 2001) Gr. K-2

Summary: Alex bosses Three J and Gabby, and then they all work together to clean a corner lot.

1. After Alex wonders what is wrong with Three J and Gabby, ask: Why do you think Three J and Gabby are upset?

2. After reading the book, ask: What lesson did the Corner Kids learn about cooperating? Ask students if they can think of a time when a boss is necessary.

3. What could we do together as a class to cooperate in keeping an area of our school or grounds clean?

Growing Vegetable Soup, by Lois Ehlert
(San Diego: Harcourt Brace Jovanovich, 1987) Gr. P-3

Summary: A child and his or her dad plant the vegetables, harvest them, and make vegetable soup.

1. This is the story of a child who helps his or her dad grow vegetables for soup. What did the father and child have to do to raise a vegetable garden and then make the soup?

2. Many children do not live where they can have their own garden. If you were going to make vegetable soup, what steps would you and your family take?

3. At the end of the book there is a recipe for vegetable soup. Students could, to the degree possible, participate in making vegetable soup.

Jack and Rick, by David McPhail
(New York: Green Light Readers, 2003) Gr. P-1

Summary: Jack the Rabbit and Rick the Bear figure out a way to cross the river and play together.

1. How did Jack and Rick help each other?

2. Jack and Rick worked together. Tell how you and others worked together in your cooperative activities for this lesson.

3. Can you think of a time when you worked together with someone? Tell us about it.

Rooster Can't Cock-a-Doodle-Doo, by Karen Rostoker-Gruber
(New York: Dial Books for Young Readers, 2004) Gr. P-2

Summary: A comical story of a farm that oversleeps because Rooster has a sore throat. The other animals help Farmer Ted finish the chores before dark.

1. Tell why Farmer Ted and the other animals needed Rooster's help each day.

2. How did the animals work together to wake up Farmer Ted?

3. How did they help Farmer Ted get the chores done before dark?

4. Tell how you are needed so that our classroom is a happy place.

5. What are ways you can be helpful to your family?

It's Mine, by Leo Leonni
(New York: Dragonfly Books, 1996) Gr. P-1

Summary: Three frogs spend all day bickering about what is theirs. When a bad storm comes, they realize they need to share to survive.

1. How did the frogs talk to each other?

2. After reading the book, ask: Have you ever had an argument like that with a friend? Ask students to share stories.

3. If you were a fish, what would you say to the frogs?

Different Feelings

Emotional Literacy

CASEL SEL COMPETENCIES

SO Social Awareness

RS Relationship Skills

Gathering: I Feel Happy When…

(Note: *Before doing the lesson, you may want to consider expanding the lesson over several periods, using the four-workshop format discussed on page 31.*)

Have the students make a circle. Review the use of the Talking Object as a way of knowing whose turn it is to talk and as a reminder to listen to the person speaking. Explain that when each person receives the object, she should just hold it quietly in her lap. Briefly review the good listening that everyone should be able to observe when it is her turn.

Before you begin, ask students to think to themselves about when it is that they feel happy. **When it is your turn, I would like you to finish the sentence, "I feel happy when… ." Others in the group will listen and try to remember what each person said.** Depending on how well they know each other and whether or not there are any newer students, you can have them also share their names. Give several examples of how you yourself might finish the sentence by saying something like: **I love going to the beach, so I might say, "I feel happy when I go to the beach." I also feel happy when I get to hold a baby. I feel happy when I am with my family and everyone is safe and enjoying themselves, so I could say, "I feel happy when I'm with my family."** Model by saying your name and then choosing one way to finish the sentence. Pass the object to the person next to you and ask her to say her name and when she feels happy. Prompt students, as needed, by repeating the sentence stem.

Agenda Check

Today we are beginning some lessons that will help us learn more about feelings. We can have lots of different feelings. We started our lesson today by saying when we feel happy (Gathering). **Did we all say the same thing? Are there some things that we probably all feel happy about? Next, we will make a chart with as many feelings as we can think of** (Different Feelings). **Then we will play a game in which we'll pretend to make a soup with a lot of different feelings** (Feelings Soup). **We'll end our lesson by singing a song** (Closing).

Activity: Different Feelings

1. Ask: **Can you give me the name of one feeling?** As the feeling is contributed, write it on the chart.

Workshop Agenda

- Gathering: I Feel Happy When…
- Agenda Check
- Activity: Different Feelings
- Activity: Feelings Soup
- Closing: "If You're Happy and You Know It"

Materials

- Workshop agenda, written on chart paper and posted
- Talking Object
- Chart paper and markers

Learning Outcome

- Students will be able to identify and name different feelings.

2. Ask: **When you feel that way, how does your face look?** Have students make a face that expresses that feeling. As you all make a face to express that feeling, help students identify what actually happens. (Does the mouth go down or up? Are the muscles tight or loose? How do the eyes look? What about the eyebrows? etc.)

3. Ask: **What does the rest of your body do? What do you do when you are feeling _____?** It can be helpful to add a quick illustration next to the feeling on the chart, if possible.

4. Ask for another example of a feeling and discuss, as above. Continue until ideas are exhausted or interest wanes. Try to have the four major feeling families (happy, sad, mad, scared) represented. Save the chart for use in Lesson 7.

Activity: Feelings Soup

1. Designate an area as the "soup bowl." An area rug is perfect, but any space large enough to hold all the students standing around it will do.

2. Have students form a circle around this area.

3. Explain that you are making "Feelings Soup" and you want to put different feelings in it. Choose a feeling, such as happiness. Ask students to show you how happiness looks.

4. Take three of the students from the circle and put them in the soup by bringing them into the center of the soup bowl space. They should continue their happy looks and movements, even when other ingredients are added to the soup.

5. Choose another feeling and ask the remaining children to show you how it looks. Then choose a few students and add them to the soup.

6. Continue until all the children are in the soup.

7. At the end, invite students to notice all the different feelings and point out that in any group, there is usually a variety of feelings present at the same time.

Closing: "If You're Happy and You Know It"

Have students re-form in a circle. Say: **Today we have talked a lot about feelings. What feeling do you think you like best?** After students have participated, tell them you're going to end the lesson by learning and singing the song ,"If You're Happy and You Know It, Clap Your Hands."

If You're Happy and You Know It

If you're happy and you know it, clap your hands *(clap, clap)*.

If you're happy and you know it, clap your hands *(clap, clap)*.

If you're happy and you know it, then your face will surely show it.

If you're happy and you know it, clap your hands *(clap, clap)*.

If you're happy and you know it, stomp your feet *(stomp, stomp)*.

If you're happy and you know it, stomp your feet *(stomp, stomp)*.

If you're happy and you know it, then your face will surely show it.

If you're happy and you know it, stomp your feet *(stomp, stomp)*.

If you're happy and you know it, shout, "Hurrah!" *(Hurrah!)*

If you're happy and you know it, shout, "Hurrah!" *(Hurrah!)*

If you're happy and you know it, then your face will surely show it.

If you're happy and you know it, shout, "Hurrah!" *(Hurrah!)*

If you're happy and you know it, do all three *(clap, clap, stomp, stomp, Hurrah!)*.

If you're happy and you know it, do all three *(clap, clap, stomp, stomp, Hurrah!)*.

If you're happy and you know it, then your face will surely show it.

If you're happy and you know it, do all three *(clap, clap, stomp, stomp, Hurrah!)*.

Extensions and Infusion Ideas

Extending the Lesson into Four Workshops

If at all possible, repeat the lesson for each of the major feeling families (happy, sad, mad, scared). Repeat the gathering, using a different emotion each time. For the Different Feelings activity, have students generate a chart of feelings that belong in that feeling family you are focusing on by saying, for instance, **Today we are learning about the feeling called *scared*.** Write the word *scared* on the chart. **What are some other words that people can use to describe the way they feel when they are feeling scared?** Chart the words that come up. Have students show with their faces how they would look for each of the words. Lead a discussion that is appropriate for the level of your students about the differences in various feelings that are in the same family. Before ending, demonstrate and have everyone show how they would walk if they were experiencing one of the charted emotions.

Other activities to include could be drawing pictures of the feeling and listening to books that highlight that emotion. (See other ideas below.) At the end of the series of workshops, students could participate in Feelings Soup and assemble Feelings Books, books made of their drawings and pictures of examples of feelings cut from magazines. (See pages 32 and 33.)

Centipede

Tell students that they are going to play a walking game called Happy/Sad/ Mad or Scared Centipede. They are going to make a centipede that is going to move around the room expressing a particular emotion. Briefly explain that a centipede is an insect with many feet. Have students form a line, holding the waist of the person in front of them. Then have them move around the room showing the chosen emotion.

Books about Feelings

There are many good books written expressly to illustrate feelings. The following is a sampling of some that might be useful.

Today I Feel Silly: And Other Moods That Make My Day, by Jamie Lee Curtis
(New York: HaperCollins, 1998)

This book, with rich watercolor illustrations, is a favorite. It introduces a lot of feeling vocabulary words and at the end makes the point that, "I'd rather feel silly, excited, or glad than cranky or grumpy, discouraged or sad. But moods are just something that happen each day. Whatever I'm feeling inside is okay!"

My Many Colored Days, by Dr. Seuss
(New York: Alfred Knopf, 1996)

Published five years after his death and illustrated by Steve Johnson and Lou Fancher, this book relates moods to different colors. "Some days are yellow. Some are blue. On different days I'm different too. You'd be surprised how many ways I change on Different Colored Days."

Feelings, by Aliki
(New York: Farrar, Straus and Giroux, 1996)

This book is really a collection of about 20 short poems, stories, and cartoons that could be used with any age.

This Is Me Laughing, by Lynea Bowdish
(New York: Farrar, Straus and Giroux, 1996)

In this enchanting poem, the whole house, as well as the entire neighborhood, becomes possessed by contagious, irrepressible, thoroughly delightful laughter.

Wemberly Worried, by Kevin Henkes
(New York: Greenwillow Books, 2000)

A great book that explores a single emotion, feeling worried. Wemberly worries about everything. When it is time for school to start, Wemberly worries even more. When Wemberly finds a friend like her, she goes back to her normal level of worry.

There's a Nightmare in My Closet, by Mercer Mayer
(New York: Dial Books for Young Readers, 1968)

A classic book that helps children learn how to confront and accept their feelings. By facing his fear, the protagonist comes to a place where he empathizes with his fear and happily welcomes it into his bed.

Class Feelings Book

Each week as you are studying a different feeling, have students find and cut out pictures from magazines that illustrate that particular feeling. These images can then be glued onto a single page for a large class book of feelings. By the end, the book will illustrate all the feelings the class has studied.

Personal Feelings Books

This is an art and literacy project that can be spread over a longer time period than the Class Feelings Book extension. The goal is that each student produces a personal book of feelings. Create class sets of title pages that might say, "I Have Many Different Feelings," with a place for the student's name, and class sets of pages that have at the top, "Sometimes I feel _____," filled in with one feeling (happy, sad, worried, angry, etc.), or "I feel ___ when ___." Working on one feeling at a time, have students draw a picture that illustrates that page for them. (You could also write or dictate an additional sentence for each page.) Collect each session's pages, and when the books are complete, bind them and give them to students to take home.

Connecting to Literature

Sometimes, by Keith Baker
(San Diego, CA: Green Light Readers, 1999) Gr. P-2

Summary: Shows an alligator in a variety of situations, with different feelings, liking himself, and what he does.

1. What are some of the ways the alligator feels?

2. Are all of his feelings fun?

3. Name one way you sometimes feel. Is that feeling comfortable or uncomfortable? Show what you look like when you feel that way.

I Feel Happy and Sad and Angry and Glad, by Mary Murphy
(New York: Dorling Kindersley Publishing, Inc., 2000) Gr. P-1

Summary: A variety of situations and the corresponding feelings.

1. Name some of the feelings Ellie and Milo had while they were playing.

2. Name at least two feelings you have already had today.

3. Is it a good thing to have more than one feeling in a day? Why?

The Feelings Book, by Todd Parr
(Boston: Little, Brown and Company, 2000) Gr. P-1

Summary: The variety of feelings that someone can have should be shared with a loved one.

1. The children in this book have lots of feelings. Name some of those feelings.

2. Sometimes the children tell what they feel like doing. Tell what feeling you might have if you feel like:

   a. standing on your head

   b. reading a book under the covers

   c. celebrating your birthday even though it's not today

   d. looking out the window all day

e. holding hands with a friend

f. making mudpies

g. you have a tummy ache

h. staying in the bathtub all day

i. camping with your dog

j. crying

k. trying something new

l. doing nothing

m. yelling really loud

n. eating pizza for breakfast

o. dressing up

p. kissing a sea lion

q. being a king

3. Why does Todd say we shouldn't keep our feelings to ourselves? How can we share our feelings?

Recognizing Feelings

 Emotional Literacy

CASEL SEL COMPETENCIES

SA   Self-Awareness

SO   Soical Awareness

RS   Relationship Skills

Gathering: I Feel Sad When…

Have students gather in a circle. **In the last lesson, we shared stories about times when we were happy. Some feelings make us feel comfortable; feeling happy is a comfortable feeling. Not all feelings are comfortable, though. Today we are going to start our lesson by talking about what it is like when we feel sad. Before we start, think for a minute to yourself: When are you sad? It might be when you have lost something important to you. It might be when you are all alone with no one to play with. I feel sad when I hear or see people being mean to each other. You may also feel sad if somebody teases you or calls you a name.** Tell students they will each finish the sentence, "I feel sad when… ." Remind students about good listening skills and about the use of the Talking Object, and then model by finishing the sentence before passing to the next student. Prompt when needed. Encourage students to share, while reminding them that everyone has the right to pass.

Agenda Check

How can you tell if a dog is happy? Do dogs get angry? How can you tell if they are angry? Knowing how a dog feels can be important. If a neighbor's dog were growling or snarling, we would know to stay away. It is even more important to know how another person is feeling. Why do you think that would be important? (Facilitate a brief discussion about the importance of empathy.)

Today we are going to practice recognizing feelings in others (Guessing Feelings). **Then we will do an activity to see if people always feel the same or if they can have different feelings about the same thing** (Alike and Different). **Then we will finish our lesson as always with a closing** (Closing).

Activity: Guessing Feelings

1. Read through and review the list of feelings created during the last lesson.

2. Say: **I am going to choose one of these feelings and then make my face look like it would if I were feeling that feeling. Your job is to try and guess how I'm feeling. Raise your hand if you think you know my feeling.**

3. Choose a feeling from the list and show that emotion by your facial expression. After someone has correctly guessed the feeling, have a brief discussion about what they noticed that physically indicated that feeling.

Workshop Agenda

- Gathering: I Feel Sad When…
- Agenda Check
- Activity: Guessing Feelings
- Activity: Alike and Different
- Closing: Summary

Materials

- Workshop agenda, written on chart paper and posted
- Feelings Chart from Lesson 6
- Talking Object

Learning Outcomes

- Students will begin to develop empathy by being able to recognize and name feelings in others.
- Students will recognize that there are similarities and differences in how people show their feelings.

4. Continue with several more feelings.

5. Tell students that the game is going to change a little. This time, when you choose a feeling, you will act out how someone might perform an activity if they were feeling that emotion. Pick an activity, like sharpening a pencil or sweeping the floor, that you can pantomime.

6. Choose a feeling, act it out, and have students raise their hand if they can guess that feeling.

7. Repeat with several feelings.

8. Demonstrate the feeling with just your tone of voice. Either ask students to close their eyes briefly, or to turn away. In a tone that expresses the feeling, say a neutral sentence, like "Today is Tuesday."

9. Conclude by saying: **Now that we've had some practice "reading" feelings, let's play another game to see if we all have the same feelings about the same thing.**

Activity: Alike and Different

1. Introduce the activity by saying: **Earlier, we said that *happy* was a comfortable feeling and that *sad* was an uncomfortable feeling. What are some other feelings that are comfortable? (excited, proud, content, etc.) What are some uncomfortable feelings? (sad, mad, scared, embarrassed, etc.)**

2. Go through the list and have students indicate which feelings are comfortable and which are uncomfortable.

3. Explain: **In this game, we are going to use our thumbs to show if we would have a comfortable or an uncomfortable feeling about something. In a minute, I'll ask you to gently close your eyes and think about how you would feel in different situations. If you would have a comfortable feeling, you would make a thumbs-up sign.** (Show them a thumbs-up and have them all make one.) **If you would have an uncomfortable feeling, like scared, sad, or mad, you would show that with a thumbs-down sign.** (Have them show and practice thumbs-down and thumbs-up.)

4. Ask them to gently close their eyes and then say: **Imagine that you are at a park, and there is a big dog there. Show with a thumbs-up or a thumbs-down whether you would have a comfortable or uncomfortable feeling.**

5. When everyone has their thumbs out, ask them to open their eyes and look around at everyone in the group.

6. Ask questions about what they notice, such as: Are we all feeling the same or do we have feel different feelings about being with a big dog? Ask individual students to name feelings they would have.

7. Continue with the following situations. Add others if you would like.

    - Someone gives you a box. When you open it there is a little snake inside.

    - You are on a giant roller coaster.

    - You are at a huge circus.

    - You are out on the playground all by yourself.

Closing: Summary

We did a lot today. How can you tell how someone else is feeling? Does everyone always feel the same about a particular thing? One of the reasons it is important to be able to "read" or tell how someone is feeling is that sometimes he may feel very differently about something from the way we would. Why else could it be important to know how someone else is feeling?

We started the lesson today talking about when we felt sad. To close our lesson today, I would like you to think about something. What could you do if you saw a friend, someone in our class, who was sad? What kind of things help you when you are feeling sad? This could be shared as a go-round, or popcorn style, with fewer students sharing.

Extensions and Infusion Ideas

Guess-the-Feeling Game

Post and review the list of feelings created in Lesson 6. Explain that students are going to try to guess how someone is feeling by the way they look and sound. The person won't use a feeling word. One student will stand up at the front, choose a feeling from the chart, then turn and demonstrate the feeling to the class without using the word. He will show the feeling with his face, his body, and his voice as he says a neutral sentence like, "Today is Tuesday." The class should listen carefully to his tone of voice, and pay attention to his facial expression and body language. Remind students how actors and actresses demonstrate feelings and encourage expression.

Choose a student to start the activity. Have him choose a feeling without saying what it is, turn, face the class, and act out the feeling while saying "Today is Tuesday." Students should raise their hands when they think they know what the feeling is. The student acting out the feeling could call on students to guess, or you could choose among volunteers.

Action Charades

This is similar to the previous activity, but this time students will demonstrate a feeling by performing an action in a manner that shows that they are experiencing that emotion. Choose an action and ask students to demonstrate different emotions while performing the same action.

This can be done as pantomime or with real props. Students may need a lot of coaching to be able to act convincingly.

Suggestions for actions:

- sweeping the floor
- sharpening a pencil
- eating something
- walking

Feeling Masks

For this activity, you will need the following art supplies: construction paper, markers, felt and other scraps of material, glue, clear tape, yarn, string, or ribbon.

Review with students the list of feelings created in Lesson 6. Have each student pick one feeling, and, using the materials provided, create a mask that shows what this feeling looks like. Encourage students to pick a variety of feelings.

After all the masks are completed, gather the students in a circle and lead a discussion with the following questions:

- How did you choose the expression to put on your mask?
- Did you think of a time when you felt the feeling you chose?
- Did you picture what someone looks like when they feel that way?
- Did you choose certain colors to mean something? If so, what?
- Can someone show a feeling by looking a certain way on the outside, but have a different feeling on the inside?
- Can you think of feelings that are sometimes hard to show other people?

Connecting to Literature

All good literature is rich in emotion. As you read stories or books together, point out the feelings that are being expressed. Have students identify feelings and articulate what makes them think the character is experiencing that feeling. Have them see if they can tell what triggers the feeling, what the characters do with the feeling, and what the results are of the character's behavior. Help students see how feelings change as stories progress and what things help them change.

What Makes Me Happy?, by Catherine and Laurence Anholt (Cambridge, MA: Candlewick Press, 1994) Gr. K-2

Summary: A small child's range of emotions.

1. After reading each pair of pages, ask : When you feel this way, is it a comfortable feeling?

2. You have seen that there are many reasons for having the same feeling. When do you feel excited? Sad? etc. After a student answers, ask: How many of you feel that way? When the response is not unanimous, point that out and affirm all responses, reminding students that people respond differently to the same situation.

A to Z: Do You Ever Feel Like Me?, by Bonnie Hausman
(New York: Dutton Children's Books, 1999) Gr. P-2

Summary: Clever list of situations describing feelings to be guessed.

1. At any feeling page, ask: How do you look when you feel ___ ?

2. What feelings were new to you?

3. Which feelings were easiest to guess? Which were hardest to guess?

4. Ask students to role-play various feelings and have the class guess which feelings are being expressed.

GRADE K, LESSON 8
Handling Anger

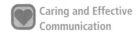 **Caring and Effective Communication**

CASEL SEL COMPETENCIES

SA   Self-Awareness

SM   Self-Management

RS   Relationship Skills

Gathering: It Bugs Me When

Have students sit in a circle. Using the Talking Object, introduce the gathering by saying something like: **We've been talking about feelings. Today we are going to be talking about the feeling that is the hardest for most people to deal with, anger. Sometimes we say that things we get angry about "bug" us. What does it mean if something bugs you?** Establish that things that bug us make us mad. **Today I want you to think about things that bug you. For the gathering, I'm going to ask you to tell us what one of those things is.** Model by telling students something that bugs you. (It might be best to share something that won't also be cited by others in the group to discourage "copying the teacher." For example, "It bugs me when my teenage son forgets to give me telephone messages.") Comment on the good listening you observe in students, and remind them to listen as well to each other. Pass the Talking Object to the next student and use the sentence stem to prompt as needed.

Agenda Check

We just finished talking about things that bug us (Gathering). **Everybody gets angry, even your parents and your teacher. Knowing what to do when you are angry can be hard. Today you are going to tell a partner about a time when you got really angry** (A Time I Was Angry). **Then we'll talk a little about what people do when they're angry and what can happen. Next we'll learn what to do when you're angry so that you and everyone else can feel happy afterwards** (Using Words). **Then we'll end our lesson with a closing** (Closing).

Activity: A Time I Was Angry

1. Pair students with a partner. (See Teaching Tools for ideas about pairing or just have them turn and face a student next to them.)

2. Explain that each of them will tell their partner a story. To prepare, you may want them to close their eyes gently as they go over the memory in their mind at first. Say something like: **I'd like you to think about a time when you got really, really mad. Don't say anything yet out loud while you listen to these questions. Who were you mad at? Where were you? What did you get mad about? What happened? What did you do? What did the other(s) do? How did you feel afterward? How did it end?**

Workshop Agenda

- Gathering: It Bugs Me When
- Agenda Check
- Activity: A Time I Was Angry
- Activity: Using Words
- Closing: A Place I Really Like

Materials

- Workshop agenda, written on chart paper and posted
- Talking Object
- Chart paper and markers

Learning Outcomes

- Students will learn words to use when they are angry and practice using words in role-plays.
- Students will be able to say how being angry affects them physically and what behaviors are connected to anger.

3. Have students tell their partner about a time when they were angry. Remind them to try to tell it as a story, including the details your questions just prompted. Have them decide who will go first. (You may want the first speaker to raise her hand to insure that each pair has decided.) Give them a short amount of time, and when it looks like most are finished, ask the second person to tell her story.

4. Regroup in a circle.

5. Ask students if they can tell if their bodies feel different when they are angry. What does angry behavior look, sound, and feel like? (You may or may not want to chart responses.) Have them make their bodies look angry and ask them to look around the group and notice how other people's bodies change.

6. Ask what they did when they were angry. (Again, you may or may not want to chart.)

7. Ask what the results were for different behaviors. Summarize things brought up during the sharing.

8. Conclude by saying: **Everybody gets angry at times. Although there is nothing wrong with feeling angry, sometimes we feel like being mean when we are angry. It's okay to be angry, but it's never okay to be mean.**

Activity: Using Words

1. Introduce the activity by saying: **What does it mean to be strong?** Acknowledge responses about muscle strength as relating to being strong on the outside. Continue: **People can also be strong on the inside. People who are really strong don't let others or their own feelings boss them around. They learn to use words when they are mad so that their angry feelings don't control them and lead them to do mean things. What are some strong words people could use instead of acting mean?** Facilitate a discussion and chart responses that include things such as:

   • "Stop that!"

   • "I don't like it when you ___."

   • "That makes me angry."

   • "I feel mad when you ___."

2. Explain that they will practice using words to be strong by doing some role-plays. If students are unfamiliar with role-plays, explain that they are going to be actors and actresses and pretend to be in a situation in which someone gets mad. Then the person who is mad will think of a way of expressing her angry feelings by using words.

3. Ask what story students would like to role-play and decide on a scenario. This could be either one of the stories that was recently read or the kind of situation that often elicits angry feelings.

4. Choose students to role-play and give them made-up names unrelated to anyone in the class. (It's important in role-plays to distinguish clearly that this is make-believe.)

5. Have the students role-play the scenario and stop as someone begins to feel anger.

6. Instruct the audience to point out what they see happening, how they know if a character is getting angry, and what might happen if she doesn't stop, think, and use words to express her feelings. Help the character choose an appropriate sentence to express her feelings and then have her finish the role-play.

7. Discuss the positive results and compare them to what could have happened.

8. Do several other role-plays as long as time and interest permit.

Closing: A Place I Really Like

If people are getting angry, and feel as if their anger might begin to take over, a good way to handle that problem is to take a break and do something fun. How do you feel when you are someplace where you really like to be or doing something that you really like to do? Sometimes, just thinking about a special place or something you like to do can help you calm down or cool off.

In a minute, I am going to ask you to gently close your eyes. When I do, I would like you to think about a place where you would like to be, or something you would like to be doing. Imagine that your thoughts are like a movie of you in your special place or doing your special thing.

Gently close your eyes and let the movie in your imagination begin. Allow a brief time for students to try to picture a calming place or activity. As you gently open your eyes, how does your body feel right now?

Using the Talking Object, have students share what they imagined either as a go-round or popcorn style.

If we are getting too angry and need to calm down, we might not always be able to do what we would like to or go someplace special, but we can always imagine these things the way we just did.

Extensions and Infusion Ideas

More Role-Plays

Have students continue role-playing until everyone has had an opportunity to practice using words to express angry feelings.

As real conflicts in the classroom occur, after students are calm, invite them to role-play the situation and practice substituting words for any negative behaviors that occurred.

Art and Writing

Have students draw a picture of their "A Time I Was Angry" stories, and dictate briefly whom they were angry with, what happened, and how it ended.

You could also have them draw a second picture showing how they would use words to solve the problem in a more positive manner.

Ballooning and Draining

"Ballooning" is basically deep breathing. Have the children stand, and tell them to take slow (not deep) breaths and fill themselves up with air as if they were balloons. Then have them slowly let the air out of the "balloons." Repeat a few times and have the children notice the way they feel.

"Draining" is consciously tensing and relaxing the muscles in the body. Again, have the children stand. Ask them to tighten all the muscles in their bodies and hold them tight until you say to let go. After a few seconds, say: **Now relax slowly and let all the anger drain out of you. Imagine a puddle of anger at your feet. How did you feel when you finished ballooning/draining? When might you use these exercises? Could you balloon or drain so that people couldn't tell you were doing it?**

Anger Thermometer

Explain to students that there are different levels of anger. You can be a little bit angry, just plain angry, or very, very angry. Anger can go up or down like an escalator or a thermometer. The higher anger goes, the hotter it gets and the more difficult to handle. (See Grade 1, Lesson 12) You could make or draw a picture of a thermometer on a chart, and simplify it by using three levels of anger: *Annoyed* or *Irritated* to represent the lowest level; *Angry* for the middle; and *Furious* for the top. During role-plays point out and ask students what level they think their character is at.

Teachable Moments

When you notice students are upset or getting angery in a situation, ask them where they are on the anger thermometer and what they can do to cool down and express their anger strongly, but calmly.

Connecting to Literature

When Sophie Gets Angry — Really, Really Angry, by Molly Bang (New York: The Blue Sky Press, 1999) Gr. K-3

Summary: When Sophie gets angry, she runs and climbs her favorite tree until she is calm.

1. Name some of the things Sophie does when she gets angry. For each, ask: Does it help Sophie feel better?

2. What can you do to help yourself feel more comfortable when you are angry?

When you notice students are upset or getting angery in a situation, ask them where they are on the anger thermometer.

I Was So Mad, by Mercer Mayer
(New York: A Golden Book, 1983) Gr. P-2

Summary: Little Critter is mad enough to leave home – until his friends ask him to play.

1. Name some of the things Little Critter wanted to do, and tell why he wasn't allowed to do them.

2. Why did Little Critter stop feeling mad?

3. Name a time when you felt mad because you couldn't do something. Then name something you could have done to feel better.

Being Kind

 **Caring and Effective Communication**

CASEL SEL COMPETENCIES

SO Social Awareness

SM Self-Management

RS Relationship Skills

Gathering: Someone Kind

Have students sit in a circle. Introduce the gathering by saying something like: **As a gathering for our lesson today, we are going to talk a little about what it means to be kind. What does it mean to be kind?** Facilitate a discussion that arrives at a definition of kind — of being friendly, doing good rather than harm. **In a minute I am going to ask you to describe someone you think is kind and why you think she or he is a kind person. This person could be someone in your family, a friend, someone you know at school, or around the neighborhood.** Model by talking about someone you think of as kind, perhaps someone students know who works in the school.

Agenda Check

In the last lesson we talked about angry feelings. When we are angry, we often feel like doing mean things, but how do mean things make us and others feel? When we do mean things, we usually feel even more mad or sad afterward, and other people feel bad, too. On the other hand, how do we feel when people are kind to us? How does it feel to be kind to others? No matter how we are feeling, we can always try to be kind. By choosing kind behavior, we almost always end up feeling happier.

Today we are going to make a list of words and actions we can choose in order to be kind (Kindness Chart). **Then we will start an art project building a rainbow that celebrates the kind things we have done for others** (Helping Hands). **We'll end our lesson with a closing** (Closing).

Activity: Kindness Chart

1. Introduce the activity by saying: **We can show kindness and respect for others by what we do and by what we say. We're going to make a chart of as many ways as possible to be kind.**

2. Create a two-column chart labeled *Actions* and *Words*. Have students read and discuss the difference. Then ask: **What is something we could do or something we could say that would be kind?**

Workshop Agenda

- Gathering: Someone Kind
- Agenda Check
- Activity: Kindness Chart
- Activity: Helping Hands
- Closing: Appreciations

Materials

- Workshop agenda, written on chart paper and posted
- Talking Object
- Chart paper and markers
- Colored construction paper cut into squares large enough for the handprint of a student (red, orange, yellow, green, and blue squares, one for each student)
- Large sheet of mural paper
- Pencils, scissors, and paste

Learning Outcomes

- Students will identify and talk about someone who is kind.
- Students will be able to identify qualities of kindness.
- Students will be able to name times when they have been kind.

3. Write contributions in the appropriate column, phrased as simply as possible. (You may want to include a visual symbol to represent the words.) Have the class read and discuss each item as it is added.

4. End the activity if students run out of ideas or lose interest. Post the chart somewhere in the classroom and let students know they can add more ideas at a later time.

Activity: Helping Hands

It may be useful to have more adults around to help with this activity. If you are the only adult, providing another activity for students to be engaged in while they are waiting for you can be helpful.

1. Prepare the following ahead of time:

    Spread out mural paper. In pencil, draw one large arch on the paper to form a rainbow. Continue drawing arches below or above this one until you have a rainbow with five arches. Label each section of the rainbow with the words *red, orange, yellow, green, and blue.* You may want to use colored markers for this if you have students who cannot read. Hang the rainbow on the wall where children will be able to reach it.

2. Give each student a construction paper square and a pencil.

3. Have students trace their hands on the paper and label the paper with their names.

4. Have each child tell you of an act of kindness he or she performed. Write this on the palm of the paper hand with a marker.

5. Have students cut out the hand and paste their "helping hand" on the appropriate color of the rainbow.

6. Repeat the process over the next week or so until the entire rainbow is filled in with "helping hands."

Closing: Appreciations

One important way of being kind is telling someone something you really like about them or saying thank you for something that they have done for you. These are sometimes called *appreciations* because they tell someone something that we appreciate or like about them. For our closing today, we are going to have a chance to share an appreciation we have for somebody in our class.

To help give students ideas, you can prepare them for the activity by brainstorming a list of compliments and/or things people would be happy to hear. Another way to prepare them would be to model appreciations by going around the group and giving a compliment or thank you to each child before inviting students to share.

The sharing could be done as a go-round using the Talking Object, or popcorn style, by asking: **Who has an appreciation they would like to give someone in our group today?**

Extensions and Infusion Ideas

Kindness Campaign

You will need a box of several hundred objects to use to signify acts of kindness. Many things can be used: dried macaroni or bow-tie pasta; large dried beans, such as lima beans; uniform, medium-sized pebbles, etc. You could put the objects in a jar, or they could be glued onto a large poster, perhaps a heart, until the heart becomes filled with symbols of the kind actions of students.

Show the children the box of objects and the glass jar and explain that any time you see someone being kind to someone else, you will put an object from this box into the glass jar. **What are some examples of words I might hear people using with each other that would be a reason for me to put an object in the jar? What kinds of actions could I see that would lead me to put an object in the jar?**

Start the campaign. Each time you put an object in the jar, describe to the children the kind words you heard or act you saw. After a few days, invite the children to take part. Have group meetings and ask the children to describe any acts of kindness they have seen. Each child who saw an act of kindness gets to put an object in the jar.

Friendship Necklaces

For this activity you will need macaroni and other pasta shapes with holes, paints and brushes for painting pasta, and yarn.

Divide the children into pairs and explain that the pairs are Partner Pals. Explain that the purpose of the activity is for everyone to make a gift for his or her Partner Pal.

Have children paint the pasta. Set the painted pasta aside on trays marked with each child's name. Allow plenty of time for the painted pasta to dry (usually one day).

When the pasta is dry, give children pieces of yarn on which to string their "beads." As children finish stringing the pasta, circulate and tie the ends of the yarn. When both Partner Pals are finished, they can present their Friendship Necklaces to each other.

Encouraging Gentleness

For this activity you will need to arrange for a visit by a small, tame pet like a rabbit, guinea pig, or hamster.

Being gentle is one way of demonstrating kindness. Ask students to tell you what it means to be gentle. Discuss when people might need others to be gentle with them, and ways that people can be gentle with each other.

Bring the pet into the circle and explain that this is an opportunity for the students to show how gentle they can be. Pass the pet around the circle, helping where needed and commenting on the gentle, kind behavior you observe.

Allow children to pass if they would rather not hold the pet and gently take the pet from anyone who is handling it too roughly. Any sudden movements of the animals can startle children and they may react aggressively. Without scolding the student, identify inappropriate handling and suggest alternative ways for the student to deal with the pet's behavior.

Environmental Projects

Explain to students how important it is for people to be kind to nature and to their environment. Help them see that by tending to plants or cleaning up a park or playground, they are behaving kindly.

Choose a project that the whole class can be involved in and wants to participate in. Ideas include:

- Growing plants from seeds or seedlings.

- Agreeing to water any plants on the school campus that may need attention. (During recess time, pairs of students could rotate responsibility to take water to the plants.)

- Have a litter collection campaign.

The Flower, the Cloud, and the Wind

With the students sitting in a circle, say: **We're going to tell a story with our hands. I'll tell the story. You help me tell it by using your hands to show what's happening.**

Once upon a time there was a flower that lived on a hill. (With one hand make gestures resembling the petals of a flower. Ask the students to do the same.)

It was a wonderful, beautiful flower because it got lots of water to drink from the rain. But as it happens sometimes, it didn't rain on that hill for two whole weeks. The flower got thirsty, and there was no water. When there is no water, flowers droop and wilt. (Discuss meanings of *droop* and *wilt*. It was a very sick flower. Teacher and students show the flower wilting and drooping with one hand.)

One day, one white cloud drifted by. (Form a "cloud," drifting, with the other hand. Move the "cloud" over the "flower.")

It looked down on the hill and saw the little wilted flower. "Oh, no!" the cloud thought. "If that flower doesn't get some rain it's going to die! I cannot let that happen. I cannot forget. I won't pass it by."

The wind saw how upset the cloud was, and said, "Why are you so sad, white cloud in the sky?" (Make the blowing sound of the wind.)

The cloud said, (Use the cloud hand in expressive ways during the next few lines – showing concern, drifting on the wind to the river, drinking up water from the river, raining and sprinkling water on the flower.) **"Oh, I never want that flower below to die. See how it is thirsty, see how it is dry.**

I cannot forget. I won't pass on by.

Oh my friend the wind, take me to the river.

I'll drink up the water so I can rain and sprinkle. When that tiny flower feels the rain from above

I'll be smiling back my smile of love."

So the flower drank up all the rain from the loving cloud above and came back to life. Use a big, celebratory gesture that encompasses the whole body to show the flower coming back to life.

Lead the class in a big round of applause for all their hand gestures. Then lead a discussion with the following questions:

- Why did the flower wilt?

- What did the flower need?

- How did the cloud show caring?

- What did the cloud do to help the flower?

- Who helped the cloud get the water for the flower?

- How did the cloud feel at the end?

- How did the flower feel at the end?

"Song of the Cloud"

The story of the cloud and the flower is based on the song called, "The Song of the Cloud," by Adrian Ramirez Flores and Robert Diaz, and can be found in the book *Linking Up!* and on the *Linking Up!* CD, Track 22. It's a very simple tune that can easily be sung to the class. Have the children listen to the song and at the same time do the hand gestures they learned above.

Connecting to Literature

Selfish Sophie, by Damian Kelleher
(Minneapolis: Picture Window Books, 2003) Gr. P-2

Summary: Sophie won't share anything, and has no friends, until a classmate shares his umbrella.

1. What does this story tell us about sharing?

2. How did Sophie learn that sharing could be fun?

3. Can you think of times when it is hard to share?

4. How can we help each other have fun sharing?

5. Tell about a time when someone shared something with you. Tell about a time when you helped someone else.

Oh, Bother! Someone Won't Share!, by Betty Birney
(Racine, WI: Western Publishing Company, Inc., 1993) Gr. K-3

Summary: Rabbit refuses to share his vegetables until an early frost brings the help of the others.

1. One of the ways to be kind is to share. Name some ways Rabbit's friends shared with him.

2. Why did Rabbit enjoy sharing?

3. Name something you can share with your friends.

Cherries and Cherry Pits, by Vera B. Williams
(New York: Mulberry Books, 1986) Gr. K-3

Summary: Bidemmi draws pictures of people feeding cherries to others and then planting the pits.

1. This story is full of examples of ways to be kind. Name some ways people in the story are kind to each other.

2. When Bidemmi plants the seeds, is that an example of kindness? How?

3. Tell about times when you can use food to do something kind.

GRADE K, LESSON 10
Helping Others

Gathering: Something I'm Good at Doing

Have students sit in a circle. Holding the Talking Object, introduce the gathering by saying something like: **Everyone is good at some things and not so good at others. For our gathering today, I would like you to think about something you are good at doing. There might be some things that we are all good at, but I would like you to think just about you. What is something you can do well?** Model by telling students something you do well and then passing the Talking Object to the next student.

Agenda Check

In our last lesson we talked about being kind. Today we are going to focus on how we can help others. Really helping and doing things for others is what most kindness is all about. First we are going to do a fun activity that will allow us to help and lead (Beanbag Partners). **Each of us has special gifts that we can use to help each other. We will see what those special things are and make a chart to show the different things that each of us knows how to do and that can help those of us who may need help** (Helper Chart). **Then we'll end our lesson with a Closing** (Closing).

Activity: Beanbag Partners

1. Explain the activity by saying: **In this game, each of you is going to have an opportunity to help and coach your partner and an opportunity to be helped by your partner. One person in each pair will get a beanbag. The goal is to walk around with the beanbag on your head. If you are the person with the beanbag, you will put the beanbag on your own head, but you cannot touch it after that. You may not keep the beanbag from falling, or pick it up if it falls on the floor. Your partner's job will be to help you. If the beanbag falls, she can pick it up and give it to you to put back on your head. Your partner can also help you learn to balance the beanbag better by giving you advice like, "I think it might work better if you put the bag a little further back on your head," or "I think you're doing great, but it might help to turn more slowly."**

2. Group students in pairs.

3. Have them decide who will be the "helper" first and give each pair a beanbag. Give them enough time to experience their roles and then have them switch places.

Workshop Agenda

- Gathering: Something I'm Good at Doing
- Agenda Check
- Activity: Beanbag Partners
- Activity: Helper Chart
- Closing: A Time I Helped Someone

Materials

- Workshop agenda, written on chart paper and posted
- Talking Object
- Beanbags (at least one for each pair of students)
- Chart paper and markers

Learning Outcomes

- Students will be able to identify personal strengths and skills.
- Students will be able to apply their skills in a practice exercise in which they help one another.

4. Have the students re-form in the circle and have them discuss their experience by asking questions such as:

- How did it feel to help your partner?

- What was hard about helping? What was easy?

- When you had the beanbag, what kinds of things did your partner do that were helpful?

- How did it feel to be helped by your partner?

Activity: Helper Chart

1. Prepare a chart ahead of time that lists classroom tasks at which not all students are equally proficient. Icons can also be used. Include things that some students sometimes ask for your help with, but that other students can perform. Some possible tasks include:

- Tying shoelaces

- Zipping and buttoning jackets

- Writing letters

- Cutting with scissors

- Washing paintbrushes

- Caring for class animals

- Drawing objects

- Putting together puzzles

- Building with blocks

2. Introduce the activity by saying something like: **In the gathering, we all talked about things that we can do well. We all have different talents. We've also seen that helping others can be very fun. When we are in a group, we should help each other by sharing our special talents. To help us do that better, I thought we could make a chart that would show the things we are good at so we would know who we could ask for help if we needed it. I call it the Helper Chart.**

3. Show students the chart and explain that you have already listed some tasks that students might be able to help each other with. Say: **I'm going to read the different things I've already put on the chart. Then we'll go back and see who might volunteer to put her name next to something that she can do well, so that people who need help with that task will know who to ask. Then we can add some other tasks that you think of to the chart and put up the names of people who can help with those tasks, too.**

4. As you read through the chart, ask students to be thinking about what task they are good at and where they think their name should go. The second time through, have discussions about what names to put next to each task. It is probably best to keep the list of names to two or three for each task.

5. Elicit other tasks that could be added to the chart. Try to elicit enough different tasks so that each child can have her name next to at least one thing on the chart. For students who could qualify to help others with many tasks, you might choose or ask them to choose the two things they could be most helpful with.

6. When the chart is completed, post it prominently somewhere in the room and encourage students to consult it when they need help.

Closing: A Time I Helped Someone

We started out today talking about things we can do well. Then we got a chance to help a partner in the beanbag activity, and finally we made a chart of things we can help others with. How does it feel to help others?

For our closing today, I would like you to think about how you have helped others in the past. Maybe you have a baby brother or sister that you help with all the time. Maybe you'll think of something you have done to help a parent. I've noticed many ways people have helped each other in class or have helped me.

This can be done as a go-round or popcorn style. Have students share a concrete example of a time they helped someone. What kind of help was needed? What did they do? What happened in the end? How did people feel?

Extensions and Infusion Ideas

Classroom Problem Solving

When a problem comes up in the classroom, ask students to meet and help you solve it. For example, if you notice you are spending more and more time waiting for the class to line up, you could tell them that you have a problem and ask if they might be willing to help you solve it.

For example, explain that you have been feeling _____ (annoyed, irritated, grouchy) lately when the class lines up because it seems to take so much time. **Sometimes, when I am feeling this way, I am not as kind as I would like to be. Sometimes I even think I sound a little mean, and I don't feel good about that. I was wondering if you have some ideas to help me solve my problem.**

Invite students to brainstorm and problem-solve things that could be done to speed things up. Discuss the pros and cons of different ideas, decide on which idea seems best to try, and get a commitment from the class to see if it will work. (More information about class meetings is available at Operation Respect *Don't Laugh at Me* Teacher Guide: http://www.operationrespect.org.)

Food Drives

Find out about organizations in your community that collect food for the hungry. Make arrangements with one of them to have your class participate in a food drive.

In a letter to parents, describe the food drive and give them information about the date you plan to invite students to bring one can or box of food to school for your local organization. Discuss with students the different ways people in a community help each other; for example, by sharing things they have that are needed by people who are less fortunate. Tell students that some families and children do not have enough food to eat and are hungry. Suggest different types of food that are needed and discuss the importance of nutritious food. Tell students about the letter you are sending home to their families asking them to donate a can or box of food that their children can give to the hungry. On the day of collection, you might give students a can or box of food if they didn't bring any from home. It would be great to have someone from the organization come to school to pick up the food and talk with the students about the organization's work, or if you can manage it, have your class deliver the goods themselves.

Frozen Beanbag

This is a more complex, advanced version of Beanbag Partners. For this activity, you will need a beanbag for every student.

Give each student a beanbag to put on her head. Each student then moves around the area. If the beanbag slips off a child's head, she is "frozen" and must stop moving. The child should stand like a statue in the position she was in when the beanbag fell. Students who see someone frozen should try to help that person by picking up the beanbag and putting it back on the frozen student's head. If the helper's beanbag falls off while she is helping, then she is frozen as well. Soon everyone will be frozen.

Wizards and Gelflings

Mark off a boundary ahead of time. For a running tag game, set off a large area; for a walking tag game, keep the area smaller.

Explain this cooperative tag game to the children by saying: **We are taking a trip to a very special land where there are two types of people, Wizards and Gelflings. The Wizards want everyone in the land to be like them, so they use their magic powers to freeze the Gelflings. The Gelflings like themselves the way they are. To fight off the Wizards, they must cooperate.**

Ask for two volunteers to be the Wizards. Their goal is to tag all the Gelflings. Once a Gelfling is tagged, she is frozen and cannot move. The rest of the group are Gelflings. The Gelflings' goal is to stay away from the Wizards.

If a Gelfling is tagged and frozen, they can be helped. But help can only be given if a frozen Gelfling asks for it. Once she has asked for help, two unfrozen Gelflings can help by making a ring around the frozen student with their arms and saying, "Be free, Gelfling!" This unfreezes the frozen Gelfling.

Show the students the area for play, and tell them that all players must stay in bounds. The game continues for as long as it is still fun for all (or until all the Gelflings are frozen).

Connecting to Literature

As you read books and stories, help students see where and how characters help each other and what the results of their efforts are.

Big Al and Shrimpy, by Andrew Clements
(New York: Simon & Schuster Books for Young Readers, 2002) Gr. K-3

Summary: When Big Al gets caught in the Big Deep (the ocean), a tiny fish coordinates his rescue.

1. How did Shrimpy and the other little fish help Big Al?

2. Shrimpy showed that you don't have to be big in order to help others. Is there a way that you can help the bigger children in this school?

Chicken Chickens, by Valeri Gorbachev
(New York: North-South Books, 2001) Gr. P-2

Summary: Unlike his companions, who tease the little chickens for being scared of the slide, Beaver helps them go down.

1. After Beaver says he has an idea, ask: What do you think Beaver's idea is?

2. After reading the book, say: Beaver was a helpful friend. Name some ways you can be helpful friends to each other:

    a. on our playground

    b. in our classroom

    c. in our cafeteria

Swimmy, by Leo Leonni
(New York: Alfred Knopf, 1963)

Summary: Swimmy is the lone survivor of a school of fish who have been eaten by a big fish and must find a new group to swim with.

1. Why were the red fish swimming in the dark shade?

2. Where did they want to swim?

3. How did Swimmy help the fish?

4. How did the fish help each other?

Further Suggestions

Peach & Blue, by Sarah Kilborne
(New York: Dragonfly Books, 1998)

Summary: A beautiful story of a frog who helps a peach see the world. It gently makes the point that helping others who are disabled in some way can bring as many benefits to the helper as it brings to the person being helped. It also gently brings up the inevitability of death and the importance of reaching out to others in the present.

Miss Tizzy, by Libba Moore Gray
(New York: Aladdin, 1998)

Summary: The story of an eccentric old lady whom the neighborhood children adored. Together, they do all kinds of fun things, including making pictures full of sunshine and butterflies for folks who had stopped smiling. When Miss Tizzy becomes ill, the children know just what to do to let her know she is missed and loved.

Strong Listening

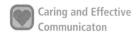
Caring and Effective Communicaton

CASEL SEL COMPETENCIES

SO   Social Awareness

RS   Relationship Skills

Gathering: Zoom

Have children sit or stand in a circle. Explain that the goal of this game is to pass the word *ZOOM* around the circle. **I will start to say the word *ZOOM* and keep saying the beginning of the word until I have made eye contact with the person on my right, who will say the word next. As soon as our eyes meet, I will finish saying the word. I have just "passed it" to the next person. That person will start to say the first part of the word, turn to the next person, make eye contact, and finish saying the word.**

Begin the activity. Say, "**ZZZZZ...**" and turn your head to the child on your right. Look that child in the eyes. When you have made eye contact, finish saying *ZOOM*. That child then begins to say *ZOOM* and then turns to the child to his right, makes eye contact, and so on. Reverse the direction and send *ZOOM* the other way.

Agenda Check

Today we are going to be talking about listening. It is probably the most important skill anybody can have. You need it to learn. It is very important in being able to help others, and you must have it in order to do a good job of solving problems and getting along with others. Being a good listener is one of the most important things that makes us strong as a person. (Review the difference between physical strength and inner strength.)

What did we have to do in order to pass the word, *ZOOM*, around the group? We are going to look at how these things and others make up good, strong listening (Good Listening). **Then we will practice in an activity called Listening Circles** (Listening Circles). **We'll close our lesson by talking about what we did and singing a song** (Closing).

Activity: Good Listening

You will need to find another person, preferably another adult, to tell you a story about a vacation, or what they like to do on weekends as you demonstrate good listening. If another adult is not available, the exercise can be done with a student as the speaker. Choose a verbal, self-assured student and tell him beforehand what you will be doing.

1. Introduce the activity by saying: **We are going to create a Good Listening chart that includes all the important things a strong listener does. Then you will get to test me on my listening skills.**

Workshop Agenda

- Gathering: Zoom
- Agenda Check
- Activity: Good Listening
- Activity: Listening Circles
- Closing: Summary

Materials

- Workshop agenda, written on chart paper and posted
- Chart paper and markers
- Several Talking Objects, one for every group of three students

Learning Outcomes

- Students will identify effective listening skills.
- Students will be able to listen and paraphrase what is being said.

2. Facilitate a discussion about what comprises good listening and chart specific behaviors that come up in the discussion. Icons that illustrate the simple words can be great. The chart will probably include some of the following:

   - Making eye contact
   - Keeping body still
   - Sitting up
   - Paying attention (or thinking about what the speaker is saying)
   - Not interrupting

3. Through creative questions, you might get a more advanced group to acknowledge the usefulness of nodding, smiling, asking a good question about what the speaker said, or repeating what was said.

4. Once the group has come up with a chart, ask them to use it to test your listening. Invite the other adult or the student who is going to tell you a story to come up to the front of the group. Have him start talking.

5. Model both attentive listening (following all the things on the chart) as well as poor listening (glancing around the room, yawning, looking bored, laughing inappropriately, interrupting, changing the subject, etc.) Freeze the exercise frequently and ask the class what they notice and whether or not they think you are doing a good job of listening.

6. Ask the speaker how he felt when you were listening carefully and how he felt when you were not listening carefully.

Activity: Listening Circles

1. Introduce the activity by saying: **One of the ways we can let someone know that we are listening carefully is to say back, or repeat, what the person said. We are now going to participate in a game where we can practice doing this. Doing all the things on our Good Listening chart will help us be able to do this well.**

2. Choose three students to come and sit in a small circle in the middle of the group. Show the class what you are going to use as a Talking Object, and give one to one of the students in the small group. Remind them that only the person with the Talking Object will talk.

3. Suggest one of the following topics (or make up your own) for the children to talk about:

   - Describe your favorite game.
   - What do you like to do on the playground?

4. Have the student holding the Talking Object speak to the second child on the chosen topic. Then hand the Talking Object to the second child.

5. The second child repeats to the third child what the first child said and hands the Talking Object to him or her.

6. The third child then tells the description back to the first child. Things get mixed up if the children didn't listen well!

7. Briefly discuss what just occured in the demonstration group.

8. Have all students sit in groups of three and give one student in each group a Talking Object.

9. Repeat the same directions, with all students participating.

10. Repeat the game with the second child in each group speaking first, then with the third child speaking first. Children may now be listening better and recognize more of the original description.

11. Play the game again, with a new subject and new groups of children.

Closing: Summary

Good listening can be hard work. What was one thing you learned today about listening? What's one thing that you do that makes you a good listener? How does it feel when someone listens to you well?

Since the feelings that will be shared in response to the last question are usually "Good," "Great,"and "Happy," you could end the lesson by singing, "If You're Happy and You Know It" (See pages 30 and 31).

Extensions and Infusion Ideas

Listening Web

For this activity you will need a ball of thick, brightly colored yarn.

Have students stand in a circle. Explain: **In this game, we will get to make a web with this ball of yarn while we practice being a strong listener. Before we start, I would like you to think to yourself, without saying anything out loud, what your favorite food is. Then one person at a time will tell us what that food is, but before they do that, they have to repeat what the last person said his favorite food was.**

Give the end of the yarn to a student. Ask that student to hold the end without letting it go. Ask him to tell the group his favorite food (or color, game, storybook character, etc). Take the ball of yarn, unraveling it as you walk into the center of the circle and ask who can tell you what the first person said. Choose a student, stretch the yarn over to that person and ask him to hold on to the section of yarn that just reaches him. He should say the first person's name and repeat what he said, and then tell the group his own favorite food.

Take the ball of yarn over to another student across the circle, have him share the last person's name and favorite food and then share his own. You will have to carry the ball of yarn around to the next student from the outside of the circle unless you can crouch underneath the web as it crosses back and forth. Continue until everyone has had a turn and the group has created an intricate, colorful web of listening.

Listening without Ears

- Tell students you would like to see if they can understand something that is being expressed without using any words. Share several common nonverbal hand signals, like hello, come here, stop, etc.

- Have students watch part of a movie or television program with the sound off. Have them guess what is being communicated by the actions and facial expressions of people on the screen.

- While others observe, try directing a group of students, or the entire class in some simple movements around the class without using any words. Discuss what students observed and what they learned from the above activities.

Mirrors

This is a good activity to use to help students learn to tune in and focus on another person. It can also be a good calming-down activity.

Tell students they are going to play a game of mirroring. Have a volunteer come up to help you demonstrate what they will all be doing. Ask the volunteer to stand facing you and ask him to copy all your movements, just as if he were a mirror. Tell students the goal is to work together so that someone just coming in the room will not be able to tell who is initiating the movements. Point out that the person initiating will need to move slowly in order for the game to work. Divide students into pairs, facing one another. (See Teaching Tools for suggestions about pairing students.) Have pairs choose one person to be A and one to be B. Person B reflects all the movements initiated by Person A, including facial expressions. After a short time, call "Change," so that the positions are reversed. Ask: **Was it difficult to mirror someone? What did it feel like? Did you feel you worked together well enough so that an outsider would not know which one of you was the mirror?**

Connecting to Literature

Oh, Bother! No One's Listening, by Nikki Grimes
(New York: A Golden Book, 1997) Gr. P-2

Summary: No one listens to Rabbit's directions for planning a picnic, and they show up with the wrong things – but they work out a solution.

1. After Rabbit asks if there are any questions, ask: How would you feel if you were Rabbit, trying to plan the party?

2. After reading the book, say: Name some things that Pooh and his friends were doing instead of listening to Rabbit.

3. What would have happened if Pooh and his friends had not listened the second time?

Mean vs. Strong

Caring and Effective
Communication

CASEL SEL COMPETENCIES

SM Self-Management
RS Relationship Skills

Gathering: Favorite Story

Have students sit in a circle. Explain: **In a minute, we will use the Talking Object to share with each other something that, for now, I just want you think about. The question is this: "What is your favorite story, and why?" You have read many different fairy tales, books, and stories, as well as seen movies of stories you have read. What is your favorite story, and why?**

You may want to model by talking first, or if you think your students know how to do go-rounds well, you might ask a student to start. This avoids the temptation for some children to be influenced by your story choice and allows students more of a leadership role.

Agenda Check

In our last lesson we studied how to be a strong listener. Today we are going to talk a little more about what it really means to be *strong*. **We got to tell each other about our favorite stories in the gathering** (Gathering). **Today we will participate in a story about the sun and the wind** ("The Sun and the Wind"). **Then we will look at the differences between being "mean" and being "strong." We'll end our lesson with a closing that will allow you to see how much you've learned about being strong** (Closing).

Activity: "The Sun and the Wind"

Prepare for this activity by learning the story, "The Sun and the Wind," which follows, as well as the Sun's song.

1. Explain that you are going to tell them a story called "The Sun and the Wind." There are two parts in this story. Say: **When the Wind speaks, we will wave our arms in the air and make whooshing sounds. When the Sun speaks, we will spread our fingers wide and hold our hands with our thumbs pointing towards our ears.**

2. Teach the children the song the Sun sings. Use the tune of the song, "You Are My Sunshine."

   I am the sunshine. I am the sunshine.

   I spread happiness. Oh, yes I do.

   I shine with kindness, I shine with caring.

   You can be like sunshine, too.

3. Tell the story, giving the Wind a harsh voice and the Sun a gentle one.

Workshop Agenda

- Gathering: Favorite Story
- Agenda Check
- Activity: "The Sun and the Wind"
- Activity: Mean vs. Strong
- Closing: Open Fist

Materials

- Workshop agenda, written on chart paper and posted
- Talking Object

Learning Outcomes

- Students will be able to distinguish between aggressive communication and assertive communication.
- Students will discuss the advantages of assertive communication.

The Sun and the Wind

The Wind had been blowing its cold, prickly breath all morning long and was feeling very, very strong. (Make a whooshing sound. Wave arms around.)

The Sun had been shining its bright light all morning long and was also feeling strong. (Spread hands wide, thumbs pointed at your ears.)

The Sun sang to itself as it shone.

> I am the sunshine. I am the sunshine.
>
> I spread happiness. Oh, yes I do.
>
> I shine with kindness, I shine with caring.
>
> You can be like sunshine, too.

The Wind thought it was better than the Sun. "When I blow my cold, prickly breath I am more powerful than you," hissed the Wind to the Sun. (Make a whooshing sound. Wave arms around.)

"No, you're not," smiled the Sun, and shook her head with glee. (Spread hands wide, thumbs pointed at your ears.)

"You are not stronger than I, for..." and the Sun began to sing its song.

> I am the sunshine. I am the sunshine.
>
> I spread happiness. Oh, yes I do.
>
> I shine with kindness, I shine with caring.
>
> You can be like sunshine, too.

The Wind did not like the Sun's song. Scowling and wagging its finger at the Sun, the Wind argued back, "No. No. I am more powerful than you!"

"No, you're not," smiled the Sun. (Spread hands wide, thumbs pointed at your ears.)

"Yes, I am."

"No, you're not"

"Yes, I am."

"Okay. Let's see who is the strongest," challenged the Sun. "Do you see those children waiting for the bus to take them to school? They all have on their winter coats, hats, mittens, and scarves. Let's see which one of us is powerful enough to get the children to take off their winter clothes."

"Okay," said the Wind. "I accept your challenge."

So the Wind began to blow its cold, icy breath at the children. (Make a whooshing sound. Wave arms around.)

It blew and blew for all it was worth. It pushed and pushed at the children. It pulled and pulled at them.

But the more the Wind blew and pushed and pulled, the more the children held their coats, hats, mittens, and scarves closer and closer to their bodies. The Wind tried and tried and tried, but it could not get the children to take off their winter clothes.

"Now it's my turn," smiled the Sun. (Spread hands wide, thumbs pointed at your ears.)

The Sun shone sunny beams all over the children's faces and bodies. The children began to feel warm. The Sun shone brighter and brighter. The children felt warmer and warmer and warmer. They began to unbutton their coats. They took off their scarves. They took off their mittens. They took off their hats. They took off their coats.

"You are not more powerful than I," said the Sun.
"I see that you are right," replied the Wind.

The Sun sang its song. As the children waited for the bus, holding all their winter clothes in their arms, they sang the Sun's song, too. And the Wind decided to join in by dancing gently around the children as they sang...

We are the sunshine. We are the sunshine.

We spread happiness. Oh, yes we do.

We shine with kindness, we shine with caring.

You can be like sunshine, too.

Activity: Mean vs. Strong

1. Explain: **Most of the time when we think of being strong, we think about "muscle" strong. But we have been learning that there are other ways to be strong. How do we show that we are strong listeners? What are strong ways of dealing with angry feelings?**

    The Wind definitely used more force than the Sun, he had more muscle strength. But it was the Sun, spreading happiness and sunshine, who turned out to be stronger in the long run.

    It's not good to be weak, to let other people do wrong things, to hurt you, or to always let them get their way. But no one has to be mean when she is standing up for something. The story helped us see that being strong is *very* different from being mean. Even though it is hard to learn, you can always be kind, even when you are being strong.

    Now we are going to learn and practice being strong in different situations.

2. Choose a situation and tell students what the situation is and who you are going to pretend to be. Possible situations:

    · Child telling a parent they don't like something

    · Child telling a friend they want to play a different game

- Child telling a sibling that they want them to not touch something they've built

- Student telling a classmate that it's his or her turn at something

3. Communicate the situation in an aggressive, mean way and ask students if that was mean or strong. Ask questions about tone of voice, choice of words, facial expressions, and body actions that go with being "mean." Then communicate the same message in a strong, authoritative, but respectful way. Have students analyze specific qualities (tone, words, expression, actions) that make the message strong.

For example: **You are a student and your tablemate has spread his things over on your side of the table leaving you no room for your things.** (Face very angry and voice very loud.) **You are such a pig! Get this junk off my side of the table!** (Pretend to violently push things away.) Discuss with class. Then role-play in a strong way. (Face neither angry nor happy, tone of voice firm, at a normal volume level.) **John, I need more room for my things. Please move your things to your side of the table.** Discuss with class.

4. After students have analyzed and labeled the examples of mean and strong communication that you have role-played, choose another scenario. Ask students what a *mean* response might sound or look like. Ask how they would communicate the same message in a *strong* way. Help students craft strong statements, both in words and tone of voice as well as body language and actions. (As students contribute responses, you can role-play the recipient of the message, helping them see the resistance to *mean* messages and the effectiveness of *strong* ones.)

5. Repeat as long as time and interest support more practice.

Closing: Open Fist

We've done a lot of good work today. What do you think is the most important thing we have learned? As a closing, I have a challenge. Let's see how much we have learned about being strong. (Make a fist with one hand, palm side up, in front of the students.) **If I asked you to try and get my fist open, how might you try to do it in a mean way?** Acknowledge responses (hurting, force, rude speech). If you would like, you could have someone come up and try to pry your hand open (as long as you know you could keep it closed). Then ask: **What's a strong way someone might try to get me to open my fist?** Acknowledge responses, and invite a student with one of the strongest verbal requests to come up and use it. Open your hand, of course! Summarize by saying something like: **You can be strong without being mean or violent.**

Extensions and Infusion Ideas

Weak or Strong

This activity is designed to help students who may have difficulty because they are "too nice" when asserting. It allows students to practice communicating messages with strong voice inflection and body language.

Review the difference between being mean and strong by choosing one of the following assertive statements and delivering it first in a mean way and then a strong way. Have students identify which is which and point out differences in voice tone, volume, and body language. Then ask students: **What's wrong with this message?** Deliver the same statement, but in a very passive, weak way. (Body slumped, head downward, voice very low, mumbling and/or using an overly sweet tone.)

Help students identify what makes the statement weak. Have them take turns practicing one of the statements below in a strong manner.

- "I don't like that."
- "Leave me alone."
- "I don't want you to bother me any more."
- "Stop that!"

Teachable Moments

When dealing with individual student behavior or conflicts between students, help students reflect on "mean" ways they have attempted to fulfill a need. Challenge them to brainstorm "strong" alternatives they could have used. Have them role-play and rehearse effective responses. When appropriate, help guide their ability to deliver strong messages to each other. When there is physical aggression or a threat, sometimes a simple reminder to "Use your words" can accomplish the goal. Of course, students need to have already learned how to "use strong words," but they have to have many opportunities to practice, practice, practice. You can help by taking the role of a coach instead of solving issues directly as the adult.

(Note: *It is always important to make sure a student is calm enough for a learning experience. If they are really angry or upset, they will need an adequate time to cool down before a "teachable moment" can be effective.*)

When there is physical aggression or a threat, sometimes a simple reminder to "Use your words" can accomplish the goal.

Connecting to Literature

Move over, Twerp, by Martha Alexander
(New York: Dial Books, 1981) Gr. K-3

Summary: Big boys take Jeffrey's seat on the school bus. He tries unsuccessfully to fight back and then uses humor to settle the fight.

1. In this story, Jeffrey is shown on three different bus rides. Tell how he acted and talked on each one. Why did he get to keep his seat on the last ride? Was Jeffrey mean or strong?

2. How did the other kids on the bus act the first two times? The last time?

3. What could Jeffrey do if he thinks the bigger kids might hurt him?

The Berenstain Bears and the Trouble with Friends, by Stan and Jan Berenstain (New York: Random House, 1986) Gr. K-3

Summary: Sister meets Lizzy Bruin, who is "bossy and braggy." After a fight, they make up and decide to take turns.

1. When Lizzy wanted to be the teacher, she and Sister used mean words with each other.

    a. How did their argument get worse?

    b. What strong words could they have used instead?

2. Why did Sister and Lizzy find it hard to play together at first?

3. How did Sister and Lizzy learn to play well together?

Mufaro's Beautiful Daughters, by John Steptoe (New York: Amistad, 1987) Gr. K-2

Summary: Based on an African folktale. Mufaro has two beautiful daughters, but one is mean and selfish and the other is kind and considerate. When the King decides to consider both girls for marriage, he cares about more than just beauty.

1. Are you like Nyasha in any ways?

2. If Nyasha saw someone being unfair in a game, what do you think she would say?

3. If Nyasha saw someone being teased, what would she do?

4. Do you ever act like Manyara?

5. Nyasha showed her strength in the way she helped others. Have any good things happened to you when you have been kind to other people?

Conflicts and Problem Solving

CASEL SEL COMPETENCIES

SM   Self-Management

DM   Responsible Decision Making

RS   Relationship Skills

Gathering: If I Were an Animal

Have students sit in a circle. Explain: **Before we start our lesson today, I would like you to think about something. In a minute, we will use the Talking Object to share with each other the answers that you come up with. The question is this, "If you were an animal, what kind of animal would you be?" Just take a moment to think what animal seems right for you.**

If you would like, you could brainstorm a list of many different animals to help students think. Choose one student to start, or model by saying what animal you would be. Have each person share what animal he thought best represented him and a brief reason, if possible.

Agenda Check

Today we are going to be talking about problems and conflicts. An example of a conflict is a fight or disagreement. Who has a pet at home? Does your pet always get along with other animals? If there are problems, what kind of things can cause them? What do animals do when they get into conflicts? How do they solve them? What's the difference between animals and humans?

People have conflicts and problems with each other all the time. Today we are going to look at problems or conflicts we can get into and how we deal with them. We will look at and discuss some pictures (Problem Pictures) **and then we'll talk a little bit about conflict** (Conflicts). **We'll end by sharing some stories about conflicts we've had and how we have solved them** (Closing).

Activity: Problem Pictures

See pictures on page 75, 76, 77, and 78. Pictures can be photocopied and enlarged before hand.

1. Explain the activity by saying: **We're going to look at some pictures and talk about the problems we see.**

2. Show students the first picture (page 75) and have them describe what they see, or make up a brief story, giving names to the students in the picture. Have students verbalize what emotion they think is being expressed.

Workshop Agenda

- Gathering: If I Were an Animal
- Agenda Check
- Activity: Problem Pictures
- Activity: Conflicts
- Closing: Recent Conflicts

Materials

- Workshop agenda, written on chart paper and posted
- Talking Object
- Problem Pictures
- Chart paper and markers

Learning Outcomes

- Students will be able to identify and describe conflicts.
- Students will be able to identify more than one solution to a problem.

3. Say: **The conflict is that both boys want to look at the same book.**

   What would be a mean way they might use to try and get what they want? If they did that, what do you think would happen? How could they talk about their problem in a strong way, instead? What are some ways they could solve their conflict?

4. Show the next picture (page 76) and have students describe what they see. Summarize: **Here, the problem has been caused by an accident.** (The middle child, who has fallen off her chair, has accidentally broken the other student's cat creation.) Help students see how the student who caused the accident is feeling. Ask: **What might happen if one of the children yells at her in a mean way?** Have students articulate strong ways the children in the picture could handle the situation. Help them see that if the middle child apologized, that would be an example of being strong.

5. Discuss the third picture (page 77). This is an opportunity to talk about the importance of patience and what students can do when they need to wait for a long time. If the child at the fountain is playing around, what can the other students say or do that would be a strong way of confronting the problem? Say: **Here the conflict can happen because someone is acting selfishly and not considering others. Could a conflict start between two students who are waiting in line? What if, because everyone is feeling annoyed and impatient, someone bumps into the person in front of him? How could a fight start? What could the person who was bumped say, in a strong way, which might help resolve the conflict?**

6. Show the last picture. Define the problem as a disagreement over what game to play with the ball. The two people on the right want to play one game and the other children want to play a different game. Say: **Being mean would just make the problem worse. We are going to try and think of as many different solutions as possible. What is one thing they could do to solve their conflict in a strong way?** If someone suggests a solution that would not be good for everyone, ask how the losing students would feel and if they think the solution is mean or strong. After a positive solution is offered, ask how one of the students in the picture could suggest the idea in a strong way. Have a volunteer role-play what he would say. The goal is to give students practice using strong communication to suggest positive solutions to conflicts.

7. Acknowledge the first solution as one of several that are possible and then ask for others. You might want to chart ideas. The goal here is for students to experience brainstorming and to see that there are many possible win-win solutions to conflicts. Briefly discuss each idea and have students role-play how this idea could be communicated to others in the situation.

Activity: Conflicts

1. Explain: **Today we have been talking about conflicts.** (You may want to write out the word, have students sound it out, or say the word together.) **A conflict is a problem in which people's "wants" don't go together very easily. Sometimes we call conflicts arguments or fights.**

   It would be helpful to illustrate the concept with examples of conflicts that happened in the class recently, as long as individuals are not put on the spot.

2. Ask: **Who are some of the people we have conflicts with? Do friends sometimes have conflicts? What about brothers and sisters? There are many conflicts between parents and children. What is a conflict you've had with a parent?**

3. Say: **Wanting to do something that someone else doesn't want you to do is one thing that can cause a conflict. The pictures we just looked at showed some other things that could start a conflict. Think about a conflict you've had recently. What else could cause a conflict?**

4. Continue: **Conflicts happen everyday. When they start they can either get worse and get stuck or they can get better and/or be solved. Again, think about a conflict you've had recently. What makes conflicts get bigger or worse?** (Not controlling our own feelings, saying things in mean ways, aggressive actions, etc.) **What helps make a conflict better?** (Staying calm, acting and talking in strong ways, considering everyone's views and needs.)

Closing: Recent Conflicts

For the closing today, I would like you to think about a conflict or problem you have had recently and how you solved it. Have students share stories either as a go-round with the Talking Object, or popcorn style, with as many students sharing stories as you would like.

Extensions and Infusion Ideas

Role-Plays

Have students role-play the situations depicted in the Problem Pictures, and help them to use strong listening and communicating skills.

Art – Puppets

(Note: *For this activity you will need small paper bags for each student, yarn and glue for hair, scissors, crayons and markers.*)

Have students create puppets using the paper bags, yarn for hair and eyebrows, and crayons, and markers for drawing faces on the puppets. Have students use the puppets to role-play conflict resolution strategies.

The Hating Book

Explain: **Mistakes in communication can cause conflicts. These kinds of mistakes can be called *misunderstandings*. When we get the message clearly that someone sends to us, we say we "understand." Sometimes we think we get the message right, but we don't. We call that a misunderstanding.** Share an example of a misunderstanding that has recently happened in the classroom.

Read *The Hating Book*, by Charlotte Zolotow (New York: Harper Collins, 1969), to students. This short book tells the story of two friends who get into a feud as the result of a misunderstanding.

Discuss the story by asking the following questions:

- How did the conflict get started? What happened?

- What was the misunderstanding? Why was her friend acting mean to her?

- What was she feeling?

- The little girl did not want to ask her friend, "why?" What was bothering her?

- What happened when she finally did?

Divide students into pairs and ask them to try to think of examples of conflicts they have been involved in that were caused by misunderstandings. Ask them to take turns telling their partner a story about what happened, who was involved, where and when it happened, how they felt, how the other person felt, and how it ended.

Ask for volunteers to share their experience with the class, asking *who*, *what*, and *how* questions to help them tell their story. **How can conflicts like those we've been talking about be prevented? What can we do to resolve a misunderstanding?**

"Two in the Fight"

The song "Two in the Fight," can be found in the book *Linking Up!*, by Sarah Pirtle, and on the *Linking Up!* CD, Track 26. The music and lyrics can be found at the end of the lesson. The lyrics can also be read in a singsong way without knowing the music. Use your index fingers to act out this story. Ask the students to click their fingers with you and to join in on the chorus (it repeats each time) initially. As they hear the song more times, they can sing along with more and more words.

ABCD Problem Solving

If you want to continue this lesson by exposing your students to a format they can use to work through problems, you may want to teach them the ABCD Problem Solving process that can be found in Grade 1, Lesson 9.

Connecting to Literature

Almost all literature contains conflicts that drive the story. As you read books and stories, have students analyze and describe different types of conflict. Discuss how the characters in the story feel about it and how they are dealing with the conflict. Have students notice if the conflict gets worse or better.

Friends, by Kim Lewis
(New York: Walker Books, 1999) Gr. P-2

Summary: Sam and Alice gather an egg and then fight over it – and then gather another.

1. How did Alice and Sam's conflict start?

2. What made the conflict get worse?

3. How did Sam and Alice get over their conflict?

Two in the Fight

© 1997 Words by Sarah Pirtle, Music Traditional

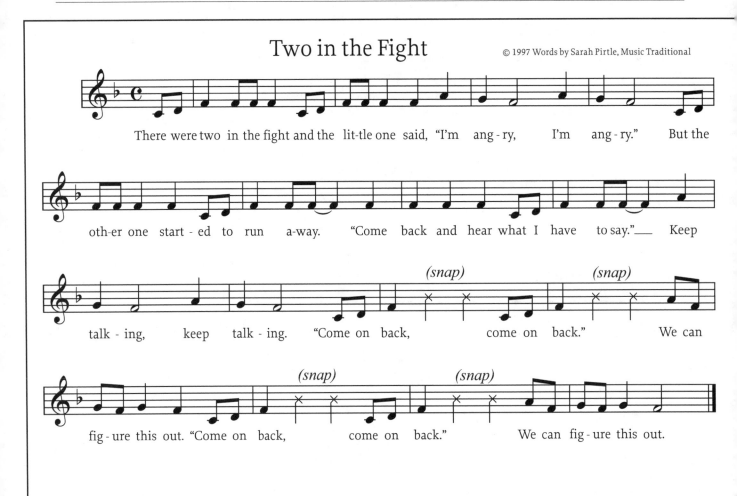

Two in the Fight

There were two in the fight

And the little one said,

"I'm angry, I'm angry."

But the other one started to run away.

"Come back and hear what I have to say."

Keep talking, keep talking.

Come on back, *(click, click)*

come on back, *(click, click)*

We can figure this out.

Come on back, *(click, click)*

come on back, *(click, click)*

We can figure this out.

There were two in the fight

and the other one said,

"I'm angry, I'm angry."

But the little one did not run away.

"Tell me what you have to say."

Keep talking, keep talking.

Talk it out, *(click, click)*

talk it out. *(click, click)*

We can figure this out.

Talk it out, *(click, click)*

talk it out. *(click, click)*

We can figure this out!

© 1997 Words by Sarah Pirtle

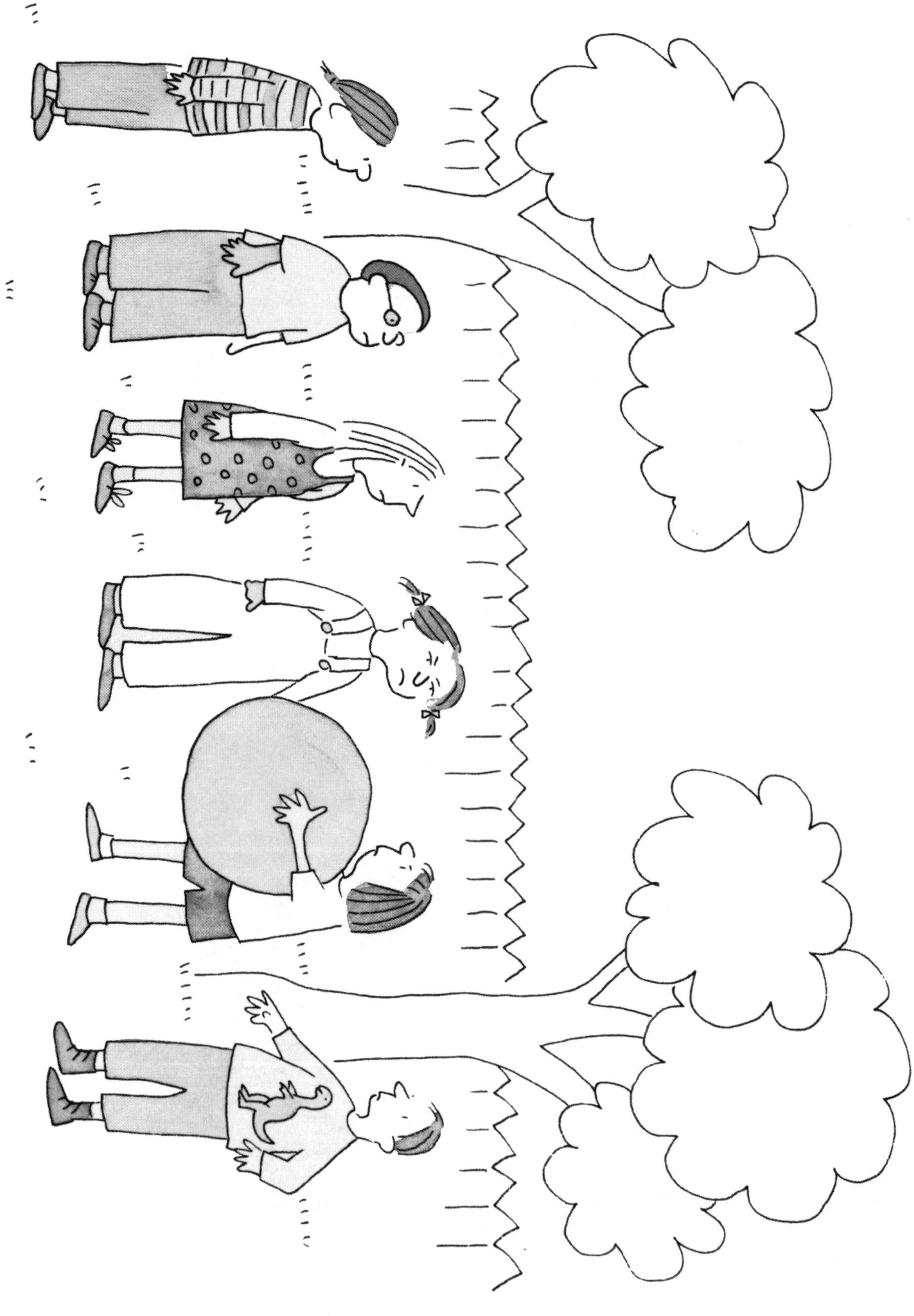

Win-Win Solutions

⏸ Conflict Management and
Decision Making

CASEL SEL COMPETENCIES

SO Social Awareness

DM Responsible Decision Making

RS Relationship Skills

Gathering: Sitting Circle

Ask students to stand in a circle, shoulder to shoulder. Have them all turn to their right and then ask them to take one step to the left in order to make the circle smaller. When everyone is very close together in a tight circle, have them all sit down at the same time. Students will be sitting on the lap of the student behind them.

Agenda Check

To accomplish what we just accomplished took teamwork. We all won together. Today we are going to be looking at how conflicts can get stuck when one person tries to win and make the other person lose. A lot of conflicts need to be settled in a win-win way – in a way that lets both people feel they have won. In the lesson we are going to hear a story about two donkeys (Two Donkeys). **Then we will make a chart of some things we can do to get to win-win solutions** (Win-Win Ways). **At the end, we will close our lesson by thinking of some conflicts we sometimes have, looking at the list of win-win ideas we came up with and choosing which ones might help us with our conflict** (Closing).

Activity: Two Donkeys

The pictures on pages 84 and 85 can be photocopied beforehand.

Use Picture 1 and Picture 2 to tell the story, "Two Donkeys," up to the point where it says, "They he-ha'd and he-ha'd and he-ha'd until they were tired. And also very hungry."

1. Tell the story.

Two Donkeys

Once upon a time, there were two donkeys tied together in a barn. Each of the donkeys had its own pile of hay, one pile on the left and one on the right. The donkey on the left wanted to eat from the hay pile on the left. The donkey on the right wanted to eat from the hay pile on the right.

At the same time, both donkeys went to eat from the pile of hay that they wanted, but the rope tying them together was too short. Neither donkey could reach its pile of hay.

Workshop Agenda

- Gathering: Sitting Circle
- Agenda Check
- Activity: Two Donkeys
- Activity: Win-Win Ways
- Closing: Ideas for Solving Conflicts

Materials

- Workshop agenda, written on chart paper and posted
- Chart paper and markers
- Talking Object

Learning Outcomes

- Students will be able to define win-win solutions.
- Students will be able to identify a win-win solution to a particular problem.

"Ow," they both said at once. "Let me get at my hay," they both cried.

"You aren't letting me eat," said one.

"You aren't letting me eat," said the other.

"Be nice."

"No, you be nice."

They argued. They pulled to get their way. They whined. They bawled. They he-ha'd and he-ha'd and he-ha'd until they were tired. And also very hungry.

2. Stop and lead a discussion using the following questions:

    - How do you think the donkeys are feeling?

    - What is their conflict?

    - What can they do about their problem? What do you think they will do?

3. Tell the rest of the story, using pictures 3 and 4.

    Well, let's see what happens. The donkeys were bawling. They were tired and hungry. Suddenly, one of the donkeys said, "This is stupid. If we keep this up, neither of us will eat."

    "You're right. Let's not fight."

    "Let's cooperate!"

    "If we put our heads together, we might know what to do."

    So that is what they did. They sat down and rested. They put their heads together. They thought and thought.

    "I know," said one.

    "What?" said the other.

    "Let's share! You can help me eat my pile. Then we can both eat yours."

    "What a brilliant idea. I love it."

    So the donkeys ate the hay together until their stomachs were full. They lived happily ever after.

4. Lead a discussion using the following questions:

    - How do you think the donkeys felt at the end of the story?

    - Did the donkeys cooperate with each other?

    - How did they cooperate?

5. Summarize the point of the story by saying: **We call the kind of solution that they came up with in the end a win-win solution. In a conflict, people can either win or lose. We say people win if they can get what they need and feel good about things. In the first part of the story, was either of the donkeys winning? Usually when we try to win without helping the other person also win, we both end up losing and no one**

feels good about things. When people work together and think about how everyone feels, they can often find win-win ways to deal with problems.

Activity: Win-Win Ways

1. Introduce the activity by saying: **We're going to make a chart of some things to do or ideas that would be useful in getting to a win-win solution. What's one thing that people can do to solve a problem so that everyone is happy at the end?**

2. Ask students for contributions, asking probing questions and suggesting scenarios to solicit ideas. As they share ideas, ask for examples of each strategy or behavior.

3. Record the ideas on the chart, with a quick iconic sketch, if possible. If students suggest something that wouldn't lead to a win-win solution, remind them that you are looking for ways to solve conflicts that allow everyone to be happy about the outcome.

   Some things that are likely to come up or that you might want to elicit:

   - Apologize
   - Share
   - Take turns
   - Talk it out
   - Listen to each other
   - Use strong, not mean, words
   - Walk away to cool down
   - Let it go — Find something else
   - Rock/Paper/Scissors
   - Ask someone to help

4. Post the list prominently in the classroom and tell students that it is there to remind them of ways to solve conflicts that come up in class.

Closing: Ideas for Solving Conflicts

Today we have learned about solving conflicts so that everyone feels good about the solution. We learned that that kind of ending is called a win-win solution. What happened when each donkey tried to get what it wanted without thinking about the other one? Both donkeys were unhappy. For the closing, I would like you to think about conflicts that you sometimes have at school, at home, or at other places, like day care. Then look at the list of ideas we came up with and choose one you think would be most helpful in getting to a win-win solution. Remind students about the use of the Talking Object. Begin by starting with a conflict you have and then think about what you might do that would be helpful.

Extensions and Infusion Ideas

What Can I Do When ...?

For this activity, you will need a blank book and a marker or pens.

This activity can be an ongoing way of inviting students to think about win-win strategies for specific issues.

Explain: **I would like you to help me write a book called *What Can I Do When ...?* This book will be about what to do when there is a problem. The more ideas we have, the better the book will be, so I want you all to think of a lot of different ideas.**

Prop up the book so that it faces the children. Turn to the first page and write, "What can I do when I want something someone else has?" Read the sentence as you write.

Ask if anyone has an idea of what you could do. If someone offers an idea, ask the students: **Would this work? If not, how could we change it to work better?** If no one volunteers, get things rolling with an obviously bad idea like, "I can walk up and take it."

When children agree on a good idea, write it in simple words and draw a quick sketch. Keep adding to your book, but stick to one problem per session.

Alternative Endings

Have students discuss and rewrite endings to stories and fairy tales that you read and discuss in class. For each story, have students identify the conflict that the characters had and how they solved it. Then have them brainstorm alternative ways the conflict could be resolved.

Have students draw pictures of the characters resolving the conflict in a win-win way. Collect the pictures and display them on a bulletin board, or put them together in a class book.

Win-Win Puppets

As you read stories and books throughout the year, draw or copy pictures of the main characters involved in conflicts onto a sheet of paper. Have students cut out the characters, color, and then paste onto sticks to make puppets. When the puppets are finished, the students can then act out the main conflict of the book. Have them stop and analyze what is happening and create different, win-win solutions to the conflicts.

Connecting to Literature

My Friend and I, by Lisa Jahn-Clough
(Minneapolis, MN: Sagebrush Bound, 2003) Gr. P-1

Summary: A simple story of a girl and boy who play together until they fight over a toy bunny. Later, each is miserable and they get together and mend the toy and their friendship.

1. What started the conflict? What made it worse?

2. What did the boy and girl do after their conflict? How did they feel?

3. How did they mend their friendship?

4. Have you had a conflict with a friend? What was helpful in settling it?

The Rainbow Fish and the Big Blue Whale, by Marcus Pfister
(New York: Scholastic, Inc., 1988) Gr. P-2

Summary: Rainbow Fish and the others get suspicious and afraid of the Big Blue Whale, who retaliates. Rainbow Fish talks to the whale and they become friends and work together.

1. How did the conflict between the whale and the small fish begin?

    a. Why did the whale look at the fish?

    b. Why did the fish become afraid of the whale?

    c. What did the whale do when he became angry?

    d. What happened to the tiny fish that were their food, the krill?

2. Rainbow Fish talked to the whale.

    a. What strong words did Rainbow Fish use?

    b. What did Rainbow Fish and the whale tell each other?

    c. Did one of them apologize? Explain.

3. Was there a solution that was good for everyone?

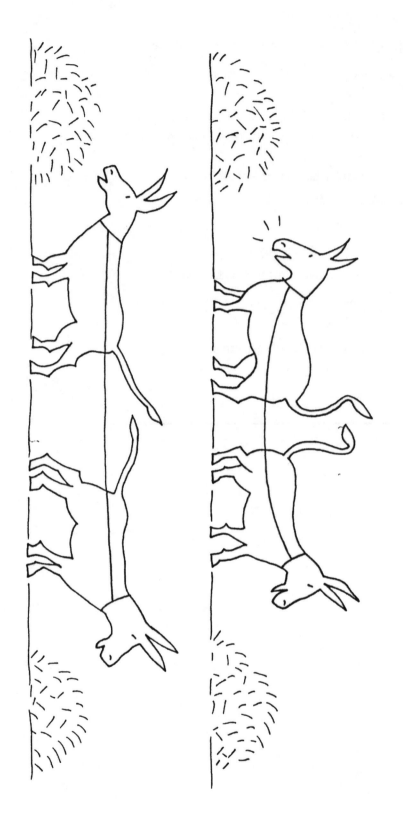

TWO DONKEYS PICTURES

TWO DONKEYS PICTURES

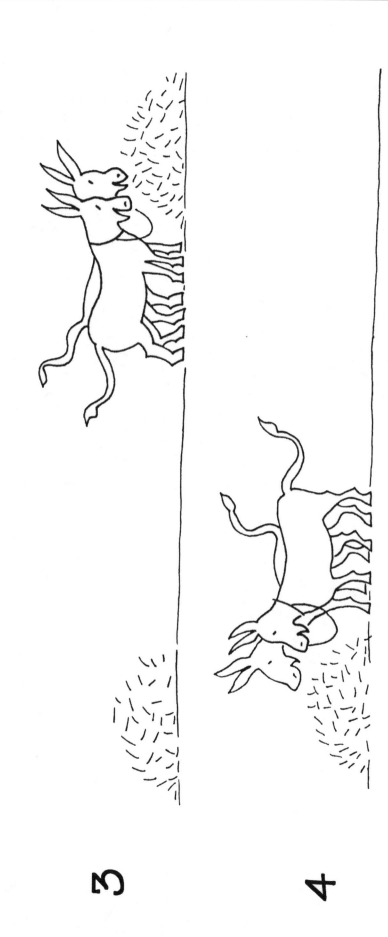

3

4

Practicing Being Strong and Dealing with Bullying

Caring and Effective
Communication

CASEL SEL COMPETENCIES

SO   Social Awareness

RS   Relationship Skills

Gathering: Heroes and Sheroes

Explain: **Heroes are people who are admired for their achievements and strong and good qualities. Girl heroes are called heroines; some people call them** *sheroes.* **Heroes and sheroes are people who are brave and strong in standing up for others or in doing what is right.** Share some examples of people your students will have heard of – people from stories they've read recently, national heroes like Martin Luther King, Jr. or Abraham Lincoln. **Heroes can also be people we know in our families or in our neighborhoods. The important thing about heroes and sheroes is that they always try to help others, acting in strong ways that are never mean.**

Who is someone you think of as a hero or shero and why? Ask students to think to themselves for a minute. Suggest possible people most in the class are familiar with and talk about what it is about that person that might make him or her a hero. Holding the Talking Object, begin by discussing someone you admire and explaining why. Then pass the Talking Object to the next person. As always, allow students to pass if they choose to, and acknowledge that it is always more difficult to speak at the beginning of the circle. Assure them you will come back at the end to see if they have something to share.

Agenda Check

Today we are going to be talking about something called *bullying.* Bullying is being mean to someone or picking on someone to try to get something that you want or to make someone feel bad. People who bully usually pick on someone they think is weaker than they are. Bullying can make the person who is bullying feel "big" for a little while, but it usually doesn't last very long. It is important to be able to be strong when someone is bullying you, but it is not easy. We all need help from others sometimes, and when people are being bullied, they often need help from people who are nearby. They need heroes who have the courage and strength to help them. Today we are going to learn how we can all be heroes. First, some puppets will show us what bullying can look like (Bullying). **Then we are going to practice being heroes and think of some strong ways to stand up to bullying behavior** (Acting Strong). **We will end our lesson, as usual, with a closing** (Closing).

Workshop Agenda

- Gathering: Heroes and Sheroes
- Agenda Check
- Activity: Bullying
- Activity: Acting Strong
- Closing: "Speak Up"

Materials

- Workshop agenda, written on chart paper and posted
- Talking Object
- Two puppets

Learning Outcomes

- Students will be able to describe bullying behavior.
- Students will practice how to intervene effectively when someone else is being bullied.
- Students will be able to identify ways of confronting bullying behavior.

Activity: Bullying

1. Introduce the two puppets and have them act out a brief scenario in which one puppet is being bullied by the other one. Suggested scenarios include:

   - Making fun of the other puppet's name

   - Not letting the other puppet play on the monkey bars because he or she wants the whole structure to play on

   - Teasing the other puppet about his or her hair, clothes, accent, etc.

   - Threatening the other puppet, i.e. "You better get out of here or I'll throw this dirt in your face."

2. Before the puppet being teased responds, stop the action and ask students: **What's going on here? What is ___ (the bullying puppet) doing? What does he want? Is this a mean or strong way to try to get what he wants? How do you think ___ (the other puppet) is feeling? Can anyone think of a strong way** (he or she) **could respond?**

3. Have students think of strong ways the puppet could respond to the bullying behavior. Have students who offer an effective response come up and role-play that response by taking the puppet that was being bullied and using it to act out their strong response.

4. Repeat with different scenarios as time and interest permits.

Activity: Acting Strong

1. Introduce the activity by saying: **Sometimes, when you are the person being bullied, it's hard to think of something strong to do because you have many feelings at the time. If you see someone else being bullied, though, you are sometimes in a very good position to help out.**

2. Tell students you are going to replay one of the scenarios with the puppets, or that you are going to have the puppets play out a new scenario, and ask them to think about how a hero might intervene.

3. Have the puppets role-play a scenario, and have the puppet being bullied seem overwhelmed. Ask: **If you were standing nearby and heard what was going on, what could you say or do to be a hero? What is a strong way you could help?**

4. Have students brainstorm strong ways of intervening. Examples include:

   - Saying things to the person who is bullying like: "Stop that!","I don't like what you're doing.","You shouldn't ___," or "We don't say things like that at this school."

   - Saying things to the person who is being targeted like: "You don't have to listen to that," "I like your ___," or "Why don't you come play with me?"

   - Putting your arm around the person being targeted.

5. Have students who offer an effective response come up and role-play that response with the puppets. (They can either role-play directly, or use a third puppet to act out the response.)

6. Repeat with several different scenarios.

Closing: "Speak Up"

Today we have learned the importance of acting strong and speaking up when someone is being teased or bullied. For our closing, we'll learn and sing a song about how important it is to stand up to people who are bullying. We all need to speak up when anyone is bullied. Teach students the song, "Speak Up." It can be found in the book *Linking Up!*, by Sarah Pirtle, and on the *Linking Up!* CD, Track 17. The music and lyrics can be found at the end of the lesson.

Extensions and Infusion Ideas

King of the Playground

This extension can also be presented before doing the lesson.

King of the Playground, by Phyllis Reynolds Naylor, (New York: Aladdin, 1994) is a story about Sammy, a boy who is afraid to go to the playground because Kevin is there. Talking with his father helps Sammy figure out how not to let Kevin bully him.

Read the book up to the point where Sammy shouts, "You can't play here! I'm King of the Monkey Bars," and then tells Kevin what he would do if he saw him there again. Lead a discussion using the following questions:

- How do you think Sammy is feeling?
- What is Sammy's problem?
- How do you think he can solve this problem?
- What do you think will happen next in the story?

Read the rest of the story, and then lead a discussion using the following questions:

- How does Kevin stand up for himself?
- Do you think Kevin chose a good solution to solve his problem?
- Did Kevin and Sammy find a win-win solution?

Involve the children in a dramatization of the story. Choose one child to play Kevin, and one child to play Kevin's father. Reread the story for the dramatization (if necessary, say each child's lines first, and have the child repeat the lines after you).

Ask the class: **If someone were bothering you in the way Sammy was bothering Kevin, what could you do?**

List the children's ideas, then ask: **Which of these are win-win choices?**

Role-Play Practice

During the role-plays, you may want to make a simple chart of Strong Ways to Intervene that students can use when they observe bullying behavior.

Have students brainstorm possible bullying situations, or suggest a scenario. Select students to play the different parts: the person who is bullying, the person being targeted, and several bystanders who will practice intervening. Have students role-play the scenario. If the bystanders get stuck, ask other students for suggestions or prompt with something from the list of Strong Ways to Intervene. Repeat with other students. You can also role-play a situation in which someone being bullied handles the situation in a strong way.

Strength to Ignore

Introduce the activity by saying something like: **We've been talking about handling bullying in strong ways. Many times heroes show their strength by taking action, but sometimes it is what a hero *doesn't* do that shows his real strength. Sometimes the strongest thing to do is to ignore something. Does anyone know what *ignore* means?** Lead a brief discussion to define the word. **Usually, not listening might be a way to get into a fight with someone, but sometimes not listening can keep you out of trouble. When someone is trying to make you mad, not getting drawn in when they call you a name can stop people from bullying.**

Have the group practice saying the word *Mookie* in different voices and manners. Have them say it as a sergeant would, then a grandma. How about a cow, or a cat, a vampire, or a rapper? Develop as many different and playful ways as possible.

Have the group form two parallel lines, facing each other. Ask for a volunteer to walk slowly down the middle without cracking a smile. All the while the other students will be doing their best Mookie calls, trying to distract the walker and get him to smile. Repeat this many times, encouraging variations of Mookie calls.

After the activity, have the class sit in a circle and lead a brief discussion with questions such as the following:

- What was one reason why this activity was hard?
- How did it feel to be part of the crowd?
- How did it feel to walk down the center?
- When might it be a good idea to ignore something at school?

Connecting to Literature

The Berenstain Bears and the Bully, by Stan and Jan Berenstain (New York: Random House, 1995) Gr. K-3

Summary: After a girl, Tuffy, beats Sister up, Brother teaches Sister self-defense. Sister avoids Tuffy but hits back when Tuffy hits her. The principal and psychologist deal with Tuffy, who is getting hit by her parents.

1. Why did Brother leave after he talked to Tuffy?

2. Was it a good idea for Sister to hit Tuffy? Why or why not?

3. Why was Tuffy hitting other people?

   a. Did that make it okay for Tuffy to be bullying others?

   b. How did the adults help both Sister and Tuffy?

Dog Eared, by Amanda Harvey
(New York: Doubleday Books for Young Readers, 2002) Gr. K-3

Summary: Dog is bullied and feels bad about his long ears until his owner says she likes them.

1. When the big dog said, "Out of my way, Big Ears!" to Otis, how do you think Otis must have felt? What did Otis start to think?

2. How did Lucy's words help Otis feel better?

3. When the big dog called Otis "Fat Face," how did Otis act?

4. Have you ever been called a name? What was it like? If you are called a name, how can you be strong?

5. If you hear someone called a name, what can you do to help?

Speak Up

©1997. Words and Music by Sarah Pirtle
Discovery Center Music, BMI

Speak Up

Speak up, we need your voice.

Speak up, we need your voice.

Speak up, we need your voice

in our world.

Speak up when something's not fair.

Speak up and show that you care.

Speak up when something's not right.

Speak up and follow your light.

Speak up, we need your voice.

Speak up, we need your voice.

Speak up, we need your voice

ringing strong...Speak up!

GRADE K, LESSON 16
Concepts of Peace

Cultural Competence
and Social Responsibility

CASEL SEL COMPETENCIES

SA   Self Awareness

Gathering: I Feel Good About Myself When…

Have students sit in a circle. Explain: **We often feel good about ourselves when we have helped others, or worked hard at something, or when others have shown they love and care about us.** Using the Talking Object, tell students that each person will get a turn to complete the sentence: "I feel good about myself when ___." Model by completing the sentence yourself and then go around the circle.

Agenda Check

We have learned a lot this year about being strong and kind, about dealing with our feelings and getting along with others. Today we're going to be talking about peace. We often have a feeling of peace when we are doing a good job of handling our feelings and getting along well with others. First, we'll talk a little about what peace is (Peace Is…). Then, we will think about a time when we felt peaceful and draw a picture of that time (Drawing a Time of Peace). We'll end our lesson by sharing our pictures with each other (Closing).

Activity: Peace Is…

1. Write the words *Peace is* on chart paper. Explain that you are going to write down some things they can think of that make them feel peaceful.

2. To expand students' ideas of peace, give an example or two from your own life, such as: **I feel really peaceful when it's a summer day and I'm sitting in the sand at the beach. So I would say, 'Peace is playing in the sand.' Or, I feel peaceful when I get a nice hug from a child I love. So I would say, 'Peace is getting a good hug.'**

3. Go around the group, asking students to complete the sentence. Depending on the results, you may want to go around the group a second time. You can write either a few key words or whole sentences beginning with "Peace is"

4. You may want to post the chart in the room so that students can refer to it later.

5. You can also read *The Peace Book*, by Todd Parr (New York: Little, Brown, 2004), which illustrates many different ideas of peace.

Activity: Drawing a Time of Peace

1. Distribute drawing materials.

2. Ask students to be quiet and think of a time when they felt peaceful. Encourage them to bring concrete details into their mental picture by asking such questions as: **What were you doing? Who were you with? Where were you? What were you wearing? Was it cold or hot? Could you smell anything? How were you feeling?**

3. Ask students to draw a picture of the scene they imagined, including as many concrete details in it as possible. You may wish to play some quiet music during this time.

4. Have students write or dictate a caption for their picture.

Closing: Sharing Peace Pictures

Have students form a circle. Ask a few volunteers: **What did you like most about today?** Go around the group and ask students to show their picture and tell something about the peaceful time they drew.

Extensions and Infusion Ideas

Peaceful Family Times

Have students tell about, draw pictures of, or write about peaceful things they do with their families.

Science

Have students find pictures of animals at peace or in peaceful environments.

Music

When students are listening to different music, ask them to identify parts that sound peaceful to them. Help them articulate what it is about the music that sounds peaceful.

Teachable Moments

Throughout the year, acknowledge times during class that feel peaceful to you. Point out concrete things that contribute to the peaceful feeling of the experience, such as the class working cooperatively together, quiet tones of voices, and students sharing politely with each other. Periodically, ask the students to assess whether or not the tone in class seems peaceful to them.

Connecting to Literature

When I Feel Good About Myself, by Cornelia Maude Spelman
(Morton Grove, IL: Albert Whitman, 2003) Gr. P-1

Summary: A little guinea pig tells all the ways she is accepted and feels good about herself.

1. After reading "Somebody likes what I paint or make," ask: Why is the little guinea pig feeling good about herself?

2. After reading "... and I like learning new things," ask:

    a. Why does the guinea pig feel good?

    b. Who are some of the people you help?

    c. Who are some new friends you have met?

    d. What new things have you learned to do?

3. After reading the book, ask: Can you still feel good about yourself if you make a mistake?

4. How can you help others feel good about themselves?

Talk Peace, by Sam Williams
(New York: Holiday House, 2005) Gr. P-2

Summary: A book that sends the poetic message that we can talk about peace anywhere, anytime.

1. What does it mean to "talk peace"?

2. Name some places where you can talk peace.

3. What are some ways you can talk peace?

GRADE 1, LESSON 1
Making Connections

Gathering: A Favorite Place to Go

Have students form a circle. Explain that we use the Talking Object so that we know whose turn it is to talk, and as a reminder to listen to the person speaking. Explain that when each person receives the object, they should just hold it quietly in their lap.

Then ask students to think quietly about a special place they like to go. Suggest a variety of ideas by saying something like: **Some people really like going to a park. Others may like going to the beach or a pool better. You may think of a special relative's house, a grandparent or aunt or uncle. Some people like to go to movies, others prefer going to the zoo.** Explain that when it is their turn, you would like them to say their name and a special place they like to go. Others in the group will listen and try to remember what each person said. Model by saying your name and someplace you like to go. Then pass the object to the person next to you and ask him to say his name and a special place he likes to go. After going around the circle choose a few students to stand up. Ask the others if anyone can remember the special place each person standing likes to go.

Agenda Check

Our class will be together all year, so it is very important that we all get to know each other and learn to respect each other. Everyone wants to be respected. Being respected means being treated by others the way we would like to be treated. It means being cared about. Really listening well to each other is the most important skill that is part of respecting each other. Today we are going to work on our listening skills and get to know each other better while we are doing it.

In some ways, we are all the same, and in some ways we are very different. Differences sometimes can cause problems, but they are also what make being in a group really fun. This year we will discover many similarities in the class as well as many differences.

Now I am going to talk about the agenda for the lesson. Does anyone know what *agenda* means? Agenda means the plan for today, or what we're going to do together as a class.

Workshop Agenda

- Gathering: A Favorite Place to Go
- Agenda Check
- Activity: Good and Poor Listening
- Activity: Good Listening Practice
- Summary
- Closing: Stand Up If

Materials

- Workshop agenda, written on chart paper and posted
- Talking Object
- Chart paper and markers

Learning Outcomes

- Students will know each other's names.
- Students will begin to learn something about each of their classmates.
- Students will be able to identify and demonstrate good listening behavior.

Connections to Standards

Behavioral Studies

- Understands that people are both different and alike
- Understands that people learn from each other in many ways

Health

- Understands individual differences (in appearance, behavior)

Language Arts

Writing

- Prewriting: discusses ideas with peers

Listening and Speaking

- Makes contributions in class and group discussions
- Asks and responds to questions
- Follows rules of conversation
- Recites and responds to familiar stories, poems, and can relate them to own life

Connections to Standards, cont.

Working with Others
- Engages in active listening
- Makes eye contact when speaking

We have already done a gathering, which brought us all together and started our lesson. Next we will look at what good and poor listening are (Good and Poor Listening), **and then do some practice** (Good Listening Practice)**. We will summarize what we learned** (Summary)**, and then do a closing game to practice even more and find out other ways we are the same as well as different from each other** (Stand Up If)**.**

Activity: Good and Poor Listening

For this activity it is best to role-play with another adult. If another adult is not available, the role-play can be done with a student as the speaker. Tell the student beforehand what you will be doing.

1. Explain that you are going to demonstrate listening while your partner tells you about a special vacation or experience he enjoyed. Tell the students that for this example, instead of listening to the speaker, you want them to pay attention to what you are doing as the listener.

2. Ask your partner to start telling you his story. Although you have told the class you are demonstrating listening, deliberately demonstrate poor listening. While the other person talks, illustrate poor listening with such actions as glancing around the room, moving your body, yawning, looking at your watch, looking bored, laughing at an inappropriate place, or interrupting.

3. Stop the role-play and discuss with the class.

    -   What was happening here? What did I do as the listener that was an example of poor listening?

    -   Does anyone remember a time when someone didn't listen carefully to you?

    -   How do you feel when people don't listen to you? Can someone remember a time someone listened to you really well?

    -   How do you feel when someone listens to you well?

4. Repeat the role-play, modeling good listening: face the person, nod encouragingly, smile, if appropriate, and listen attentively.

5. Ask the speaker to describe how he felt this time compared to the time you demonstrated poor listening.

6. Make a chart labeled Good Listening. Talk about the body signs of good listening. Elicit students' help by asking them to recall what they noticed you did that demonstrated good listening. A possible list of guidelines might include:

    -   Look at the speaker

    -   Keep body still and quiet

    -   Pay attention (think about what the speaker is saying)

    -   Don't interrupt

    Save the chart to keep posted in the classroom.

Activity: Good Listening Practice

1. The class will now have a chance to show how well they can listen to each other. Explain that one or two other students will get to tell about a fun trip or time they have experienced. (How many share an experience is up to you. You may want to say that there will be other "practice" times later, if you would like to give each child a turn to share.) Explain that the important thing is for all of them to practice good listening.

2. Choose a student to describe a fun vacation/trip/experience he had. Remind students who are listening to try to exhibit all the behaviors on the list you have just created. When appropriate, without interrupting the student who is speaking, remark on good listening as you observe it.

3. Ask the student who was speaking: **How did it feel to have people paying attention to you? How could you tell if people were listening?**

4. Depending on the concentration of the group and the amount of time you would like to spend, have one or more other students share an experience.

Summary

Ask: **What was one thing you learned today about listening?** Continue soliciting responses until you have summarized the contents of the Good Listening chart that was created. **Why is it important to listen to each other? How does it make us feel when people listen carefully to us?**

Closing: Stand Up If

Sometimes we can "say" things without using words. Bring up examples, like waving hello or smiling at someone. **We are going to play a game that will let us get to know some ways that we are the same and some ways that we are different from others in the class. This is a game with NO TALKING. The game is called Stand Up If. The way we will show that we are the same or different is either by standing up or by staying seated. We will "listen" by looking to see who is standing and who is sitting. How could we say** *yes* **or** *no* **without talking?** Elicit that they can answer *yes* by shaking their heads up and down, and *no* by shaking their head back and forth.

For the first statement, say something that will get everyone to stand, such as: **Stand up if you have two ears.** After they are all standing, ask if this is a way that we are all the same and elicit a *yes* nod. Continue with a variety of topics that will be of interest and will show similarities and differences between different students. Encourage students to observe who is standing and who is sitting, who is the same and who is different from them. Occasionally ask them to nod *yes* or *no* to questions like: **Is this a way that we are different from some students in our class? Are we all alike in this way?** Some possible topics: number of siblings, if they are the youngest or oldest child, number and types of pets, likes and dislikes in areas such as food, games, etc.

Extensions and Infusion Ideas

Name Game with Ball

This is a great activity to do at the beginning of the year to help students learn everyone's name. You will need a soft ball and an empty space large enough so that the whole class can stand in a circle. It is a great activity to do outdoors.

Organize the students into a standing circle. Holding the ball, stand in the center of the circle and explain: **I am going to go around the circle and throw the ball to each of you. When you catch the ball, I would like you to say your name in a nice, loud voice. Then I would like you to throw the ball back to me. When I catch the ball, everyone will say your name at the same time. As we all look at the student and say his or her name together, we will be starting to learn each other's names.**

Throw the ball to a student and prompt him, if necessary, to say his name loud enough to be heard. Then ask him to throw the ball back to you while the class says his name. Keep the pace and rhythm going fairly quickly, with the ball going gently from you to each student, and back to you. Repeat the direction that each student gets to say his name alone first, and then everyone says it together. By keeping the rhythm going the game becomes a name chant.

Name Game with Movement

This activity provides another way to help students learn each other's name while also inviting self-expression and practicing focused listening. Each student performs a movement of his choice and says his name. The whole class then performs that same movement while saying that students' name.

Gather the class in a standing circle. Ask the students to follow your lead. Start a rhythm of simple movements performed in twos, such as claps, taps on shoulders, twists, arms reaching up, etc. Use movements that students can easily copy, appropriate for their developmental level.

While you are performing the movements, say: **We are going to play another name game, this time with movements. There are lots of movements we can do. These are some.** (Demonstrate.) **There are lots more you may know. While we do these movements, think of one that you like a lot. Or think of one that you can make up. Choose a movement that you want to be yours to share with everyone – a movement that will go with your name. When it's your turn, you will do your movement and say your name like this… .**

To demonstrate, do a movement in the twos rhythm and say your own first name. Then say: **That was my movement and my name. I say it alone and do it alone. Now everyone will do my movement and say my name like this.** Demonstrate, getting everyone to join. Review, repeating the instructions: **First I do my movement and say my name, and then everyone does my movement and says my name.** Repeat the practice. **Who would like to try first? When it's your turn, say your own name and do your own movement.** Choose one child to try, clarifying any confusion. **Now everyone should think of a movement to do when it's your turn. You can do one**

of the movements I showed you (demonstrate) **or make one up. We'll go around the circle starting with** _____ (the child who demonstrated). **He'll go first.**

Check to see if the next few children around the circle are ready to go. Try to keep up the rhythm so it can become a name song and dance. If one student is stuck, let that student pass, saying that you'll come back to him later. Keep the pace lively so attention does not lag. When everyone has had a turn, applaud.

Right, Left, and Me

Gather everyone in a circle with you. Start this game by giving the Talking Object or a small, soft ball to one of the students in the circle. That person must say the name of the person to his right and pass the object to the right. Once the Talking Object has been passed all the way around the circle, toss it to a student and have that person say the name of the student to his left. The object then gets passed to the left. Finally, the object will go around the circle a third time. Give the object to a student and have him say three names, first the name of the person to his right, then the name of the person to his left, and then his own name. Have that student pass the object to his right. The next person says the names of the people to his right and left, then his own name, and passes the object to the right. Continue passing and naming until everyone has had a turn.

A fun variation once children have the knack of the game is to try timing it. What world record speed can the group achieve? Encourage the group to beat their own score, and then try doing it with eyes closed.

Spend a few moments marveling at the speed at which the class was able to go around the circle. Ask a few questions before moving on, but don't spend too much time here. Some questions might be:

- Which created a better time? Eyes closed or open?

- Was it difficult to be the beginning person? Why?

Connecting to Literature

Franklin's New Friend, by Paulette Bourgeois
(New York: Scholastic Inc., 1997) Gr. P-2

Summary: Franklin overcomes his fear of Moose and they become friends.

1. After reading "During recess, Moose stood alone as Franklin and his friends played soccer," show the picture of Moose under the tree and ask:

   a. Why do you think Moose said he didn't want to play?

   b. Why did the other animals feel better when Moose didn't play with them?

2. After reading the book, ask: What did Franklin learn about the way Moose was really feeling at school?

3. When Franklin and Moose spent time working together, what do you think they heard from each other?

The Mixed-Up Chameleon, by Eric Carle
(Hong Kong: HarperCollins, 1975) Gr. P-2

Summary: A chameleon tries to take on the characteristics of many zoo animals and finds it cannot function unless it is itself.

1. Name some of the things the chameleon likes about the other animals.

2. When you look at your classmates, you probably see many things you like about them. Name some of those things. Name some qualities that cannot be seen (like kindness). Name some of the things you like about yourself.

3. What did the chameleon learn about being himself?

GRADE 1, LESSON 2
Creating a Positive Classroom Environment

 Making Connections

CASEL SEL COMPETENCIES

SA Self-Awareness

SO Social Awareness

Gathering: Friends

Have students form a circle. Ask students to think about what they like to do with their friends and what it is that they like about having friends. Share something you like about a friend or friends of your own. Pass the Talking Object to the next student and ask her to share. Demonstrate and then review good listening behaviors. Comment on specific good listening behaviors you notice. Help students realize how they feel when others listen carefully to them.

Agenda Check

Today we are going to think about how we can make other people feel respected and feel good about themselves. Summarize things that may have come up during the gathering about how friends are nice to each other. **Being careful of what we say and do to others is important in creating a respectful classroom. What do we mean by respect? What does respect look like and feel like? What behaviors show respect?** (For example, being nice, caring for others, treating others the way we would like to be treated.) **We want to create a classroom where we all feel comfortable and respected. First, we'll talk about put-downs and put-ups** (Put-Downs and Put-Ups), **then we'll hear a story about how put-downs and put-ups can make us feel** (Maria's Story). **We'll think back about what we learned today** (Summary) **and then close our lesson with a song** (Closing).

Activity: Put-Downs and Put-Ups

1. Explain: **Sometimes people say or do hurtful things to others. These are called put-downs. Put-downs tell people that they are not good or important. They can make people feel "less than" or not as good as other people.**

2. Ask for several examples of put-downs. **How do those statements make people feel? Why do you think we say them? If people in our class used put-downs very often, what would happen?**

3. Ask the class to think of examples of put-ups, kind and friendly things that people can say or do. These may be compliments, but they can also be words of encouragement or support. List the contributions on chart paper.

Workshop Agenda
- Gathering: Friends
- Agenda Check
- Activity: Put-Downs and Put-Ups
- Activity: Maria's Story
- Summary
- Closing: "I Like You"

Materials
- Workshop agenda, written on chart paper and posted
- Talking Object
- Chart paper and markers
- Two large hearts cut out of construction or chart paper
- A story about a child experiencing put-downs

Learning Outcome
- Students will be able to identify and describe positive and negative classroom behavior.

Connections to Standards
Language Arts
Reading
- Makes simple inferences regarding the order of events and possible outcomes
- Knows main ideas or theme of a story

Working with Others
- Demonstrates respect for others
- Displays empathy with others

How do these things make people feel? What would our class be like if we used these put-ups instead of put-downs?

4. Save the list of put-ups for future reference.

Activity: Maria's Story

1. Explain that you are going to tell a story about someone and what happens to her during one morning in her life.

2. Hold one of the cutout hearts in front of your chest. Read the story below or create one similar to it. Try to choose a name that is not connected with any students in your class. When the child receives a put-down, rip off a piece of the heart and drop it to the floor. By the end of the story, the heart will be in shreds.

Maria's Story

One morning, Maria didn't get up right away when her mother called her. Finally, her father came in shouting, "You're so lazy, get out of bed!" *(Rip.)* She got up and put on some of her favorite clothes. She wanted to dress like a dancer today. However, her big sister came into the room and said, "You can't wear that to school! You look stupid." *(Rip.)*

Maria took off her dancer's costume and put on pants and a top she guessed must be all right for school since she wore them before. Then her mother called that she had to hurry up because she was going to be late. She put on her shoes very fast and rushed to the kitchen table for breakfast. As she came in, her brother grabbed her favorite cereal and put the last of it in his bowl. *(Rip.)* Then looking at her, he said, "You dope, you've got on two different kinds of shoes." *(Rip.)* Knowing that she was late, Maria poured a small bowl of another cereal, but as she quickly tried to pour some milk, she spilled some on the table. Her mother said, "You're worse than your baby sister! I don't have all day to clean up after you." *(Rip.)*

When she got to school, everybody had already gone inside. When she got to her class, her teacher had already written the number of boys and girls who were in school on the board. As she saw Maria, her teacher wrote "LATE" in big letters on the board and wrote down Maria's name. *(Rip.)* "Somebody was a slowpoke this morning," she said. *(Rip.)*

During reading time, the teacher called on Maria to read out loud. When she said one of the words wrong, some children in the class laughed. *(Rip.)* At recess, as students were lining up, Raymond gave Maria a poke in the back. *(Rip.)* "Slowpoke, slowpoke," he chanted. *(Rip.)*

3. Ask: **How do you think Maria is feeling now? When she feels like this, do you think she can learn as much as when she is feeling good about herself?**

Maria is usually a very good sport if someone accidentally bumps into her on the playground. Do you think she will be as pleasant today if someone bumps into her? What would happen to her if she were treated like this day after day?

4. Hold up the other heart. Tell the students you are going to retell the story, but this time, instead of including put-downs, you would like them to think of put-ups that the people in the story could give instead.

5. Retell the story, stopping at each put-down and asking the class for suggestions of possible put-ups. After hearing a few, use a colorful marker to put a star on the heart. At the end of the story, point out that even though she had the same problems, the way people treated her added a sparkle instead of tearing at her heart.

6. Ask: **How do you think Maria is feeling now? How much do you think she will be able to learn today? How do you think she will act if someone accidentally bumps into her?**

Summary

What did we learn today? Lead a brief discussion of the effects of put-downs and put-ups on people. **What do we always want to remember to do in our class?**

Closing: "I Like You"

Teach the song, "I Like You," to the tune of "Skip to My Lou."

I Like You

I like you; there's no doubt about it.

I like you; there's no doubt about it.

I like you; there's no doubt about it.

You are my best friend.

You like me; there's no doubt about it.

You like me; there's no doubt about it.

You like me; there's no doubt about it.

I am your best friend.

I like me; there's no doubt about it.

I like me; there's no doubt about it.

I like me; there's no doubt about it.

I am my best friend.

Teach the song with gestures, as follows:

Verse 1

"I" *Point to self with finger or both hands.* **"like you;"** *Point to other with finger or both hands.* **"there's no doubt about it."** *Move finger back and forth, to the left, then right.*

"You" *Point to other with finger or both hands.* **"are my"** *Point to self with finger or both hands.* **"best friend."** *Cross hands over chest like a hug.*

Verse 2

"You" *Point to other with finger or both hands.* **"like me;"** *Point to self with finger or both hands.* **"there's no doubt about it."** *Move finger back and forth, to the left, then right.* **"I"** *Point to self with finger or both hands* **"am your"** *Point to other with finger or both hands* **"best friend."** *Cross hands over chest like a hug.*

Extensions and Infusion Ideas

Ongoing Recognition of Put-Ups

When you hear students using put-ups, recognize them verbally and label the behaviors you observe. You can also create a visual acknowledgement by creating a bulletin board that includes the put-ups you notice. One teacher found a creative way of using all the bows she had saved from gifts. After putting a large cutout heart on the board, she then added a bow to the heart when she heard a put-up she wanted to acknowledge. The very colorful, full heart became a reminder to students about the importance of supporting each other.

Other bulletin board ideas include using seasonal themes to frame put-ups that you and the students notice. For example, in the fall, you could start with a tree trunk and a supply of various colors of die-cut leaves. Write put-ups on the leaves as you hear them and add them to the tree. In February, display a bulletin board with the put-ups written on die-cut hearts or snowmen for a winter theme; in spring, use flowers. Use words that most students can read and the board can become an additional reading incentive.

Car Wash

Explain: **The purpose of a car wash is to help cars get clean and sparkling. Just as cars collect dust and dirt from being out in the world, we people sometimes can feel "dirtied" by the put-downs we get over the course of a day. Receiving put-ups can be a way of helping us remember our positive qualities and helping us feel great about ourselves again.**

Select one or more students to "go through the car wash." Review what put-ups are and ask students to think of some put-ups for the students who are going to go through the "wash." Have the other students form two lines facing each other, with enough room for a student to walk between. Students proceed slowly through the "car wash," with students on either side giving them a put-up as the "car" briefly pauses in front of them.

ABC I Like Me!

ABC I Like Me!, by Nancy Carlson (New York: Viking, 1977) is a brightly illustrated alphabet book in which a pig, a frog, and a mouse all celebrate their
own wonderful qualities, letter by letter.

Introduce the activity by telling students that it is just as important to give
ourselves put-ups as it is to give put-ups to others. Have students form a circle.
Say: **Today we are going to read a book in which we are going to meet a pig,
a frog, and a mouse, and some of their friends. With each letter of the alphabet, they will tell us about themselves. Listen closely to find out what
each of them says about themselves. As you listen to this book, think
about what words might describe you. Later you will get to tell a partner
what you are like.**

At several points in the book, ask the class questions like: **What quality did
pig say he has? What did frog say about himself? What qualities does
mouse have?**

After you read the book, pair students with partners. Once the students
have partners, tell them to ask their partners what words they thought of to
describe themselves. Depending on your class, you may want to structure
which student goes first by a random method, such as "the person with the
shortest hair" or "whoever is sitting closer to the door." After the pairs have
shared with each other, have them get permission to share with the rest of the
class the qualities their partners told them. Have the class come back into a circle. Ask for volunteers to tell what they found out from their partners – what
qualities the partner has. Acknowledge feelings and things that come up
during the sharing.

Connecting to Literature

When reading books and stories, point out put-ups and put-downs. Have students identify and discuss the effects of these statements on the characters in
the story.

How to Lose All Your Friends, by Nancy Carlson
(New York: Viking, 1994) Gr. P-2

Summary: A list of ways to lose your friends.

1. Before reading the last page, ask: What could the girl do to be happier?

2. After reading the book, ask: This book gives six directions for losing
    friends. Can you think of six directions for *making* friends?

3. Write your own directions for "How to have a Happy Classroom."

So What?, by Miriam Cohen
(New York: Bantam Doubleday Dell Books for Young Readers, 1998) Gr. K-3

Summary: Elinor Woodman from Chicago teaches Jim that ranking
does not matter.

1. What did Jim think about himself in the beginning?

2. Why did Jim want to start a club? Did it help him be popular?

3. What did Elinor Woodman mean when she said, "So what?"

4. Was the class the same after Elinor left? If someone in our class moved away, how would we be different as a class?

Elmer and the Kangaroo, by David McKee
(New York: HarperCollins Publishers, 2000) Gr. K-3

Summary: Elmer teaches a kangaroo, who can only bounce, that he can jump and win the contest. Strangers become friends.

1. How did Elmer, Lion, and Tiger help Kangaroo win the contest?

2. What does the story tell us?

3. What could you say to the white kangaroo after Kangaroo made the winning jump? Make a list of put-ups you could say to your classmates. (The list can be posted as a resource.)

4. Is there something you would like your friends to help you learn to do?

GRADE 1, LESSON 3
Exploring Our Diversity

Cultural Competence and
Social Responsibility

CASEL SEL COMPETENCIES

Sa Self-Awareness

SO Social Awareness

Gathering: Something I Like To Do

Have students make a circle. Ask them to think about an activity they like to do or a hobby they have. Remind students how to use the Talking Object and how to demonstrate respectful listening. Model by sharing something you like to do. (This works best if it is something different from the activities you think they might say. This avoids the temptation for students to say the same activity in order to be like the teacher.)

After you have modeled, pass the object to a student next to you and ask him to share something he enjoys doing. When appropriate, without interrupting the student who is speaking, remark on good listening as you observe it, pointing out specific behaviors.

Remind students to look around at the whole class while they talk. Occasionally, ask the student who was just speaking questions such as: **How did it feel to have people paying attention to you? How could you tell if people were listening?**

Agenda Check

Summarize and discuss what occurred during the gathering. The goal is to get students to recognize that their classmates had different things to share. Say: **Raise your hand if someone shared something different from what you shared, but something you also like to do. Raise your hand if someone else shared something they like to do that you don't enjoy doing. There are many ways we are alike as well as ways we are different. Today we are going to explore other similarities and differences we have with each other. First, puppets will help us talk about similarities and differences** (Diversity Puppets). **Next, you will have an opportunity to discover ways you and another classmate are the same and ways you are different** (Comparing Partners). **We'll end by summarizing what we learned** (Summary) **and then do a fun activity at the end** (Closing).

Activity: Diversity Puppets

1. Introduce the puppets to the students, saying something like: **These two puppets are friends. They are going to help us learn about things that people have in common – things that are the same about us – and things that are different.** Have the puppets introduce themselves. Names should not be those of people in the class.

Workshop Agenda
- Gathering: Something I Like To Do
- Agenda Check
- Activity: Diversity Puppets
- Activity: Comparing Partners
- Summary
- Closing: Person-to-Person

Materials
- Workshop agenda, written on chart paper and posted
- Talking Object
- Two puppets with different physical characteristics

Learning Outcome
- Students will identify ways in which they are similar to and different from one another.

Connections to Standards
Behavioral Studies
- Understands that people are different and alike
- Understands that people learn from each other in many ways

Health
- Understands individual differences (in appearance, behavior)

109

2. Through the mouths of the puppets, explain: **In a few minutes, the teacher will ask you to pair up and notice what is the same and what is different about each other. But before that happens, let's look at "us"** (the puppets). **We are partners. What do we have in common? How are we different?**

3. Listen actively as the students notice differences in skin color, hair, eyes, facial characteristics, gender, and clothing. Then ask them to say what the puppet characters have in common.

4. After they have identified traits that can be seen, ask them if there are some other things that could be the same or different about them, things that cannot be seen. Through a discussion, come up with such things as: kinds of families, numbers of brothers and sisters, hobbies and interests, favorite color, food, etc.

Activity: Comparing Partners

1. Have students partner with a classmate. (See Teaching Tools for suggestions about pairing students.)

2. Ask students to notice what they have in common with their partners and what's different. Tell them they should try to think of as many things as possible, but that they need to find out at least one way that they are the same and one way that they are different that are not things the rest of the class can see. Give them several minutes to do this. Circulate and help pairs that are experiencing difficulty think of at least one non-obvious way that they are the same and one non-obvious way that they are different.

3. Have students make a circle again, sitting next to their partner. Go around the circle and ask each pair to describe a difference or similarity that they learned about each other. Highlight and encourage the similarities and differences that the rest of the group cannot see. Through this process, elicit a variety of ways in which we are similar to each other and different from each other.

Summary

Today we learned about ways that we are different from each other as well as things we have in common with others in the class. How many of you found out something about someone else that surprised you? How did it feel to discover a way that you and someone else were alike? What do you think it would be like if all of us were exactly the same? Fortunately, although we share many things with others, each of us is different – unique. No one is just like each of us. Differences are wonderful, but could they sometimes cause conflicts? What could we remember to help us deal with these conflicts?

Closing: Person-to-Person

Have students stand and face their partners. As you call out the name of a body part, ask partners to connect those parts. For example, when you call out "knees," partners touch knees. As a variation, call out two body parts for people to connect, for example, one elbow to one knee.

Extensions and Infusion Ideas

Different Ways to Play

Ask the class if they all like to play. The chances are they will all agree that they do. Point out that liking to play is one thing they all have in common. Tell them that children and grownups all over the world love to play, but that people play in different ways.

Ask the students to choose partners and talk with their partners about their favorite games. Give them two or three minutes for this.

Ask volunteers to share their favorite games. Make a list of the games students name.

Discuss: **What's similar about the games on the list? What's different?** Ask students if they always agree with their friends on which games they will play. Invite them to tell about a time when they disagreed with a friend about which game they would play. How did they feel about not wanting to play the same game as their friend(s)? How does it feel to like different things? Do your likes and dislikes make you different? How does that feel?

Family Banners

(Note: *In this activity it is very important to create a safe climate in which students can describe their own families. Give consideration to particular issues that may come up with individual students. Many students, and most of the students in some class-rooms, do not live in traditional families. There are many family structures, including same-sex and single-parent families. Be sensitive to those students who may be in foster placements, who live with extended family members, or who have one or more impor-tant people missing in their lives because of legal or medical reasons.*)

Start the activity with a class discussion that could begin something like: **There is a lot of variety in families today. Our families can be very differ-ent from each other.** Then ask: **How are our families the same? How could they be different?** (You may want to make a list of these.) **We've all learned that there is nothing wrong with being different, but that we can feel sad if we are treated badly because of our differences.**

Tell students that they are going to make a special banner with pictures and words that represent their families.

Distribute paper and markers. Explain that you want students to make a ban-ner showing things that are important to their families. First, ask them to put their family's name on the paper. Next, ask them to add words or pictures that tell more about their families.

They might put names or pictures of people in their families, something about holidays, things members of their families like to do together, places where their families live, etc.

If you feel your students need more structure, you could divide the paper into a number of spaces and ask students to fill in each space with a particular category. For example, a picture of their family in the first space, something their family does in the evening in the second space, and a favorite food their family likes to eat in the third space. Be sure to choose categories that all students will feel comfortable responding to.

Ask students to find a partner. Give the partners a few minutes to show their family banners and describe them. Ask two or three volunteers to show their family banners to the class and describe them. Display all the banners on a bulletin board.

Connecting to Literature

Meet the Barkers: Morgan and Moffat Go to School, by Tomie De Paolo
(New York: G. P. Putnam's Sons, 2001) Gr. P-2

Summary: The Welsh terrier twins are introduced. Moffie gets gold stars and Morgie makes friends. Then they learn to diversify.

1. How are Morgie and Moffie the same? How are they different?

2. How are you like Morgie? Like Moffie? Is one better than the other? Why or why not?

Five Creatures, by Emily Jenkins
(New York: Farrar, Straus and Giroux, 2001) Gr. P-2

Summary: This story shows many ways the parents, daughter, and their two cats are alike and different.

1. Tell the ways some of the creatures in this story are alike. How are they different?

2. Select a pair of pages in the book: Think of every creature who lives with you. What statements can you make about the creatures in your house? What is something they all need?

All the Colors We Are, by Katie Kissinger
(St. Paul, MN: Redleaf Press, 1994) Gr. 1-4

Summary: Relates the three ways we get our skin color: parents, sun, and melanin.

1. What are the three ways we get our skin color?

2. Think about your own skin color. Do you think your ancestors came from a sunny place or a cooler place?

3. Slowly read the paint swatch colors on p. 30. Then pass the Talking Object, giving children the option of sharing which color best represents his or her skin color.

Respecting Differences

Cultural Competence and
Social Responsibility

CASEL SEL COMPETENCIES

SA   Self-Awareness

SO   Social Awareness

Gathering: A Favorite Food

Have students make a circle. Explain that one of the important reasons that gatherings are done in circles is so that everyone is in a position that enables them to use all of their good listening skills as each person takes a turn. Remind them that a key part of good listening is being able to face people and look at them as they are speaking.

Explain: **How do people feel when the people they are talking with use good listening skills while they are speaking? That kind of listening is probably one of the biggest put-ups we can give and helps us build a respectful classroom. Today we are going to tell each other about our favorite food. Before we start, think of a food that you really like.**

Point out that they are not all thinking of the same food at this point. Tell students about a food that you like that will be different from many of the other students' choices (fish, a certain vegetable, etc). Explain that you may also like a food that almost everybody might like – for example, pizza or ice cream – but it wouldn't be very interesting if everyone said the same food. Students should be familiar with go-rounds, and you may decide to have a student start, instead of modeling a response first. Sometimes there is a tendency to want to please or be like the teacher that may influence students' choices. Go around the circle, prompting if needed.

Agenda Check

We've started to look at ways we're alike and different. We practiced ways of listening well to one another and talked about how important it is that we respect each other so we can trust each other enough to speak freely. In today's lesson, we'll talk about what an opinion is (Opinions) **and then we're going to find out if we have different ideas about things by playing a game** (Corners). **We'll ask some questions about what we learned** (Summary) **and end the lesson with a song** (Closing).

Activity: Opinions

1. Introduce the activity: **Lots of times people have different ideas about things. When people believe that their idea is true, we call that having an opinion. For example, it is Marco's opinion that you should always color the sky blue in your picture. Keisha's opinion is that it is all right to color the sky pink or gold if you want to. Even though people have different opinions, they can still be friends.**

Workshop Agenda

- Gathering: A Favorite Food
- Agenda Check
- Activity: Opinions
- Activity: Corners
- Summary
- Closing: "I Like You"

Materials

- Workshop agenda, written on chart paper and posted
- Three signs labeled *Agree, Disagree, Not Sure*
- Masking tape

Learning Outcome

- Students will understand that people, even friends, may not agree with each others' opinions.

Connections to Standards

Behavioral Studies

- Understands that people are both different and alike
- Understands that people often choose to do the same things as their friends, but also may do things their own way
- Knows that disagreements are common, even among family and friends

2. Ask the students who think cats make the best pets to raise their hands. Say that all of those people who raised their hands *agree* on something – that they think cats are good pets. Show them the sign labeled *Agree*. Say that this word shows we have the same opinion about something.

3. Ask which students don't think cats make the best pets and would not want to have a cat. These people disagree with the idea that cats make good pets. Show students the sign labeled *Disagree*. The people who don't think cats make good pets disagree with the people who do.

4. Show the sign labeled *Not Sure*. Ask if there are people in the room who don't know whether they think cats make good pets. Maybe these people will have an opinion about whether or not cats make good pets at some time in the future, but right now they are not sure.

Activity: Corners

1. Tape the three signs to the wall in three different corners of the room. In the next part of this activity, students will move around the room to the corners where the signs are posted. If, for some reason, having students move around the room is inappropriate for your class, tape the signs along a continuum on the chalkboard. Then, instead of having students show their opinion by moving to a corner, you can have them raise their hands. Write the count below the *Disagree*, *Not Sure*, and *Agree* signs.

2. Tell the students that you are going to make a statement. Explain: **Those people who agree with the statement should stand by the *Agree* sign. Those who disagree should stand by the *Disagree* sign. Those who aren't sure should stand by the *Not Sure* sign.** Carefully define expected behavior by saying something like: **Just like in the Stand Up If game, you are going to let people know your opinion by silently moving your body to one of the three corners. It may be difficult not to talk, but it is important to remain silent.** After they are standing quietly in their groups, you can ask students who would like to to explain to the group the reason that they moved to that particular sign. It can also be helpful to acknowledge potential distractions in different corners of the room and remind students about the importance of respectful listening.

3. Read one of the following statements:

   • Vanilla is the best flavor of ice cream.

   • Red clothes look better on people than blue.

   • Children my age should be allowed to decide what time to go to bed.

   • Math, or working with numbers, is more fun than reading.

4. When they have sorted themselves out, ask a few volunteers from each group to talk about the position they chose. You might also ask if they see one of their friends standing in a different place from themselves. Emphasize that sometimes people who are friends have different opinions about something. Give lots of positive feedback about the good listening you observe.

5. Repeat with other statements. Add others as you wish. Stop before students lose the ability to focus and enjoy the activity.

Summary

Gather students in a circle. Some questions to ask: **How did you decide where to stand in the room? Were there different people in the groups for different statements? How many of you changed your mind after hearing ideas people shared about their opinions? Was it hard to be honest instead of just going to a group because your friend was there? How did it feel to be in a big group or a very small group?**

Summarize by saying something like: **Sometimes people we know think the same things we do and sometimes they don't. We can be friends even if we don't agree on everything.**

Closing: "I Like You"

Sing, "I Like You." See page 105 for lyrics.

Extensions and Infusion Ideas

Opinion Graphs

You will need to draw chart-sized tables with empty cells. The number of columns can vary, but approximately six should be enough to provide different choices. The number of rows should be enough to hold most of your students' names. You will also need cards with each student's name sized to fit into a cell.

This activity is a way for students to learn more about each other. It also reinforces students' ability to express an opinion. You can choose different topics, such as favorite color, movie, etc. This illustration uses Favorite Food for Dinner. Ask students for the names of the food they like best for dinner. Write their responses across the bottom cells. Give each student her own name card. Have students come up one-by-one and place their name card above one of the foods named, i.e. her favorite.

Opinion Graph					
William					
Phoebe					
Aaron		Anthony			
Sam		Sergio			
Latisha		Dwayne			
Carlos		Tara			
Maria	Maddison	Juan		Jose	
Toby	Elisa	Jane	Bob	Ellie	
Susie	Tom	Gina	Greg	Allan	Ken
Enchiladas	Hamburgers	Pizza	Chicken	Spaghetti	Fish

When students are finished expressing their opinion, help them reflect on the graph and what it shows. Lead a discussion that emphasizes that every choice is equally valid. This can be a great place to acknowledge that sometimes when there is a strong majority in favor of one choice, there can be a tendency to think that the other choices are not as good. If this exercise is done with different topics, students will get used to the idea of being in different groups at different times, and be comfortable with the fact that the size of their groups will change.

Math

Using the graph from the previous activity, have students count the number of people who chose each food. Write the number at the bottom of each column. Have students identify the tallest and shortest columns and the categories with the most and fewest choices. As students get into simple arithmetic, the graph can be used with addition and subtraction problems. **How many more people prefer Spaghetti to Fish? How many people preferred either Pizza or Spaghetti?**

Connecting to Literature

Look for and help students identify those places in stories and books in which characters are expressing opinions. Ask them their opinions about what they have read or about characters in the story. Examples might be: **How many of you think what Pooh just did will solve the problem? How many disagree and think something else will need to be done? How many of you think this is the best book we have read so far this year? How many disagree and like one of the ones we have already read better than this one? Which one is your favorite?** etc.

Aggie and Will, by Larry Dane Brimner
(New York: Children's Press of Grolie, 1998) Gr. K-3

Summary: These friends disagree on everything but going to the library.

1. Name some of the ways Aggie and Will disagreed. For each way mentioned, ask: What is a positive way to express disagreement?

2. How do Aggie and Will manage to stay friends?

3. What is helpful if you and your friend want to stay friends? Tell some ways you and a friend can disagree but still remain friends.

Mr. and Mrs. Muddle, by Mary Ann Hoberman
(Boston: Little, Brown and Company, 1988) Gr. 1-3

Summary: This donkey couple agrees on almost everything except that he does not want a car and she does. They are hampered in many activities until Elmer the turtle helps them find a middle way around this disagreement.

1. Name some areas in which Mr. and Mrs. Muddle agree.

2. Name some things they did not get to do because they disagreed.

3. What were their reasons for their opinions?

4. How did Elmer help Mr. and Mrs. Muddle solve their problems?

5. What do you find it helpful to do when you do not agree with someone?

GRADE 1, LESSON 5
Identifying Feelings

 Emotional Literacy

CASEL SEL COMPETENCIES

SA Self-Awareness

SM Self-Management

Gathering: Feelings Faces

Have students sit in a circle. Ask them if they have ever noticed how actors and actresses show feelings on their faces. Challenge them to see if they can show on their faces the way they would feel in the situations that you will describe. Encourage them to look around and notice each other's faces during the activity. After each statement you, too, should model the feeling.

- Today is your birthday.
- Your birthday present gets lost.
- You find it.
- There is a bee flying around your head.
- The bee lands on your arm.
- It flies away.
- You are playing with your friend.
- Your friend breaks your favorite toy.
- Your friend says she's sorry.
- It's snowing outside.
- Your mother says you can't go outside in the snow.
- She changes her mind.

Agenda Check

We have been learning things that will help us get along better with each other. Today we are going to start learning more about feelings and how we communicate them. Being able to communicate our feelings is important in helping us solve problems. First, we'll think of some words that describe feelings (Feelings Words). **Then we'll get to do some art** (Drawing a Feeling). **We'll end by summarizing what we learned** (Summary) **and sharing our pictures** (Closing).

Activity: Feelings Words

1. Now that students have shown some feelings on their faces, they will be able to think of words that name feelings. Ask students to think of words that name the feelings they just expressed in Feelings Faces. List the words on chart paper.

Workshop Agenda
- Gathering: Feelings Faces
- Agenda Check
- Activity: Feelings Words
- Activity: Drawing or Painting a Feeling
- Summary
- Closing: Sharing Pictures

Materials
- Workshop agenda, written on chart paper and posted
- Chart paper and markers
- Paper for drawings or paintings
- Drawing or painting materials

Learning Outcomes
- Students will identify words that describe feelings.
- Students will expand their vocabulary of feelings words.

Connections to Standards
Behavioral Studies
- Knows that people learn from each other in many ways

Health
- Identifies and shares feelings in appropriate ways

Language Arts
Reading
- Relates new information to prior knowledge and experience

Viewing
- Knows different features (e.g. facial expressions, body language) affect a viewer's perception of characters in visual media

2. After students have come up with an initial list, expand their thinking by reading a book that presents a rich list of feeling words. *Today I Feel Silly & Other Moods That Make My Day* by Jamie Lee Curtis (New York: Scholastic, 1999) is a good example. Read it to the students and ask them to pay attention to feelings words they may have not thought of when making the list. Tell them to try to remember the words so you can add them to the list.

3. Pick feelings from the list and ask students to think of a time they felt that way.

4. Save the chart for future reference.

Activity: Drawing or Painting a Feeling

1. Ask students to think of a feeling and picture a time they felt that way. Ask: **What were you doing? Who else was there? Where were you?** Then ask them to draw a picture of that feeling.

2. Distribute art materials for drawing or painting. While they are drawing, walk around and briefly talk with each student about their work. Have the students write or dictate the name of the feeling and/or a sentence about the feeling.

Summary

Today we've begun to learn more about feelings. Do you think that some feelings are more difficult to experience or deal with than others? Being able to use a word to describe how we are feeling can help us in many ways. It can help us communicate to others what we need and want, and it can help us understand how someone else feels.

Closing: Sharing Pictures

Have students make a circle and bring their pictures with them. Have them put their pictures face down on the floor in front of them. Explain that you are going to go around the circle and have each student, one at a time, pick up his picture to share with the others. Ask them to tell what feeling their picture is about. Remind students about good listening and the importance of not touching their picture until it is their turn. Let them know that it is okay if they would rather not show their picture; all they need to say is *pass* when it is their turn. You may want to collect the drawings to assemble into a class Feelings Book.

Extensions and Infusion Ideas

Feelings Collage

Either as an individual or small-group activity, assign a feeling to each individual or group and ask students to find appropriate pictures from newspapers and magazines illustrating it. Use the pictures to make a collage.

Be sure the newspapers and magazines are appropriate for the racial and ethnic composition of your class.

Feelings Chart

As other words that name feelings come up in daily class activities, add them to the chart begun in this lesson. Illustrate the chart with students' drawings.

Feelings Boxes

Write each student's name on a tongue depressor or Popsicle stick with a brightly colored marker, using one of six colors. Store the sticks in six small containers covered in the same six colors as the markers. Students can retrieve their sticks easily by looking in the appropriate boxes of the correct colors.

When students come into the room each day, have them find their sticks and put them into a Feelings Box to show what feelings they are having at that moment. Label boxes *Happy, Sad, Angry / Mad, Afraid / Worried, Embarrassed, Other*, and have students decorate them with faces that express those feelings. Empty, individual milk or juice containers from the cafeteria are just about the right size to hold the sticks once you cut off the tops of the containers and open them up. These can be covered with colored contact paper before being decorated.

If you like, you can ask one or two people if they feel like talking about the feeling they chose.

Connecting to Literature

As you read different books, have students identify the way characters in the story are feeling. As books or stories use feeling words that were not already listed on the chart, add them to the list.

Some Days, Other Days, by P. J. Petersen
(New York: Charles Scribner's Sons, 1994) Gr. 1-3

Summary: Jimmy is not sure he wants to get up because some days things go well and other days they do not.

1. After each pair of "Some days ... Other days ..." ask students to name some feelings Jimmy might have.

2. After reading the book, ask: Why didn't Jimmy want to get out of bed?

3. Jimmy's mother taught him an important lesson about helping the day go better. What can you do to make sure the day has some comfortable feelings in it?

How Do I Feel, by Norma Simon
(Chicago: Albert Whitman & Company, 1979) Gr. K-3

Summary: Carl tells of his twin Eddie and their family. The boys often feel differently about the same situation.

1. After each time Carl asks, "How do I feel?" stop so the students can guess how Carl is feeling.

2. After reading the book, ask: Tell about a time when you and a friend or brother or sister had different feelings about what was happening. Do you know why that happened? (Maybe one person was tired, more interested, not alert, etc.)

Communicating Feelings

 Emotional Literacy

CASEL SEL COMPETENCIES

SO   Social Awareness

RS   Relationship Skills

Gathering: Mimic the Leader

This is a simple theater warm-up exercise. Ask students to imitate the sounds and motions you make. The sillier you are, the better. Once everyone understands the exercise, give one or two students a turn at leading.

Agenda Check

Today we are going to be looking at how we communicate feelings and how we can listen to or read the feelings that others are communicating. In the gathering, we were communicating. In this lesson we're going to examine how our different facial expressions and voices communicate different feelings (Feelings Faces and Voices). **Next, we'll play a game of charades** (Feelings Charades). **Can anyone tell me what charades is?** Briefly define. **Then we'll use our words to communicate about feelings** (Sharing Stories). **We'll end by summarizing what we learned** (Summary) **and singing a song** (Closing).

Activity: Feelings Faces and Voices

1. Make your face look like it would if you were experiencing one of the feelings from the Feelings Chart made during Lesson 5. Ask students to guess the feeling. Repeat several times. Then tell students that you are going to see if they can guess the feeling from the way your voice sounds. Say the sentence, "Today is ___ (insert day of the week)." Turn your face away and say the sentence in a tone of voice that would convey one of the feelings. It is best at first to stick with the basic categories of feelings such as happy, sad, mad, or scared.

2. Use the experience to convey that feelings are communicated by facial expressions and by tone of voice. If students make mistakes guessing, it is an opportunity to point out that no one can know for sure how a person is feeling without checking it out with the person directly. It can also be an opportunity to point out that just as with any communication, sometimes the message doesn't get through clearly, which can cause or add to conflict.

Activity: Feelings Charades

1. Say: **Just as our faces and voices can let people know how we are feeling, our bodies can also communicate how we are feeling.** Explain that students will act out feelings listed on the chart from Lesson 5.

Workshop Agenda

- Gathering: Mimic the Leader
- Agenda Check
- Activity: Feelings Faces and Voices
- Activity: Feelings Charades
- Activity: Sharing Stories
- Summary
- Closing: "If You're Happy and You Know It"

Materials

- Workshop agenda, written on chart paper and posted
- Chart listing feelings from Lesson 5

Learning Outcomes

- Students will be able to describe the ways people communicate when they have strong feelings.
- Students will be able to identify physical reactions and physical behaviors related to strong feelings.
- Students will be able to demonstrate feelings both verbally and nonverbally.

Connections to Standards

Language Arts

Listening and Speaking

- Uses different voice level, phrasing, and intonation for different situations

Working with Others

- Occasionally serves as a leader in groups
- Uses nonverbal communication such as eye contact, body positions, and voice tone effectively

2. Choose a feeling from the chart – for example, *anger*. Have all students pantomime an action, for example, sweeping the floor, in an angry way.

3. Have students pantomime other actions in an angry way (sharpening a pencil, shaking hands, buttoning a shirt).

4. Ask for volunteers to choose another feeling from the chart and pantomime an action reflecting the feeling for the class to guess. Ask volunteers to show the feeling with their faces as well as with the movements of their bodies.

Activity: Sharing Stories

1. Explain: **While our faces, voices, and bodies can communicate feelings, words are an important way to tell others how we are feeling.** Tell students they will now have an opportunity to communicate feelings by talking about them.

2. Divide students into pairs. Have students take turns telling about a time when they were happy. They should include whether they let others know how they were feeling and, if they did, how they communicated the feeling. Allow one minute for each turn.

   (Note: *Some students may have trouble using their time well in pairs. If this is the case in your class, you can either adapt this lesson for the whole class or go ahead with the pairing with the understanding that it will take time and practice before your students are able to exchange time in pairs.*)

3. Ask two or three volunteers to share their experience with the group and describe the way they communicated their feeling.

Summary

Today we have learned a lot about communicating feelings. What are some ways people show what they're feeling without talking? What are some ways our bodies react when we have strong feelings? How could we tell what our classmates were feeling? Why do you think it is important to be able to tell how a person is feeling?

Closing: "If You're Happy and You Know It"

Sing "If You're Happy and You Know It." Lyrics can be found on pages 30 and 31.

Extensions and Infusion Ideas

Sharing Stories

Repeat the Sharing Stories activity with other feelings.

Feelings Walk

Gather the students in a standing circle. **We're going to play a walking game. We'll walk around the classroom like a centipede.** (Review the meaning of *centipede.*) Choose one child to be at the head of the centipede, behind you. Everyone else lines up behind her. Practice snaking around the class in this line for a few steps until the children get the technique. Then say, **This centipede's name is Pete.** (Change the name if you have a student named Pete.) **Pete's very happy today because he got new sneakers** (or whatever your students call them)! **(Bet you didn't know centipedes wear sneakers!) Let's snake around the class and show with your body how happy you are.** Demonstrate a happy walk, showing happiness in your whole body. Lead the children around in the snake walk for just a few steps, guiding them to do a happy walk.

Walk around four more times, saying each of these sentences:

- Pete's angry because Joe the Snake stepped on his sneakers.
- Pete's happy again because Joe said he's sorry.
- Pete's feelings are hurt because someone made fun of his sneakers.
- Pete's happy again because someone said his sneakers are really cool.

How Did It Feel?

For this activity, you will need a set of Feelings Cards for each team of three or four students. Create the cards using 3x5 or 5x8 cards and putting a different feeling word on each. Use words from the chart created in Lesson 5.

After reading a story or seeing a play in which characters experienced different feelings, divide students into teams of three or four.

Give each team a set of Feelings Cards. Choose a main character from the story and ask teams to choose cards that describe the way that character in the story felt at (1) the beginning, (2) the middle, and (3) the end.

Ask each group to present their cards to the class and describe why they chose their particular cards.

Have the class go over what they just did by asking questions such as: **What happened in the story that made you choose this particular feeling? At what point in the story did the feelings change? Why? What exactly was said or done to cause the feelings to change?**

Connecting to Literature

As you read books, point out the many ways emotions are communicated. Have students discuss what characters might be feeling and why they think the characters are experiencing that particular emotion.

If You're Happy and You Know It!, by Jan Ormerod, et al. (New York: Star Bright Books, 2003) Gr. P-2

Summary: Variations on the song, in which animals join in on the verses, each expressing happiness in his or her own way.

1. Each character in this book has his or her own way of showing happiness. The author says, "Do your thing." What does that mean?

2. What is one way you show happiness?

3. How do you think each character shows that he or she is sad? Mad? Scared? How do you show you are sad? Mad? Scared?

My Many Colored Days, by Dr. Seuss
(New York: Alfred Knopf, Inc., 1996) Gr. P-3

Summary: Using colors, a child describes his feelings on given days. In the end, he accepts the range of feelings he has.

1. Name some of the colors of the child's days and tell how he feels on that color of day.

2. Reread the book and stop at each color. Show how you would look when you are having a day of this color. Choose a color for today: red, blue, brown, yellow, gray, orange, green, purple, pink, black, mixed-up.

3. Maybe *your* ideas of colors are not the same as Dr. Seuss's ideas. For example, if your favorite color is purple, then you might feel really good on a purple day. If your ideas about colors are different from the ones in the book, tell what *your* colored day would look like.

Responses to Anger

 Emotional Literacy

CASEL SEL COMPETENCIES

SA   Self-Awareness

SM   Self-Management

Gathering: I Feel Happy When…

Make a circle. Using the Talking Object, tell students that they will each have a turn to complete the sentence: "I feel happy when… ." Model by completing the sentence yourself, and then go around the circle.

Agenda Check

Today we are going to be learning more about anger. Anger is an important feeling that often develops in conflict situations. While it is an emotion that we all feel, it is probably the feeling that is hardest for us to deal with successfully. We'll look at what people do when they're angry (Things People Do When They're Angry) and how we can stay calm when we get angry (Cooling Off). We'll talk about what we learned (Summary) and end by singing a song (Closing).

Activity: Things People Do When They're Angry

1. Explain: **People do different things when they get angry. You can think of some of these things by talking with a partner. Then we will make a list of things people do when they're angry.**

2. Divide students into pairs and have them listen to each other in turn. (This can also be done as a whole class.) Ask students to think of a time they were angry. What happened? What did they do? How did the situation turn out? Allow about a minute each.

3. With the students still in pairs, ask them to recall a time someone was angry at them. Ask: **What happened? How did you feel?** Allow about a minute.

4. Ask students to sum up the things people do when they're angry. List their responses on chart paper. Distinguish between constructive and destructive responses by discussing: **Might any of these things on our list hurt someone or be dangerous in some way? Could any of these get a person into trouble? Would any of these either not solve the problem or make it worse? Are there any that might hurt the person who got angry in the long run?** (Note: *If students respond, "Keep your feelings to yourself," or "Ignore it," explain that this approach may lead to a bigger problem later on.*)

5. Draw a line through those responses that might be dangerous or hurtful immediately or in the long run. The line means that these are not recommended.

Workshop Agenda

*   Gathering: I Feel Happy When…
*   Agenda Check
*   Activity: Things People Do When They're Angry
*   Activity: Cooling Off
*   Summary
*   Closing: "This Little Light of Mine"

Materials

*   Workshop agenda, written on chart paper and posted
*   Chart paper and markers
*   Talking Object

Learning Outcomes

*   Students will be able to identify how people behave when they are angry.
*   Students will be able to describe and distinguish between constructive and destructive responses to anger.

Connections to Standards

Health

*   Identifies and shares feelings in appropriate ways
*   Understands individual differences (e.g., appearance, behavior)

Language Arts

Listening and Speaking

*   Makes contributions in class and group discussions (e.g., recounts personal experiences)

6. Ask: **Will any of these responses lead to a good result?** Often there are only a few things, sometimes none that are not already crossed off. Save the chart for use in Lesson 10.

Activity: Cooling Off

1. The vast majority, if not all, of the items on the Things People Do list will probably have a line through them at this point. This can help make the point that although everyone gets angry, and there is nothing wrong with the emotion of anger, it is often very difficult for people to make good decisions about what to do when they are angry.

2. Explain that when people are angry, it can be hard to think clearly about what to do. When that happens, it's good to know some ways to cool off so we can think better about what to do. It's called cooling off because our bodies can get hot when we're angry. Examples of cooling off can be found in the Extensions and Infusion Ideas in this lesson.

3. Ask students to brainstorm all the ways they can think of to cool off. List their responses on chart paper. Stress that once a person has cooled off, he then can think about the problem more clearly. The point is not to cool off and ignore the problem, but to gain a little time in order to think. This can be a good time to introduce the concept and practice of a Peaceful Place in the classroom. See page 129.

Summary

What is one thing that you learned today? One of the important things to remember is that anger, like all feelings, is a natural part of being human. The important thing is that we learn to deal with our feelings in good ways. It's okay to be angry; it isn't okay to be mean. How can we use what we've learned in our class? (Discuss.) **Sometimes anger and the things we feel like doing when we are angry can cover up who we are inside and keep people from seeing who we really are. For the closing, we're going to learn a song that reminds us to let our light shine.**

Closing: "This Little Light of Mine"

This song can be found in *Linking Up!*, by Sarah Pirtle, and on the *Linking Up!* CD, Track 3. Music and lyrics at end of lesson.

Extensions and Infusion Ideas

More Cooling Off Strategies

Counting If students' ideas for cooling off didn't include counting, suggest counting to 10 or 20. It is surprising how many young people have not been exposed to this simple strategy. The reason it is effective is that it requires the brain to think about something different from what was triggering the anger.

Other things students could use to distract the mind could include thinking of as many different names of colors as possible, perhaps keeping track of how many with their fingers.

Deep Breathing Slow and deep breathing is another very effective way of calming down. Breathing is something we can consciously control. As we slow down and deepen our breathing, we begin to control other autonomic responses, such as increased heart rate and muscle tension. Filling up your lungs as if you were a balloon is one way to do this. Have the students fill their lungs as full as they can, while raising their arms in front to mimic blowing up balloons. Next, have them let out the air out slowly and deflate themselves. Help them to do this more and more slowly, focusing on letting their muscles become very loose as they exhale. Practice a few times.

Out-Tension the Tension Anger naturally tightens muscles. One way of getting tight muscles more relaxed is to tighten them more and then to release. It's like pushing someone in a swing – to get him to go further, you start by pulling him back first and then pushing, which allows the swing to go further.

Ask students to practice the following exercise. Have students start by curling their toes into a tight ball. Ask them to feel the tension. Then have them tighten their legs, stomach and chest, arms and hands, neck and face. As the tension builds, ask them to be aware of how their body feels. When everything is tight, have them hold it for just a few seconds.

Then tell them to RELEASE every part of their body, letting all the tension go. It can be useful to use visual metaphors, such as imagining all the tension draining out of their muscles into puddles on the floor. Ask them to picture their bodies as limp rag dolls.

Imaginary Trips Another useful tool is helping students develop the ability to use their imagination to interrupt anger responses. Have them think of peaceful places they like to be. You could even have them draw a picture of their Peaceful Place. Using guided imagery, invite them to use their imagination to visit that place.

Your exercise might sound something like this: **Now that we have all thought of a place that is peaceful for us, I want you to use your imagination to take a little vacation trip to that very spot. Find a comfortable position for your body. You will want to keep it still, so your mind can travel. You may gently close your eyes if you would like. Each person is going to be going to his own place, so it is going to be very important that nobody talks during this time. If you would rather not close your eyes, you could just look down at a place on the carpet. We want to make sure we don't interfere with anyone else's experience.**

Now, imagine being in the place that is peaceful and safe. As you use your imagination to make a picture, look around and see what you notice. Maybe you are able to hear some beautiful sounds that are associated with your special place. You may feel or smell something good. Notice if there is anyone else in your imaginary place. Pay attention to how nice and peaceful your body feels.

Know that in the future, if you are starting to get very angry and need to cool off, you can always come back and visit this special place in your mind. As you say goodbye to this peaceful place, if you have closed your eyes, you may gently open them.

Some groups may have trouble with guided imagery at first. A few students may initially feel self-conscious or silly about doing it. Your own comfort level, however, and the tone you set in this exercise will influence the way they benefit from the experience.

Writing and Art

Have students draw pictures and/or write stories about a time they were angry.

Connecting to Literature

Point out the way characters in stories and books you have read and are reading deal with angry feelings and the consequences of their choices. When a character has let his angry feelings get the better of him, invite the class to suggest things the character could have done to cool down first. Then ask students what would have been a productive way to handle the situation.

Franklin's Bad Day, by Paulette Bourgeois
(New York: Scholastic Inc., 1997) Gr. P-2

Summary: After his friend Otter moves away, Franklin is sad and grumpy. His mother helps him write a letter to Otter.

1. Name the things Franklin did because he felt angry. (For some of the responses, ask what Franklin could have done instead.)

2. Why was Franklin feeling so angry? How did Franklin's mother help him deal with his anger?

3. Can you think of a time when you got to talk about your feelings and then do something about them?

Mad Isn't Bad, by Michaelene Mundy
(St. Meinrad, IN: Abbey Press, 1999) Gr. K-3

Summary: Elf-help Books for Kids. Illustrations of elves accompany an exploration of anger, why it happens, and ways to deal with it.

1. Can anger ever be good? Explain.

2. Why is it important to figure out why you are mad?

3. How do you feel when you are angry?

4. Name some good ways to handle anger. Name some not-so-good ways to handle anger.

5. What should you do if someone is angry with you?

When I Feel Angry, by Cornelia Spelman
(Morton Grove, IL: Albert Whitman & Company, 2000) Gr. P-2

Summary: A little rabbit tells about times when she gets angry and what she can do.

1. Name some of the times the little rabbit feels angry.

2. Name some of the times you feel angry.

3. The little rabbit knows what to do when she is angry. What are some of the things you would like to do when you feel angry?

This Little Light of Mine

This lit-tle light of mine, ___ I'm gon-na let it shine.

This lit-tle light of mine, ___ I'm gon-na let it ___ shine.

This lit-tle light of mine, ___ I'm gon-na let it ___ shine. Let it

shine, let it shine, ___ let it shine.

This Little Light of Mine

This little light of mine,
I'm gonna let it shine.
This little light of mine,
I'm gonna let it shine.
This little light of mine,

I'm gonna let it shine.
Let it shine, let it shine, let it shine.

Everywhere I go,
I'm gonna let it shine. (*3 times*)
Let it shine, let it shine, let it shine.

All around this room,
I'm gonna let it shine. (*3 times*)
Let it shine, let it shine, let it shine.

(*Hold up your finger like a candle and
indicate blowing.*)
Nobody can "pfoof" it out,
I'm gonna let it shine. (*3 times*)
Let it shine, let it shine, let it shine.

GRADE 1, LESSON 8
Listening Practice and Helping with Feelings

Caring and Effective Communication

CASEL SEL COMPETENCIES

SA   Self-Awareness

SM   Self-Management

Gathering: Things We Don't Like

Make a circle. Tell students that they are going to get a chance to describe something that they don't like or that they get angry about. You might help them think of some examples by thinking out loud about a list of things that you don't like or get mad about. Try to include a wide array of things. For example, traffic jams, seeing adults yelling at children, people interrupting you, not being listened to when you're upset, or making a special trip to a store and finding it closed. Then explain: **Before you share what you don't like or what you get mad about, you have to repeat what the person before you shared.** You can do this as a go-round, or if it is possible to throw or roll a ball gently to others in the circle, you can invite students to roll or toss the ball to anyone else who has not yet had a turn. Students can indicate if they are eligible by holding their hand out in front, ready to receive the ball. Model by choosing a student to go first and then having her pass the object to you. Model by saying something like: **Jenna gets mad when people take cuts. I don't like it when I have to get up really early in the morning.** Then pass the ball/object to another student, who will repeat that you don't like getting up early and then share something that she doesn't like or gets angry about. Continue until everyone has had a turn.

Agenda Check

Today we are going to be working on what is probably the most important skill a person can have, the ability to really listen and understand others. We have been talking about feelings, how important they are, and how they are communicated. In our gathering, we practiced a very important listening skill. We are going to do another game that will allow us to practice this skill even more (Pete and Repeat). **Then we are going to have an opportunity to share a feeling with the class and practice how we can be helpful as listeners when people are expressing feelings** (Sharing Circle). **Next we will summarize what we learned today** (Summary) **and end with a closing** (Closing).

Workshop Agenda

- Gathering: Things We Don't Like
- Agenda Check
- Activity: Pete and Repeat
- Activity: Sharing Circle
- Summary
- Closing: Something That Makes You Laugh

Materials

- Workshop agenda, written on chart paper and posted
- Talking Object or soft ball
- Good Listening Chart from Lesson 1

Learning Outcomes

- Students will demonstrate active listening skills.
- Students will be able to paraphrase a simple story.
- Students will be able to articulate recent feelings.

Connections to Standards

Health

- Identifies and shares feelings in appropriate ways

Working with Others

- Engages in active listening

Activity: Pete and Repeat

1. Explain: **One of the ways to make sure we have understood what someone has told us is to repeat, or say back, what we thought we heard. This makes sure that we have heard the person correctly and it also lets the other person know we understand what they have said. This can make the speaker feel good.**

2. Have students pair off. Designate one student as Pete and the other as Repeat. Explain that whenever Pete says something, he will stop for a moment, and Repeat will paraphrase it. Pete should nod or say "uh-huh" if it is an accurate paraphrase.

3. Have all the Petes talk about things they like to do after school. After a few minutes, stop the activity and have the students switch roles. Then continue as above.

Activity: Sharing Circle

1. Have the students form a circle again.

2. Explain that when people have strong feelings – when they feel scared, or sad, or angry – it often helps to tell someone about it. **Being listened to can help us manage our feelings. Listening to people describe how they are feeling helps us to understand each other better. In this activity, we will have a chance to talk and to be good listeners for each other.**

3. Review the Good Listening Chart from Lesson 1:

   Good Listening

   - Look at the speaker.
   - Keep body still and quiet.
   - Pay attention (think about what the speaker is saying).
   - Don't interrupt.

4. Introduce the topic: A Feeling I Have Had Lately. Explain that everyone will have about the same amount of time to talk (about a minute). Be sure students understand that a person who does not want to talk can pass.

5. Model the activity by describing a feeling you have had lately. (This should be something from your life outside the classroom.) If students have trouble talking, ask questions that will help them get going. Otherwise, simply accept the stories the students tell without comment. Periodically, reflect and comment on the good listening you observe from students. Be careful not to give attention to those who might not be exhibiting all the good listening traits. Occasionally, before students start talking, ask them to look around at the whole class and notice the good listening that all the other students are doing.

Summary

How did it feel to share a feeling and be listened to so respectfully? How did it feel to be a good listener and help someone else feel good? Was it hard or easy to listen? Was it hard or easy to share? Being able to share feelings with friends and family is important. It helps deal with our feelings in positive ways. And being a good listener not only helps understand people and their feelings better, it can be very important in helping other people deal with their feelings. This is especially important in solving conflicts.

Closing: Something That Makes You Laugh

Acknowledge that sharing your feelings and listening to others share can be hard work. To end the lesson, ask students to think of something that makes them laugh. This can be done as a go-round, popcorn style, or by having students quickly partner with someone near them, share with each other, and then asking one or two volunteers to share with the whole class.

Extensions and Infusion Ideas

Encouraging Students to Help Others with Feelings

As issues come up that involve students' strong feelings, acknowledge these feelings and invite volunteers to be "listening friends" during recess or free time. Be careful not to give the impression that you yourself are not interested in the student's feelings; for certain issues you are going to want to be the person who students talk to and who helps work out anything that needs to be done. The vast majority of issues, however, are things that peers can help with just as well. By inviting and expecting this kind of support from other students, you send a strong message about your confidence in their abilities and you give them valuable opportunities to practice important skills. It also frees up time for you.

If you have instituted something like the Feelings Boxes, suggested in Lesson 5, this can be a regular way to invite students to notice peers who put their sticks in boxes like *sad* or *embarrassed* and to seek them out at recess or other time to offer a "listening ear."

Listening for Feelings

Explain that when we listen to people, we need to listen for two things. One is what they say, the other is how they feel about it.

Read the following sentences to the group in a monotone and have them identify possible feelings the speaker could be conveying. Explain that there can be more than one feeling at a time and that different people can have different feelings about the same thing.

- Look at the picture I drew.
- I can do this part by myself. I don't need your help.

- I guess it was pretty mean. I shouldn't have said it.
- I don't have any friends.
- She let me cut in line.
- The teacher said we should share.
- I got here first.
- That's mine!
- No one will play with me.
- I don't want to. It's dark in there.

Once a feeling has been suggested, say and act out the sentences in a way that communicates that feeling. Have students identify clues in your tone of voice, facial expression, and body movements that convey that emotion. Ask if someone can think of another emotion that would fit with the same words. Act out how that would look and sound and have students notice differences between the different expressions.

Student Role-Plays

Using the previous sentence stems, have a student role-play one with the particular feeling that they think is most appropriate. Coach the volunteer to say the sentence showing the emotion with their tone of voice, facial expression, and body language.

Have the other students guess what the emotion is. Once the class has identified the feeling, have them brainstorm helpful responses that the role-player might like to hear. This is a great time to practice paraphrasing as students verbalize what they see and then devise responses.

Connecting to Literature

Why is the Sky Blue?, by Sally Grindley
(New York: Simon & Schuster Books for Young Readers, 1996) Gr. P-2

Summary: When Rabbit can settle down long enough to listen, he learns from Donkey, and Donkey learns from Rabbit.

1. What are some things Rabbit learned about himself? What else might he have learned if he had listened better?

2. If you had been Donkey, how would you have felt when you tried to teach Rabbit?

Listen Buddy, by Helen Lester
(New York: Houghton Mifflin Co., 1995) Gr. K-3

Summary: Buddy Rabbit learns the hard way that for his own safety he needs to listen.

1. After Buddy leaves on his long hop, ask: What do you think might happen to Buddy now?

2. After reading the book, say: Name some of the things Buddy was doing instead of listening to his parents.

3. What happened when Buddy didn't listen to directions?

Conflicts and Problem Solving

Conflict Management and
Decision Making

CASEL SEL COMPETENCIES

SM Self-Management

DM Responsible Decision Making

RS Relationship Skills

Gathering: Sharing Sounds

Make a circle. Have a student make a sound, using a part of his body (clap, whistle, stamp, snap fingers). The next person should try to repeat the sound and add a new one. Continue around the circle, with each person repeating the sound of the one person before him and then making his own sound. Remind students that they will have to use good listening skills to be able to repeat the sound of the previous person.

Agenda Check

We have been learning about each other and how important it is to treat each other with respect. Even when we are being very nice and respectful to each other, we can still have conflicts or problems. Differences can sometimes cause conflicts. Other things can cause conflict, too. Conflicts happen everywhere – in class, at home, with our brothers or sisters. Today we are going to use some puppets to talk about what conflict is (Conflict Skit) **and learn a way to solve conflicts when they become problems** (ABCD Problem Solving). **Then we'll review what we learned** (Summary) **and end with a fun activity** (Closing).

Activity: Conflict Skit

1. Write the word *conflict* on chart paper. Pronounce the word and say that you are going to be talking about this word today. Introduce the puppets by name.

2. Perform this skit with the puppets. Situation: The puppets are siblings. They come home from school one day and they are both very hungry. There's one cookie in the kitchen and they both want it. They argue. End as the argument gets heated.

3. Ask: **What is happening? What is the matter here?** You can either have a verbal discussion or write students' responses on the chart paper. You can either list words or write sentences. Help students describe the way the puppets were feeling about the situation and what they think will happen next. Accept a range of responses rather than trying to compile a cohesive story.

Workshop Agenda

- Gathering: Sharing Sounds
- Agenda Check
- Activity: Conflict Skit
- Activity: ABCD Problem Solving
- Summary
- Closing: Y-E-S

Materials

- Workshop agenda, written on chart paper and posted
- Two puppets
- Chart paper and markers
- Problem-solving steps written on chart paper

Learning Outcomes

- Students will be able to define *conflict*.
- Students will be able to describe steps in a problem-solving process.
- Students will be able to apply a problem-solving process to a problem.

Connections to Standards

Behavioral Studies

- Knows that disagreements are common, even among family and friends
- Understands that some ways of dealing with disagreements work better than others

Language Arts

Reading

Working with Others

- Determines the causes of conflicts
- Identifies an explicit strategy to deal with conflict

4. Often, words like *fight* or *argument* will come up in the discussion. Point out that another word for what is happening is *conflict*. Help students see that a conflict can be a fight or a struggle, but it can also be looked at as a disagreement. The two puppets *disagree* about who should have the cookie. Remind students of the disagreements they experienced in Lesson 4. Help them see that a disagreement doesn't have to be a fight if people know how to resolve differences of opinion or problems in peaceful ways.

5. Explain: **There are lots of times when people disagree or want different things. That's a conflict and that's okay. Now we are going to learn a way to help us solve conflicts or problems peacefully.**

Activity: ABCD Problem-Solving

1. Show students the Problem-Solving Chart (below) and tell them that ABCD can help them remember the steps for being a good problem solver. Explain that you are going to go over the chart and use it to help the puppets find a good solution to their conflict.

2. The chart should look something like the following:

   A   Ask, "What's the problem?"

   B   Brainstorm some solutions.

   C   Choose the best solution.

   D   Do it.

3. Go over the chart. **A is to help us to remember to ask, "What's the problem?"** Ask students to describe the problem in the skit they just discussed. This step is meant to help people in a conflict focus on the problem instead of on each other. Instead of saying that the problem is that one puppet is being mean or one is being selfish, help students define the problem as, "Both puppets are hungry and want the one cookie that is left."

4. Continue: **B is for brainstorming. Brainstorming is letting our minds think of as many different ideas as possible to help solve a problem. Some ideas may be better than others, but we want to create as many as possible without judging at first if it is a good idea or not.** Ask students to think of as many different ways as possible that the two puppets could solve their conflict. You may or may not want to chart these ideas. Try to stretch the discussion beyond the initial responses to illustrate the results of brainstorming. Common suggestions include fighting, cutting it in half, or the "flipping a coin" or "rock, paper, scissors" approach. Other ideas might include finding something else to eat as well as the cookie, deciding between them who is the most hungry today, or asking an adult for help in making more cookies.

5. Continue: **C is for choosing the best solution.** Ask students which of the proposed solutions would be best for both of the puppets. Lead a discussion of the benefits and drawbacks to each of the ideas proposed. Help them come to a consensus about which one would be best.

6. **D is for do it. Once people have agreed on the best solution, then they need to try it.**

7. Have the puppets role-play the conflict again. This time, before it gets heated, have the puppets go through the ABCD process, coming up with the solution the class has selected. Ask students how they think each of the puppets is feeling at the end.

Summary

Ask students what the word *conflict* means. Remind them that conflicts happen every day and that there are many ways of solving conflicts.

Review the ABCD Problem-Solving Chart. Have them go through the steps several times until they can remember what the letters stand for. Ask them how this process helped the puppets solve their conflict. Try to help them see that this can be a great tool for helping us stay calm, as well as being creative in finding peaceful solutions to conflicts we may have.

Ask what kinds of problems or conflicts they can think of that could be solved by the problem-solving method. Help them to think of conflicts that happen in the classroom, with friends, as well as with family. Ask them to try this process with as many of these conflicts as possible.

Closing: Y-E-S

Ask students to stand in a circle and join hands. Explain that in a minute, everyone will bend over, hands almost touching the floor. The class will then begin saying *yes* together softly, drawing the word out, and getting louder as everyone slowly raises their hands into the air. The class will end with their hands as high above them as possible, completing the word energetically. Tell them that as they say *yes* together, it represents a commitment to solving conflicts and problems in peaceful ways that everyone feels good about.

Extensions and Infusion Ideas

Class Meetings

Class Meetings are regular time periods set aside for the class to solve problems, make agreements, celebrate achievements, and generally check in on how things are going. They provide a consistent place to experience the joys and responsibilities of being part of a community. They also provide an opportunity for practicing the skills of problem solving, listening, cooperation, compassion, healthy expression of feelings, and appreciation of differences. These are building blocks that nurture and sustain a safe, caring, and respectful classroom environment. If students feel that they have a say in helping to create a "caring" classroom, they feel empowered and demonstrate a greater collective will to follow through on decisions and agreements. For more information about starting and facilitating class meetings see other ESR resources at http://www.esrnational.org.

Teachable Moments

Teachable moments occur daily in classrooms. An overview of all the research around variables that impact student outcomes (such as level of teacher preparation, class size, quality of curriculum, etc.) found that the one variable that had the greatest impact on student learning was classroom management. The conflicts and problems that happen daily are valuable material that help students learn more about managing conflict and solving problems in constructive ways. As you identify and help students label issues as conflict and aid them in practicing the ABCDs, they will become much more skilled and able to resolve issues on their own. This not only gives them extremely valuable life skills, it also frees up more of your time for productive instruction.

Role-Play Practice

Have students brainstorm a list of common conflicts. Choose one of the conflicts from the list and have volunteers role-play the scenario. Stop the role-play; discuss what is happening in the conflict and how the characters are feeling. Then have the class help the characters walk through the ABCD Problem-Solving process. Applaud when a win-win solution is reached. Repeat with other actors and/or scenarios.

Connecting to Literature

Franklin is Bossy, by Paulette Bourgeois
(New York: Scholastic Inc., 1993) Gr. K-3

Summary: Bear gets tired of Franklin giving orders and they fight, but later make up. Franklin learns that he cannot always have his way.

1. How did the fight start?

2. How did Franklin and Bear end their fight?

3. Look again at the picture of Franklin and Bear going toward the bridge. Suppose Franklin and Bear decided to use ABCD Problem Solving. Role-play how you think they would have done the process.

Oh, Bother! Someone's Fighting!, by Nikki Grimes
(Racine, WI: Western Publishing Company, Inc., 1994) Gr. P-2

Summary: Tigger and Rabbit upset the other animals by arguing about what activity is best for Eeyore.

1. What did Tigger and Rabbit disagree about? How do you think their argument could have avoided becoming a conflict?

2. After Piglet helped solve the problem, everyone was feeling happy except Piglet. How did Eeyore help Piglet feel better?

The conflicts and problems that happen daily are valuable material that help students learn more about managing conflict.

GRADE 1, LESSON 10
Assertiveness

Gathering: I Feel Good About Myself When…

Gather in a circle. Tell students: **I want you to think about times when you feel really proud of yourselves, when you feel good about yourselves, when you feel really strong. What do you think it means to be** *strong*?

Briefly discuss their contributions, which will probably focus on external strength or muscle strength. Explain: **The kind of "strong" I'm thinking about is an "inside" strong. It's the kind of feeling you have when you know you have done the right thing, like told the truth even when it might have meant that you would get in trouble, or being strong enough not to eat that delicious-looking cookie that your mom said you couldn't eat until later. These things are hard, but if you are strong enough to do them, it feels great.** You might ask for a few more examples from students or share a few more yourself. The intention is to invite students to begin to think about inner strength and the good feeling that comes with self-discipline. As a go-round, ask students to complete the sentence, **"I feel good about myself when… ."**

Agenda Check

As we have learned, there is nothing wrong with being angry, but a lot of things people feel like doing when they are angry are wrong. They are wrong because they hurt others and almost always end up hurting themselves, too. They make the problem worse and that's not very wise.

In the gathering, we talked a little about what it means to be strong. Is being strong the same thing as being mean? Today we are going to learn how to be strong without being mean when we have angry feelings. First, we are going to have puppets help us look at what can happen when we get angry (Angry Puppets). Then the puppets will help us look at what we can do to be strong when we get mad (Acting "Strong" When You're Angry). Then we will look back on what we learned today (Summary) and then do a closing. How does that sound?

Activity: Angry Puppets

1. The teacher will use puppets to role-play a situation in which someone is angry. Students will suggest possible ways the situation might be resolved. The puppets will try out the various endings.

Workshop Agenda
- Gathering: I Feel Good about Myself When…
- Agenda Check
- Activity: Angry Puppets
- Activity: Acting "Strong" When You're Angry
- Summary
- Closing: Strong People

Materials
- Workshop agenda, written on chart paper and posted
- Two puppets
- Things People Do Chart from Lesson 7

Learning Outcomes
- Students will be able to distinguish between assertive and aggressive behavior.
- Students will be able to express feelings assertively.

Connections to Standards
Self-Regulation
- Identifies personal strengths and weaknesses
- Identifies basic values

Language Arts
Reading
- Makes simple inferences regarding the order of events and possible outcomes
- Relates new information to prior knowledge and experience

2. Use either a situation suggested by the students or the following: Puppet One is throwing a ball against a wall and catching it when Puppet Two comes and snatches it and runs away. He wants to play dodgeball. (Be sure to give the puppets names that are appropriate for your community and do not have any personal connections with students in the class. For this example, the names Omar and Carmelo are used.)

3. Role-play the situation using the puppets. Say: **One thing that Omar might do is to act mean.** Ask students how Omar might act if he decided he wanted to be mean to Carmelo because Carmelo was mean to him. Have students choose from the list from Lesson 7 one of the things people do when they're angry and role-play the situation using that behavior.

4. Discuss: **What happened? How might Omar feel about this solution? How might Carmelo feel?**

5. Try out other endings and discuss the results.

Activity: Acting "Strong" When You're Angry

1. Explain: **It's possible to act in a strong way when you are angry without doing something dangerous or hurtful. This means saying what you want in a calm and pleasant way.**

2. Replay the puppets' conflict with Omar acting "strong." The dialogue might go as follows:

    OMAR: *(pleasant but firm)* Stop. I want to play with that ball.

    CARMELO: You can't have it. We need it to play dodgeball. Come on, you guys. We can play now.

    OMAR: I had the ball first, and I want to play with it.

    CARMELO: Go away. We're going to play with it now.

    OMAR: I want to play with the ball.

3. Stop the puppet play. Discuss: **What is Omar doing here to act strong?** (He says what he wants firmly but without acting angrily. He repeats saying what he wants when Carmelo resists his request.) **What does he want? How might this situation end so that Omar can play with the ball?** (Carmelo could give back the ball. Omar could join the dodgeball game.)

Summary

What did we learn today? Why is being mean not a good idea? What does it mean to be strong? (Help students find words to distinguish between muscle strong and what it means to be strong on the inside.) **Strong people stand up for what is right. They let people know how they feel and what they want. They don't give in. But they never let others or their own anger make them lose control and act mean. Being in control of what we decide to do is what real strength is all about.**

Closing: Strong People

Who is someone you know who knows how to be strong without being mean? Help students think of people in their families, among their friends, in their classroom, or at school who model nonviolent strength.

Extensions and Infusion Ideas

Practicing Being "Strong"

It's important to give students the opportunity to practice strong behavior. Without practice, it is not likely to become a viable option for most.

With young students, it is probably most helpful to give them a specific sentence to say when someone is bothering them, and then give them a chance to practice it. The sentence might be, "Stop it! I don't like that!"

Role-play a situation in which one puppet is bothering another and the puppet being bothered says forcefully, "Stop it! I don't like that!" Then give the students a chance to role-play the situation with the puppets. Be sure each student has a chance to play both roles.

Connecting to Literature

When the characters in stories and books you are reading are dealing with angry feelings, ask students to analyze the character's behavior. Is the character acting strong or mean? What are the consequences of the character's actions?

The Berenstain Bears and Too Much Teasing, by Stan and Jan Berenstain
(New York: Random House, 1995) Gr. K-3

Summary: Brother gets a taste of his own medicine when his classmates tease him as teacher's pet. He then befriends the new kid Milton and helps him.

1. Why did Brother stand up for Milton?

2. How was Brother strong, not mean, when talking to Too-Tall about Milton?

3. Show the pictures where Too-Tall and his group are teasing Brother and ask: If you were one of the students in Brother's class, what strong words could you have used?

Robbie and Ronnie, by Christine Kliphuis
(New York: North-South Books, 2002) Gr. 1-3

Summary: Chubby Robbie and thin Ronnie support each other when Dennis bullies them, and they return a valuable necklace to its owner.

1. When Dennis first called Robbie and Ronnie names, explain how Ronnie's words were both strong and mean.

2. Explain why Robbie's threat to sit on Dennis and his friends could have been dangerous.

3. When Ronnie went to the lifeguard, was he tattling? Why or why not?

Win-Win Solutions

Conflict Management and Decision Making

CASEL SEL COMPETENCIES

DM Responsible Decision Making

RS Relationship Skills

Gathering: Something Fun or Difficult

Have students gather in a circle. Ask them to share one thing that has been fun or difficult during their day or week. Model by sharing one thing that was fun for you and one thing that was difficult. Have them share either a good or a difficult thing; everyone has the right to pass.

Agenda Check

We have been learning a lot about feelings and ways of solving conflicts. Today we are going to look at different ways conflicts can end and how people feel when these endings occur (Winning and Losing). **We will also look at finding ways to solve conflicts that allow everybody to feel good** (Finding Win-Win Solutions). **We'll summarize what we learned** (Summary) **and finish by learning a song that will help us remember that there is always something positive we can do when we get into conflicts** (Closing).

Activity: Winning and Losing

1. Display the card with the word *Win* written on it. What does it mean to win? **When you play a game like baseball, how do you know you've won?** (Elicit responses until someone identifies winning with having the most points, higher score, etc.) **How do you feel if you win?**

2. Show the other card, with the word *Lose*. **What does it mean to lose? How do you feel if you lose?**

Activity: Finding Win-Win Solutions

1. Prepare the following skit before class. Introduce the puppets and explain that these puppets have a conflict. Perform the following skit with the puppets:

   There is a new slide on the playground, and the puppets are very excited. Both puppets approach the slide at the same time and argue over who gets to go on it first. Have the argument intensify; end as the argument gets heated.

2. Discuss: **What happened in the skit? How did the puppets feel about the situation? What was it that they wanted? Was the conflict getting worse or better?**

Workshop Agenda

- Gathering: Something Fun or Difficult
- Agenda Check
- Activity: Winning and Losing
- Activity: Finding Win-Win Solutions
- Summary
- Closing: "There Is Always Something You Can Do"

Materials

- Workshop agenda, written on chart paper and posted
- Cards with the words *Win* and *Lose*
- Two puppets
- Possible Solutions Chart, with three columns labeled: *win-lose, lose-lose,* and *win-win*

Learning Outcome

- Students will be familiar with win-win solutions in conflict situations.

Connections to Standards

Behavioral Studies

- Understands that some ways of dealing with disagreements work better than others

Language Arts

Reading

- Makes simple inferences regarding the order of events and possible outcomes
- Knows main ideas or theme of a story
- Understands the main idea and supporting details
- Summarizes information found in texts

3. Ask: **What are some ways this situation could end?** As solutions are suggested, use the puppets to dramatize some of them. Try to elicit several win-lose situations, a lose-lose situation, and at least two win-win solutions. After each dramatization, discuss: **Did either of the puppets get what he wanted with that solution? Who won and who lost? How are they feeling about that solution?** For win-lose solutions, ask students what they think will happen later on, and if that solution would affect their friendship. Help them to see that most win-lose solutions, especially among family and friends, become lose-lose endings in the long run.

4. Summarize by saying: **In conflicts, winning is different from what it is when you are playing games. Part of the fun of games is seeing who will win. It is a contest. Conflicts with people don't have to be contests. If a conflict ends so that people get what they want, we call that "winning."** Show students the Possible Solutions Chart. **Sometimes one person "loses" while another "wins" (win-lose solutions). Sometimes in a conflict both people "lose" and neither gets what he really wants (lose-lose solutions). In the best solutions, both sides "win." We call these win-win solutions. Although win-win solutions may not always be possible, we can always try our best to find them.**

5. Ask students to think of a conflict they had recently with a sibling or a friend. Ask a few volunteers to share what happened and how the conflict ended. Try to have students talk about friends without using names. Have students name the kind of resolution contained in the story and brainstorm possible win-win solutions that might have been used to achieve a better resolution.

Summary

Today we thought about how it feels to lose or win in a conflict. We learned how we can always try to find win-win solutions so that everyone involved in the conflict gets what he needs. What are some conflicts that might happen at school that will give us a chance to practice creating win-win solutions?

Closing: "There Is Always Something You Can Do"

Teach the first verse of the song for the closing. The song can be found in *Linking Up!*, by Sarah Pirtle, and on the *Linking Up!* CD, Track 30. Music and lyrics at end of lesson.

Extensions and Infusion Ideas

"There Is Always Something You Can Do"

Teach students the other verses and chorus of the song, "There Is Always Something You Can Do." Have students discuss what the words suggest.

Role-Plays

Create scenarios involving different conflict situations. Have students use puppets or role-play different endings. Brainstorm different ways the characters in the role-play could achieve a win-win solution.

Teachable Moments

As students experience real conflict with each other at school, have them look at solving these conflicts so that a win-win solution is achieved. Help students see that win-win solutions can sometimes take more time to figure out, but that they can prevent further conflicts in the future.

Writing

Have students write a story or draw a picture about a time they had a conflict that ended with both people being happy.

Connecting to Literature

Have students identify conflicts in stories they read. Ask them to classify the outcomes as lose-lose, win-lose, or win-win solutions. If a story does not end with a win-win solution, see if students can come up with one.

Abby Cadabra, Super Speller, by Joan Holub
(New York: Grosset & Dunlap, 2000) Gr. 1-3

Summary: When Wanda Cassandra moves in, Abby is no longer the top speller. The two manage to find a win-win solution to their competition.

1. Explain how Abby and Wanda found a win-win solution to their contest.

2. Describe a way you could help someone else in spelling. For example, tell some words you could help spell, if asked.

What Have You Done, Davy?, by Brigitte Weninger
(New York: North-South Books, 1996) Gr. K-3

Summary: Davy's accidents destroy his siblings' things. He makes amends and is forgiven.

1. Name all the conflicts Davy had. What caused most of them?

2. How did Davy turn each of the conflicts into a win-win situation in which everyone felt better in the end?

Two Fine Ladies Have a Tiff, by Antonia Zehler
(New York: Random House, 2001) Gr. P-1

Summary: Siblings have a fight and then make up.

1. Explain how the tiff kept getting worse.

2. How did the girls solve the conflict so that both felt better?

3. Why do you think the girls were called "fine ladies" all through the story?

Help students see that win-win solutions can sometimes take more time to figure out, but that they can prevent further conflicts in the future.

There Is Always Something

©1997. Words and Music by Sarah Pirtle
Discovery Center Music, BMI

There Is Always Something You Can Do

There is always something you can do, do, do
when you're getting in a stew, stew, stew.

You can go out for a walk.
You can try to sit and talk.
There's always something you can do.

Whether in a school or fam'ly argument,
when you feel you'd really like to throw a fit.
Don't be trapped by fights and fists and angry
threats, reach for this ordinary plan.

There is always something you can do,do,do.
Yes, it's difficult but true, true, true.
See it from each other's eyes.

Find a way to compromise.
There's always something you can do.

You can use your smarts and not your fist, fist, fist.
You can give that problem a new twist,twist, twist.
You can see it 'round about and upside down.
Give yourself the time to find a way.

There is always something you can do, do, do
when you're getting in a stew, stew, stew.
When you want to shout and scream, find the word
for what you mean.
There's always something you can do.
There's always something you can do.

150

GRADE 1, LESSON 12
Controlling Anger

Gathering: "There Is Always Something You Can Do"

Sing the song, "There Is Always Something You Can Do." See Lesson 11, page 150 for musics and lyrics. It can also be found in the book *Linking Up!*, by Sarah Pirtle, and on the *Linking Up!* CD, Track 30.

Agenda Check

Last time, we talked about how important it is to try to find win-win solutions to conflicts. **Are win-win solutions always easy to think of?** Lead a short discussion that helps students see that thinking of win-win solutions is hard. **We need our best thinking to be able to come up with good solutions to problems.**

We have also been learning about feelings, especially anger. **Did you know that when we get *really* mad, the thinking part of our brain doesn't work as well as it does when we are calm and relaxed? How many of you can think of a time when you got really angry and did something that you later felt really bad about?** Everybody has done this at some time, including your parents and me. Some people have even said that they "lost their mind" when they got really mad. **We're going to do some fun things today to help us learn how to be better at *not* losing our minds.**

First, we're going to make an anger thermometer (Constructing Anger Thermometers) **and talk about different levels of anger. We'll have the puppets help us see how those levels of anger can go higher and higher in a conflict** (Conflicts and Angry Feelings). **We'll learn what we can do to stay in control and not let our level of anger get too high. Then we'll review what we learned** (Summary) **and do a closing** (Closing).

Activity: Constructing Anger Thermometers

1. See example on page 156. Show students one of the activity sheets and tell them they are going to make an anger thermometer. First, they will cut out two sections on either side of the paper.

2. Take a pair of scissors and cut out the two areas. Then tell students the next thing they will do is fold along the two fold lines.

3. Demonstrate. The two side sections overlap when they are folded.

Workshop Agenda

- Gathering: "There Is Always Something You Can Do"
- Agenda Check
- Activity: Constructing Anger Thermometers
- Activity: Conflicts and Angry Feelings
- Summary
- Closing: Cool Down Stretches

Materials

- Workshop agenda, written on chart paper and posted
- Anger thermometer activity sheet (duplicated on lightweight cardstock for each student)
- 2 1/4" by 11" strips of red construction paper for each student
- Scissors and tape or glue
- Puppets

Learning Outcomes

- Students will be able to identify words to describe different levels of anger.
- Students will be able to articulate the way anger intensity increases.
- Students will be able to use a "reminder" to keep anger at a manageable level.

Connections to Standards

Behavioral Studies

- Understands that people are alike and different
- Understands that some ways of dealing with disagreements work better than others

Language Arts

Reading

- Understands level-appropriate sight words and vocabulary

Connections to Standards, cont.

Self-Regulation

- Understands that everyone makes mistakes
- Uses techniques to offset the negative effects of mistakes
- Avoids overreacting to criticism

4. Tell students they will either tape or glue the overlapping pieces together. When this is done, they will insert the strip of red paper inside the thermometer.

5. Distribute activity sheets and supplies to each student. Summarize the directions again, check for understanding, and have each student construct his own thermometer.

Activity: Conflicts and Angry Feelings

1. Have students bring their thermometers and make a circle or come to a rug area. If this has not yet been covered in science, ask students if they know what a temperature thermometer is and how it works.

2. Facilitate a discussion that reviews the fact that thermometers indicate the temperature by increasing or decreasing levels of mercury. The important concepts are: that thermometers are *scales*, that they measure *different levels* of temperature by markings, that the reading on a thermometer *goes up or down* depending on the degree of temperature that is present, and that *the higher the level, the hotter the temperature is*.

3. Demonstrate the way to move the slip of red paper to register different levels of anger on the thermometer. Ask students to move their red paper up to the different words as you discuss them. **Just like the temperature, there are different levels of anger.**

4. Read and discuss the levels on their thermometers, by saying something like: **The first level of anger we call *annoyed*. If a fly landed on your arm once, you might feel *annoyed*.** Demonstrate and ask them to move their red paper so that the top of the strip is next to the word *annoyed*. **The next level of anger is be called *irritated*.** Move your paper and have them follow. **If the fly kept coming back, you might begin to get *irritated*. If it wouldn't go away after a long time and you couldn't focus on what you wanted to do, you might become *angry*. If we get more and more *angry* we call that feeling *furious*. At the top of the thermometer is where we can really lose control and go into a rage. That feeling can be called *enraged*.**

5. Have the puppets act out a conflict that escalates. The following story is provided as an example. Feel free to have the puppets act out any conflict that will demonstrate increasing levels of emotion. If using the story below, feel free to change names to make them appropriate for your class.

   This is Felipe. *(Introduce one of the puppets.)* **I want you to use your anger thermometers and show how you think Felipe is feeling during this story. This is Bernard.** *(Introduce the second puppet.)* **He is a friend and classmate of Felipe's. Bernard and Felipe share a desk in their classroom. There is one set of markers for each desk. Today they are drawing pictures. Both have decided to draw a picture of the park.**

   FELIPE: *(calmly)* Bernard, I need to use the green marker.

   BERNARD: I'll give it to you when I'm done.

FELIPE: *(becoming annoyed)* Bernard, it's been a long time. I need it now.

BERNARD: Just a minute.

FELIPE: *(irritated, but still controlled)* That's not fair. You've already had it a long time.

BERNARD: Well, I can have it as long as I like!

FELIPE: *(angrily)* No, you can't!

BERNARD: I can too! Just shut up!

FELIPE: *(more angrily)* Don't tell me to shut up.

BERNARD: I'll tell you anything I want. Don't be such a baby!

FELIPE: *(lunges at Bernard and tries to grab the marker)*

6. Discuss how the feelings escalated, getting hotter and hotter. **As Felipe's feelings went up the anger thermometer, what happened to Bernard's feelings? At this point, Felipe could be in trouble with the teacher. Did he win or lose? Bernard could also be in trouble with the teacher, but even if he weren't in trouble, since they are both friends and share a desk, he also has lost.**

7. Ask: **Do you think they were able to think with their best minds at the end? To get to a win-win solution, they both need to stay cool. When they realize they are starting to go up on the thermometer, they could say to themselves, "Stop! Don't get hot!" Then they could try to think of something to work things out. This time I want you to help them stay cool by saying, "Stop! Don't get hot!" anytime you see their temperature starting to rise.**

8. Replay the story, stopping each time the class says, "Stop! Don't get hot!" Have the puppets take a deep breath and then start again. Have them begin to go up the thermometer several times to give students practice saying, "Stop! Don't get hot!" At different points, ask students for suggestions of what a puppet could do or say to move calmly toward a win-win solution. Eventually, with help from the class, have the puppets arrive at a good resolution.

Summary

Today we have learned some different names for levels of anger. What's the lowest level we talked about? Continue to ask questions to review the vocabulary on the anger thermometer. The puppets helped us see that when our anger level increases, the whole conflict becomes more serious. It's as if our angry feelings are a motor on a conflict escalator. The higher we go on the thermometer, the less able our brain is to think clearly and make good decisions. Since we need to think clearly and calmly to stay strong and come up with good win-win solutions, it's important that we learn ways to stay cool. What are some things you could say to yourself that might keep you from getting too hot?

Closing: Cool Down Stretches

For our closing, we are going to do a little exercise that can help us keep our bodies cool.

Ask the children to stand up in the circle. Demonstrate the following exercise as you say:

- **Bend over all the way to the ground and touch your toes.**

- **As you come up slowly, take a deep, deep breath, filling up your whole chest like a balloon.**

- **Raise your hands high in the air and breathe out slowly, like a balloon, letting the air out the bottom.**

- **Let's do this again. This time, as you breathe in imagine that anger is filling you up like a balloon.** (Repeat step #2.)

- **Now breathe out and imagine that the air in the balloon is leaving, and with that the anger is all floating away.**

- **Now shake yourself out, and see how good you feel.**

Extensions and Infusion Ideas

"Triggers" and Cooling Down Strategies

As a go-round in a circle, ask: **What's something that usually makes you really mad? What used to drive you way up the anger thermometer?** This can be a great opportunity to point out that we all react differently to different things. Something that may enrage one student might not make someone else angry at all.

Next, ask students to think about something they could say to themselves or do that would help them stay calm and in control. Repeat the go-round, with students sharing the thing that can trigger their anger, this time adding what they could do to stay cool. At the end, remind students what it really means to be strong, and invite them to see if they stay cool when these things occur in the future.

Role-Plays

Have students make a list of some of the things that drive their anger up the thermometer. Then ask them to role-play scenarios based on situations on the list, with the rest of the class monitoring their level of anger. Have students remind the actors to "Stop, don't get hot!" when appropriate. The students can actually role-play or use the puppets to role-play.

Family Connection

Have students take their thermometers home to share with their families. Invite them to talk with different family members about the things that drive up their anger levels. Parents could be invited to help students notice when their anger is going up the scale and to help them practice staying cool.

(Note: *Although this kind of conversation may help parents become more aware of anger escalation, be sure students know that it is not their job to teach their parents. The purpose of this exercise is to elicit support for the students' learning about anger, not to focus on family members' feelings.*)

Connecting to Literature

As you read books and stories that involve characters getting angry, ask students to give their opinions about where the character is on the thermometer. Have students notice the consequences when feelings escalate too high.

Andrew's Angry Word, by Dorothea Lachner
(New York: North-South Books, 1995) Gr. K-3

Summary: Angry words go from person to person until they are replaced by kind words.

1. Right before the fisherman meets the woman in the market, ask: How has each character reacted to the angry words being passed around?

2. After reading the book, ask: How did kind words change the story?

3. Give an example of a situation in which you could respond as the woman in the market did.

Danny, the Angry Lion, by Dorothea Lachner
(New York: North-South Books, 2000) Gr. K-3

Summary: When he doesn't get sausages and raspberry juice, Danny's anger turns him into a lion. Good deeds and friendliness help his anger to disappear.

1. How did each character help Danny deal with his anger?

2. If you met Danny, how would you help him?

3. At the end, Danny "stuck the claws in his pocket." Do you think that was a good idea? Why or why not?

The Quarreling Book, by Charlotte Zolotow
(New York: Harper Collins, 1963) Gr. 1-4

Summary: A chain reaction of anger, down to the dog, who just plays and reverses the reaction.

1. In this story, we see that when we feel angry we sometimes spread the anger to someone else. What happened in this story when someone became angry?

2. In this story we also see that when we feel angry we don't have to stay that way. How were the characters able to stop being angry?

3. What are some things you could do to stop feeling angry?

NAME

DATE

Enraged

Furious

Angry

Irritated

Annoyed

Fold Here

Fold Here

cut out on dotted line

cut out on dotted line

cut out on dotted line

cut out on dotted line

GRADE 1, LESSON 13
Stereotypes

Gathering: Cooper Says

This is a variation of Simon Says. Give students a series of directions that they are to follow only when preceded by the words "Cooper Says." The difference between the two games is that everyone remains in the game whether they follow the instructions accurately or not. The name Cooper is derived from the word *cooperation*.

Agenda Check

We have been learning about getting along with each other and solving conflicts. Conflicts often develop when things are unfair. For example, when people are not allowed to do something, or are made fun of just because they happen to belong to a certain group, that is unfair. Today we are going to talk about groups we belong to (Groups We Belong To) **and then we are going to look at some things that are said about girls and boys** (All Boys, All Girls). **Then we'll talk about what we learned today** (Summary) **and do a closing** (Closing).

Activity: Groups We Belong To

1. **All of us belong to a lot of different groups. Our families are one important group that we are a part of. Can someone think of a group that all of us in this room belong to?** (All members of the same class, school, all are human, etc.) **What are some kinds of groups that some of us belong to and others don't?**

2. Facilitate a discussion that brings out several categories of groups. These could include ethnic, religious, age, and interest groups. **One of the groups that some of us belong to and others don't depends on whether we are a boy or a girl.**

Activity: All Boys, All Girls

1. Pair students with a partner or arrange them in groups of three. (See Teaching Tools for suggestions.) Tell students you are going to ask them to talk with their partner or small group before sharing their ideas with the whole class. This allows all students to be actively involved in the discussions. Establish a Quiet Signal. Remind students to use their best active listening skills and to make sure that everyone participates.

Materials

- Workshop agenda, written on chart paper and posted
- Chart paper and markers

Learning Outcomes

- Students will be able to define the word *stereotypes*.
- Students will be able to identify ways that stereotypes limit people.

Connections to Standards

Behavioral Studies

- Knows that there are groups people are born into and others that people join
- Knows unique features of different groups to which he/she belongs and also the overlap of these groups with others

Self-Regulation

- Is able to suspend judgment when appropriate

2. Explain: **Sometimes people say that there are things boys can do that girls can't or things that girls can do that boys can't. What have you heard people say all boys are or can do?** When students have had enough time to talk about this with their partner(s), get their attention and ask volunteers to share what came up. List examples on the board or on chart paper.

3. **What have you heard people say all girls are or can do?** Again, have students discuss and then report, listing examples on the board or on chart paper.

4. Have students respond to the following questions with their partner(s). After students have responded, ask for some examples.

   - How has this affected you?

   - Can you think of a time you acted a certain way because you thought you were supposed to because you were a boy or a girl?

   - Have you ever not done something because it was something you thought you were not supposed to do because you were a boy or a girl?

5. Point out that statements like "All boys…" or "All girls…" are *stereotypes*. A stereotype is an idea that all people in a group are the same way. It's a kind of prejudice. Go over the list of examples of things "all boys" or "all girls" are said to be or do. Ask the class to think of examples of boys or girls who are different from the stereotype. For example, ask: **Can you think of any girls who are good at baseball?**

6. Discuss: **Is it true that boys (girls) can't do these things? Is it fair to think so? What is the problem with stereotypes?**

Summary

We all belong to many different groups. Sometimes people think something is true of everybody in a certain group. That is called a stereotype. One stereotype is that all good basketball players are tall. If I were choosing a basketball team and only chose the tallest kids, would that be fair? What if the best player was not one of the tallest? How would that person feel? Would I miss out?

Closing: Stretches

Have the group stand in a circle about an arm's length apart, if possible. Explain that everyone is going to do some stretches. Begin with arms stretched out in front and wiggle fingers. Then turn hands over, palms up, and curl fingers. Then shake each hand. Make small circles with arms in front, first in one direction and then in the other. Then clap hands and thank everybody for their work and participation.

Extensions and Infusion Ideas

Different Groups

One of the major difficulties with stereotypes is that they can contribute to an "us against them" dynamic. Helping students see that we belong to many different groups that include individuals we may not initially identify with can help lessen this dynamic.

Introduce the activity by saying something like: **We belong to many different groups. Some groups are large and some groups are small. For example, the group of children in the room is larger than the group of adults. It's interesting that there are different people in the different groups we belong to. If our groups were always the same, it would get pretty boring.**

We are going to play a game that will help us see some of the different groups we belong to. This is a game with NO TALKING. The way we will show that we belong to a certain group is by standing up or staying seated. We will be able to "listen" by looking to see who is standing and who is sitting.

For the first statement, say something that will get everyone to stand, such as, "Stand up if you are a member of this class." Continue with a variety of groups that will be of interest and will show similarities and differences between different students. Encourage students to observe who is standing and who is sitting, who is in that group and who is not.

(Note: *Another way to do the activity would be to have students physically move and form different groups as you indicate categories. See the Groups activity in Grade K, Lesson 3.*)

Some possible topics: number of siblings, if they are the youngest or oldest child, size of family, how they get to school, number and types of pets, likes and dislikes in areas such as food, games, etc.

Have students come back to a circle. Process the experience by asking such questions as:

- Were the other people in your groups always the same?
- Were the sizes of your groups the same or different?
- How did you feel about being in different groups?
- Would it be fair to say that all of the people in one particular group were all alike?

Connecting to Literature

Point out stereotypes when you encounter them in books students are reading. Discuss stereotypes in cartoons and movies.

A Pig is Moving In!, by Claudia Fries
(New York: Orchard Books, 2000) Gr. K-3

Summary: The neighbors cannot believe that the new neighbor can be neat and skilled.

1. Before reading the book, brainstorm words and ideas associated with pigs.

2. After reading the book, ask: In this story, what ideas did the neighbors have about pigs? Go back to your list and decide which items are true of Theodore. Explain why we can say that the neighbors were prejudiced about the pigs.

3. Sometimes when we think we know how someone will act, we "catch them" acting the way we expected. Explain how that happened in this story.

Tomboy Trouble, by Sharon Wyeth
(New York: Random House, 1998) Gr. 2-3

Summary: Eight-year-old Georgia is constantly mistaken for a boy because she has short hair and loves sports.

1. Why did the students think Georgia was a boy? For each reason, give the associated "All boys ..." or "All girls ..." statement.

2. Some mean words hurt Georgia's feelings. How could they have been said differently?

3. Georgia said some mean words, too. However, in her letter to Mrs. Weintraub, Georgia used strong words. What did Georgia say in her letter to Mrs. Weintraub?

4. How did Robin and Georgia show that a lot of stereotypes about boys and girls are not true?

William's Doll, by Charlotte Zolotow
(New York: Harper & Row Publishers, 1972) Gr. P-3

Summary: William wants a doll, even though others tell him he would be a sissy, etc. His grandmother tells William's father that William needs a doll so he can learn how to be a father.

1. A sentence beginning, "All boys" or "All girls" is a stereotype. What stereotypes do you know about boys and girls and dolls?

2. What do you think about boys having dolls?

3. Why did William's grandmother say it would be good for William to have a doll? Do you agree?

4. Can you think of other stereotypes about toys or games and boys or girls?

Prejudice and Dislike

Cultural Competence and
Social Responsibility

CASEL SEL COMPETENCY

SA   Self-Awareness

Gathering: Things We Don't Like to Eat

(Note: *Gatherings are usually best in a circle, but since both of the following activities require students to focus on you, you may want to have them sit in a theater arrangement.*)

Ask students to think about a food that they *don't* like to eat. Call on several students, popcorn style, to share what they thought of with the class.

Agenda Check

In the last lesson, we learned about stereotypes and how they can hurt people. Stereotypes are beliefs that all the people in a group are the same. A stereotype is a kind of prejudice. If a new girl student came to in our class, and someone said she wouldn't want to play with cars because she's a girl, we would be judging the girl before we found out if she did or did not. That would be stereotyping or prejudice. Some girls like to play with cars, even if most girls don't care for them.

Today we are going to learn more about prejudice and how it can cause us to make mistakes and hurt people. First, we're going to read a book that many of you may know (*Green Eggs and Ham*). Then we'll talk about the difference between prejudice and not liking something (Dislike vs. Prejudice). We'll discuss what we learned (Summary), and then we'll get to sing a song we learned a while ago (Closing).

Activity: *Green Eggs and Ham*

1. Explain: **In our gathering, we talked about food we don't like to eat. Have you ever said, "I hate _____ (a certain kind of food)," but then you tried it and liked it?** Get responses from a few volunteers.

2. Read Dr. Seuss's book, *Green Eggs and Ham* (New York: Random House,1960).

3. Discuss the fact that the character was sure that he didn't like green eggs and ham until he tried them. Ask students why they think he made the mistake of thinking he didn't like them at first. Elicit that he judged them by the way they looked. Ask if people are sometimes judged by the way they look at first. **What if a new student joined our class, but she was a color you had never seen on a person before, maybe green? Would you know whether or not that student would be fun to play with? How might she be treated at first?** Point out that they would have to get to know the student first before they could tell if they liked playing with her.

Workshop Agenda

- Gathering: Things We Don't Like to Eat
- Agenda Check
- Activity: *Green Eggs and Ham*
- Activity: Dislike vs. Prejudice
- Summary
- Closing: "I Like You"

Materials

- Workshop agenda, written on chart paper and posted
- *Green Eggs and Ham*, by Dr. Seuss
- Two puppets

Learning Outcomes

- Students will be able to define prejudice and discuss the way it affects people.
- Students will be able to distinguish between dislike and prejudice.

Connections to Standards

Language Arts
Reading

- Understands level-appropriate sight words and vocabulary
- Knows main ideas or theme of a story
- Relates stories to personal experiences (e.g. events, characters, conflicts, themes)
- Understands the main idea and supporting details

Activity: Dislike vs. Prejudice

1. Explain: **People like some things and dislike some things. We are going to use these puppets to help us think about the difference between dislike and prejudice.**

2. To illustrate *dislike*, have a conversation between the puppets along the following lines:

    PUPPET 1: I don't like chocolate.

    PUPPET 2: Everybody likes chocolate. How come you don't like it? Did you ever taste it?

    PUPPET 1: Yes. I tried Raymond's chocolate birthday cake and I tried Shirley's chocolate ice cream. I just don't like the taste.

3. Discuss: **Puppet 1 dislikes chocolate. Does she know what it tastes like? Yes. So we could say that she dislikes chocolate. That is different from being prejudiced about it.**

4. To illustrate *prejudice*, have a second discussion between the puppets about eating spinach or broccoli. It might go along the following lines:

    PUPPET 1: I won't eat that broccoli. Ick. Look at it. Disgusting.

    PUPPET 2: Have you every tried it?

    PUPPET 1: No.

    PUPPET 2: How do you know you don't like it if you've never tasted it?

    PUPPET 1: I just know I'm not going to like it. I can tell from the way it looks.

5. Discuss: **Puppet 1 says she doesn't like broccoli. How is this different from her dislike of chocolate? We would call her not liking broccoli a prejudice. Why is this different from disliking chocolate?**

6. To illustrate *prejudice*, have a conversation between the puppets along the following lines:

    PUPPET 1: Betsy wants to play with us, but I don't like her.

    PUPPET 2: Why don't you like her?

    PUPPET 1: She's in Mr. Green's class, and all the kids in there are nasty. Everybody knows that.

    PUPPET 2: Have you ever played with Betsy?

    PUPPET 1: No, but I know I don't like her.

7. Discuss: **Puppet 1 thinks she has a good reason for not playing with Betsy. Would you call this reason a dislike or a prejudice?**

8. To illustrate *dislike* of another person, have a conversation between the puppets along the following lines:

PUPPET 1: Betsy wants to play with us, but I don't want to play with her.

PUPPET 2: Why don't you want to play with her?

PUPPET 1: I don't like her because the last time we played jump rope, she took over the game and didn't let me jump.

9. Discuss: **What do you think of this reason for not playing with Betsy? How can you tell the difference between a dislike and a prejudice?**

Summary

There is a difference between prejudice and dislike. Prejudice is an opinion formed without knowledge, while dislike is an opinion formed on the basis of knowledge. Prejudice can make us miss out and make mistakes. It can also hurt people. What would be important to remember from the lesson that would help us make our classroom and the world a better place?

Closing: "I Like You"

Sing, "I Like You." This song is sung to the tune of "Skip to My Lou." Lyrics can be found on page 105.

Extensions and Infusion Ideas

Choose a Gift

For this activity you will need a beautifully wrapped box (for example, a shoe box) with something useless inside, such as an old, worn-out rag. You'll also need something that looks worthless on the outside, but symbolically contains something of great value. An example would be a dummy check for a million dollars inside an old brown paper bag that is wadded into a ball.

Show students the beautifully wrapped box and ask if anyone would like to have it as a gift. Since everyone will want it and you only have one, pretend that you are concerned and try to find something else you could also give away. Offer the old wadded-up brown bag and ask if anyone would rather have it instead of the wrapped box. After playing this up for a while, have the students discover what is inside each.

Lead a discussion about prejudice by asking questions such as the following:

- Did you make a mistake?

- Why did you choose the wrapped box instead of the bag? (Looks pretty, size, past experiences)

- Once you knew what was inside, did you change your mind?

Partner Sharing

Have students pair up with a partner. (See Teaching Tools for suggestions for pairing students.) Ask: **Have you ever refused to play with someone because another person told you something bad about them? Have people ever kept you out of a game for no good reason? If these things have not happened to you, have you ever seen them happen to other people? How do you feel about situations like this?** Give them about two minutes each to share these experiences. Let them know when the time is half up so they can switch.

Ask for volunteers to share their experiences. Discuss: **How do people get prejudices like this? Is it fair to judge people this way? How should it be?**

The Sneetches

Dr. Seuss's *The Sneetches* (New York: Random House, 1961) is another good book to read to the class when you are discussing prejudice. In this story, the Star-Belly Sneetches think they are better than the Plain-Belly Sneetches. However, the clever Plain-Belly Sneetches soon learn how to place stars on their bellies, and then how is anyone to tell who is better than whom? Some questions for discussion: **How did the Star-Belly Sneetches learn prejudice? What can we learn from this story about how people behave?**

Connecting to Literature

The Berenstain Bears' New Neighbors, by Stan and Jan Berenstain (New York: Random House, 1995) Gr. K-3

Summary: Father Bear is worried about the new neighbors, the Panda family, because they are "different."

1. Why was Papa upset about the new neighbors?

2. What were Papa's feelings about the Pandas?

3. Sometimes when we are prejudiced we get wrong ideas about others. What was one idea Papa had about the Pandas that was wrong?

4. Papa stopped being prejudiced. What helped Papa change his mind about the Pandas?

5. What does this story tell us about not judging people before we know them?

Loudmouth George and the New Neighbors, by Nancy Carlson (Minneapolis: Carolrhoda Books, Inc., 1983) Gr. K-3

Summary: George hesitates to meet the pigs until he sees others having fun with them.

1. Why didn't George want to meet his new neighbors?

2. What were George's feelings about his new neighbors? Was George showing dislike or prejudice? Explain your answer.

3. At the end of the story is a clue that George has probably learned a lesson about prejudice. What is that clue?

GRADE 1, LESSON 15

Helping Others and Standing Up to Bullying

Gathering: Heroes and Sheroes

(Note: *This Gathering is the same as the Gathering in Grade K, Lesson 15. This is done purposefully. People need role models to look up to. The ability to identify heroes and sheroes is highly correlated with important character, social, and emotional development.*)

Have students gather in a circle. Explain: **Heroes are people who are admired for their achievements and strong and good qualities. Girl heroes are called heroines; some people call them sheroes. Heroes and sheroes are people who are brave and strong in standing up for others or in doing what is right.** Share some examples of people your students will have heard of – people from stories they've read recently, national heroes like Martin Luther King, Jr. or Abraham Lincoln. **Heroes can also be people we know in our families or in our neighborhoods. The important thing about heroes and sheroes is that they always try to help others, acting in strong ways that are never mean. Who is someone you think of as a hero or shero and why?**

Ask students to think to themselves for a minute. Suggest possible people most in the class are familiar with and talk about what it is about that person that might make him or her a hero. Holding the Talking Object, begin by discussing someone you admire and explaining why. Then pass the Talking Object to the next person. As always, allow students to pass if they choose to, and acknowledge that it is always more difficult to speak at the beginning of the circle. Assure them you will come back at the end to see if they have something to share.

Agenda Check

We have just been talking about heroes and sheroes. They are people who are strong and brave and help others. They make the world a better place. Today we are going to think about how we would like to help others. We'll get to draw a picture about that (Helping Others). **Then we'll discuss some specific things we can do to help others by standing up if we see bullying or other things that are not fair** (Being Strong). **We'll summarize what we've done** (Summary) **and then end with a song that we learned a while ago** (Closing).

CASEL SEL COMPETENCIES

SO Social Awareness

RS Relationship Skills

Workshop Agenda

- Gathering: Heroes and Sheroes
- Agenda Check
- Activity: Helping Others
- Activity: Standing Up for Others
- Summary
- Closing: "This Little Light of Mine"

Materials

- Workshop agenda, written on chart paper and posted
- Talking Object
- Chart paper and markers

Learning Outcomes

- Students will learn to identify heroes and sheroes.
- Students will review things learned throughout the year about being strong.
- Students will discuss how they will confront bullying when they encounter it.

Connections to Standards

Behavioral Studies

- Understands that some ways of dealing with disagreements work better than others, and that people not involved in an argument may be helpful in solving it

Language Arts

- Listening and Speaking
- Makes contributions in class and group discussions

Self-Regulation

- Persists in the face of difficulty

Connections to Standards, cont.

Working with Others

- Contributes to the development of a supportive climate in groups
- Identifies an explicit strategy to deal with conflict

Activity: Helping Others

1. Introduce the activity: **Heroes and sheroes make the world a better place because they care about and help others. There are many ways to help others. What are some things you could do that would be helpful in making our classroom, your families, or our school a better place to be? What can we do to help others?**

2. List students' ideas on chart paper or on the board under the title *Helpful Behavior* or *Ways to Be Helpful*. Help students think of practical, doable things such as sharing supplies with others, helping to clean up at home, not fighting with a brother or sister, etc.

3. When the list is complete, ask: **How does it feel to help others?**

4. Summarize their contributions by linking them to feeling and acting strong. **We have learned a lot about being strong this year. Helping others is one of the things that can help us feel really strong.**

5. Ask students to draw a picture of themselves doing something that helps others. You could also make this a short writing assignment appropriate for your students' abilities.

6. When finished, the pictures could be collected and made into a class book entitled *Learning to Be Strong: Helping Others*.

Activity: Standing Up for Others

1. Gather students in a circle again. Explain: **We have been learning many things this year. We have learned how to be strong in communicating, dealing with conflicts, and in handling our feelings. We have learned how we are all "different" in many ways. We've learned the problems that can happen when people stereotype and we've learned the dangers of prejudice. Today we have talked about heroes and sheroes and helping others. One of the important ways we can help others is by standing up for them if they are being teased or treated unfairly by others – if they are being bullied. If you saw someone being bullied, or someone being teased because they were different in some way, what would be some strong ways of standing up for them?**

2. Lead a discussion, eliciting different ways of confronting prejudice or bullying. You may want to chart these for future reference. The following are some responses that may come up, that you might want to prompt for, or that you might want to add yourself.

    -   Refuse to join in any teasing or bullying.

    -   Invite the person being hurt to join your group.

    -   Ask the person who was bullied if it's okay to have the bully join your group if the bully apologizes.

    -   Speak out, using an I–message. Say, "I don't like it when you treat him like that!" or "I want you to stop calling him that name!" or "I'm going to tell an adult right now!"

- Be a friend to the person who has been bullied by showing him you care about him: put an arm around him; give him a put-up, etc.

- Distract the bully with a joke or something else so he stops the behavior.

- Report bullying you know about or see to an adult.

(Note: *See Grade K, Lesson 15 and Grade 2, Lesson 15 for more ideas about dealing with bullying.*)

Summary

Heroes and sheroes can make the world a better place in many different ways. Although it is not easy, each of us has the ability to be a hero or shero, too. Being strong and standing up for others is something we can always choose to do.

Closing: "This Little Light of Mine"

This song can be found in the book *Linking Up!*, by Sarah Pirtle, and on the *Linking Up!* CD, Track 3. See page 132 for music and lyrics.

Extensions and Infusion Ideas

Role-Playing

Have students brainstorm incidences of bullying and prejudice. Using the chart from the lesson, review strategies someone could use to respond to these situations in strong ways.

Then choose students or have them volunteer to role-play characters in the scenarios. Have the audience notice whether or not the confronter is becoming "too hot." At the same time, have the students show their strength by a firm, resolute tone of voice and appropriate body language. Have the audience identify which strategies were used. Continue role-playing with different students and different scenarios.

Writing and Art

Have students write and/or draw about being heroes and sheroes. Have them think of something they have seen at school or at home that exemplifies prejudice or bullying. Then ask them to imagine that they are the kind of strong hero that can stand up to this injustice in a nonviolent way. Have them then draw and write about themselves making the world a safer and better place.

"Speak Up"

This song can be found in the book *Linking Up!*, by Sarah Pirtle, and on the *Linking Up!*, CD Track 17. Music and lyrics at the end of lesson.

Connecting to Literature

Point out and discuss if and how characters in books you are reading are being strong in standing up to bullying or prejudice. Have students identify what qualities the characters exemplify and what skills they use to accomplish their good deeds.

Somewhere Today: A Book of Peace, by Shelley Moore Thomas
(Morton Grove, IL.: Albert Whitman & Company, 1998) Gr. P-2

Summary: Ten scenarios of peacemakers in everyday life.

1. What is this book about?

2. Name some other ways to be a peacemaker.

3. Do you think it is possible to bring about peace by reading a book about peace and thinking about making the world a better place?

Making the World, by Douglas Wood
(New York: Simon & Schuster Books for Young Readers, 1998) Gr. P-2

Summary: A secret: the world isn't finished yet. Here are ways that we and all the creatures of nature help in making the world.

1. After the first paragraph, ask: What are we asked to do with this secret?

2. After reading the book, ask: When we make our classroom better, is the world better? When we help make our homes happier, is the world better?

Speak Up

©1997. Words and Music by Sarah Pirtle
Discovery Center Music, BMI

Speak Up

Speak up, we need your voice.

Speak up, we need your voice.

Speak up, we need your voice

in our world.

Speak up when something's not fair.

Speak up and show that you care.

Speak up when something's not right.

Speak up and follow your light.

Speak up, we need your voice.

Speak up, we need your voice.

Speak up, we need your voice

ringing strong...Speak up!

Peacemakers

Cultural Competence and
Social Responsibility

CASEL SEL COMPETENCIES

SA   Self-Awareness

Gathering: Peace Is…

Write the words *Peace is* on chart paper. Explain that you are going to ask them to finish this sentence and you will make a chart of their ideas. You can write either a few key words or whole sentences.

To expand students' ideas of peace, give an example or two from your own life, such as: **I feel really peaceful when it's a summer day and I'm sitting in the sand at the beach. So I would say, 'Peace is playing in the sand.' Or, I feel peaceful when I get a nice hug from a child I love. So I would say, 'Peace is getting a good hug.'**

In a go-round, ask each student to complete the sentence and fill in the chart .

Agenda Check

We have learned a lot this year about being strong and kind, about dealing with our feelings, and about getting along with others. In the last lesson, we talked about the importance of heroes and of helping others. Some heroes and sheroes are known for their efforts to create peace. We started today by talking about peace. Next, we'll explore what a peacemaker is (What Is a Peacemaker?). **Then we will think about a time when we have been a peacemaker and draw a picture of that time** (Contacting the Peacemaker within You). **We'll end our lesson by summarizing what we learned** (Summary) **and sharing one thing we can do to create more peace** (Closing).

Activity: What Is a Peacemaker?

1. Review concepts of peace from the Gathering, displaying the Peace Is… chart.

2. Ask: **What is a peacemaker? What are some examples of things a peacemaker might do, feel, want? Everybody can be a peacemaker. Simple things that we do every day can help make the world more peaceful. Who are some people in your family or at school who are peacemakers?**

3. Ask: **Can you think of a time you helped make peace?**

If students have trouble thinking of things, you can suggest the following:

Workshop Agenda
- Gathering: Peace Is…
- Agenda Check
- Activity: What Is a Peacemaker?
- Activity: Contacting the Peacemaker within You
- Summary
- Closing: Being More Peaceful

Materials
- Workshop agenda, written on the board or on chart paper
- Talking Object
- Chart paper and markers
- Paper and crayons or markers

Learning Outcomes
- Students will identify what peace is for them.
- Students will discuss how they and others can actively contribute to making peace.

Connections to Standards
Behavioral Studies
- Knows that people have different interests, motivations, skills, and talents
- Understands that people learn from each other in many ways

Self-Regulation
- Identifies basic values

Can you think of a time you:

- made a new friend?
- understood what someone else was feeling?
- shared a picture you liked with someone?
- disagreed with someone and worked it out?
- told someone something you liked about them?
- were patient?
- forgave someone?
- made someone laugh and feel better?

Activity: Contacting the Peacemaker within You

1. Have students pick out one or two of the times they acted as peacemakers and draw pictures or cartoons of them.

2. Those students who wish to can show their drawings and tell the class about the time they helped make peace.

Summary

Have students gather in a circle. Explain: **Today we have talked about how each of us can be a peacemaker.** Comment on positive things students identified in their drawings. Ask: **How are each of the things you did ways of experiencing or creating peace? What do you think our classroom would be like if we all worked at being peacemakers? How would the world be different if there were more peacemakers?**

Closing: Being More Peaceful

In a go-round, ask students: **What is something you can do today for yourself or someone else to be more peaceful?**

Extensions and Infusion Ideas

Writing

Have students complete sentences such as the following:

I am a peacemaker when I _____.

My teacher is a peacemaker when she _____.

(Fill in name of family member) is a peacemaker when he or she_____.

Social Studies

Discuss a historical peacemaker like Martin Luther King, Jr. with students. What makes them peacemakers? Make a point of identifying peacemakers whose names come up in social studies and language arts work. Help students see how peacemakers approach conflict respectfully and embody the skills students have been learning about such as strong communication, managing feelings, being aware of unfairness and prejudice, and standing up for others.

Peacemaker of the Week

To recognize how important it is that everyone work toward being peacemakers, you may want to establish a regular way of acknowledging student efforts. One way to do this would be for the class to devise guidelines for selecting a person for the Peacemaker of the Week Award. As a group, brainstorm the ways a student would need to act in order to be selected. This is a great way to review concepts like active listening, I- messages, and win-win solutions. Have nomination sheets or cards available for students to fill out during the week. Include a place for the student's name, the date, and a form that says, for example, ____ was being a peacemaker when _____.

One or two students can be selected from those nominated for the award. You could give a certificate and/or have all students' names added to a bulletin board.

Music

Many songs support being a peacemaker. "Peace Is Me Being Me," and "Carry the Candle," can be found in Linking Up!, by Sarah Pirtle (Cambridge, MA: Educators for Social Responsibility, 1998).

Connecting to Literature

One Smile, by Cindy McKinley
(Bellevue, WA: Illumination Arts Publishing, 2002) Gr. P-2

Summary: Katie smiles at a young man who had been discouraged after losing his job, and he feels more like looking for employment. He then helps a woman who has a flat tire. The kindness continues until it comes full circle.

1. What are some of the good things that happened because Katie smiled?

2. Describe a time you felt better because someone smiled at you.

I Call My Hand Gentle, by Amanda Haan
(New York: Viking, 2003) Gr. P-2

Summary: The books shows that we can choose to use our hands to make peace and not to hurt others.

1. Why do peacemakers have gentle hands?

2. In what ways do you help your hands to be gentle?

3. Suppose you are writing a new book. Finish the title, I Call My Hand _____.
    Describe what you would write in it.

Making Connections

Gathering: Name Game or Favorite Place to Go

Choose one of the following gatherings. If students do not know each other's names well, you might choose A. If students already know each other by name, you might want to do B.

A. Name Game

1. Have students make a standing circle, with you standing in the middle.

2. Explain that you are going to toss the ball gently to one student at a time. When he catches it, he should hold the ball and say his name in a nice, loud voice. Then the student will toss the ball back to you.

3. As the student tosses the ball back, all of the other students are to repeat that student's name. Explain that this will help students begin to know each other by name.

4. Toss the ball to the next student in the circle and continue until everyone has had a turn.

(See Extensions from Grade 1, Lesson 1, for additional ideas.)

B. Favorite Place to Go

1. Have students sit comfortably in a circle.

2. Explain the use of the Talking Object as a way of knowing whose turn it is to talk and as a reminder to listen to the person speaking. Explain that when each person receives the object, he should just hold it quietly in his lap.

3. Ask students to think about a place they really like to go to without saying anything.

4. Explain that when it is their turn, they should say their name and the place where they enjoy going. Others in the group will listen and try to remember what each person said.

5. Model by saying your name and a place you like to go. (It is sometimes helpful to think out loud and mention several different types of places to help give students ideas.)

   This is a useful place to acknowledge the good listening you observe. It is best to ignore students who are not exhibiting good listening. Point out the particular behaviors that comprise good listening by saying something like: **As I was talking, I could look around the group and see everyone's eyes looking at me.**

Workshop Agenda

- Gathering: Name Game or Favorite Place to Go
- Agenda Check
- Activity: Find Someone Who
- Summary
- Closing: "I Like You"

Materials

- Workshop agenda, written on chart paper and posted
- Copies of the handout
- Talking Object or small, soft ball

Learning Outcomes

- Students will be able to demonstrate interviewing skills.
- Students will be able to share similarities and differences with their peers.

Connections to Standards

Behavioral Studies

- Understands that people are both different and alike
- Understands that people learn from each other in many ways

Health

- Understands individual differences

Working with Others

- Engages in Active Listening
- Uses nonverbal communication such as eye contact, body positions, and voice tone effectively

I also noticed that most of you were very still, with your bodies sitting up and facing me. These things make me feel like you are really thinking about the things I was saying. How do you think this made me feel? Since I want all of you to feel as good as I did, I would like you to look around the group while you're talking, too, in order to notice all the respectful listening that will be going on.

6. Pass the object to the person next to you and ask him to say his name and what he likes to do.

Agenda Check

These lessons are going to help us learn more about each other and help us become better learners. We are going to be increasing our skills in getting along with others, solving conflicts, managing feelings, and making good decisions. Today we are going to be learning more about each other and finding out some things we have in common and ways we are different.

The word *agenda* means a plan for the lesson. Let's go over the agenda for today. We have already had a gathering, which brought us all together and started our lesson (Gathering). Next we are going to play a game that will help us learn more about each other (Find Someone Who). When we are through, we will look back and talk about what we learned (Summary) and then do a closing to end our lesson (Closing).

Activity: Find Someone Who

1. Tell students they are going to play a finding game in which they will learn more about each other. You will give them a short time to fill out a survey sheet. When they hear a signal from you, they stop what they are doing and don't move.

2. Distribute the handout or one you have customized based on it. Read it aloud with students first.

3. Explain that when students find someone who fits the description on the form they should ask that person if it is okay to put his name on the sheet. If the person says yes, they can write down the person's first name or have the person help by writing his own name on the form. Stress that the object is to get to know each other, and that they can briefly talk with each student to learn more about them before moving on to another one.

4. Begin the game. Move around the room and check for students who may be having trouble with the task. Continue the activity as long as it seems productive. It is not necessary for all students to complete the form. On the other hand, if the time is being well spent, you could have students find additional names for some categories if they have finished before the rest of the class.

5. Some questions to ask:

   - Who found someone wearing the same color shirt as you? What color is that?

   - Who found someone who can sing a song?

   Choose someone who responds and ask if he knows what song his classmate can sing.

6. Repeat the process with other questions as long as interest continues. Keep the pace quick and involve as many children as possible in the group sharing.

Summary

Today we began to get to know each other better. How did it feel to ask each other questions at first? Did it feel different after you were doing it for a while? What did it feel like to find out a way that you and someone else were the same? Why do you think it would help for us to know each other better? How do you think it would help us work together this year?

Closing: "I Like You"

Teach the song, "I Like You," to the tune of "Skip to My Lou." Lyrics can be found on page 105.

Extensions and Infusion Ideas

Exploring Names

Send a letter home to parents asking them to tell their child any of the following information concerning his/her name:

- Who gave him/her the name?

- Who, if anybody, was he/she named after?

- What does the name mean?

- Why was the name chosen?

- Are there any other stories or facts about the child's name?

The next day gather the students in a circle. Provide opportunities for all students to tell the story of their name in some way. Methods for sharing can include any of the following ideas:

- Ask for volunteers. Take a few volunteers at a time. During the next circle time, take a few more, and so on until everyone who wants to share has had a chance.

- If you have another adult in the class, break down the circle into smaller groups for sharing.

- Pair students with a partner. Ask each student to share what he knows about his name with his partner.

Art

Give out drawing paper. Have each student express who he is in visual form, using drawings. Remind students that artists' self-portraits can be realistic or very fanciful. They might want to express who they are by just using colors and shapes. Once pictures are finished, have them share their picture with a partner or do a go-round in a circle, inviting those who would like to share their picture to do so. Then post the pictures on the bulletin board.

Writing

Brainstorm with students the kinds of things that are interesting to know about new friends. For example, things they like to do, preferences, information about families, as well as big event experiences are all things that might be listed on a chart or on the board. Give students writing paper and pencils and help them write a few sentences about who they are. When they are finished, have them read to a partner or to the whole class.

Connecting to Literature

Willie's Not the Hugging Kind, by Joyce Durham Barrett
(NY: HarperTrophy, 1989) Gr. K-3

Summary: When Willie's friend Jo-Jo says hugging is silly, Willie stops hugging his family and then misses it. Finally, he let them know that he is the hugging kind.

1. Why do we hug people? Willie found out that not all of his classmates liked to hug. What did Willie do when he found out Jo-Jo thought hugging was silly?

2. What happened to Willie when he tried not to be "the hugging kind"?

3. Name some other ways that you and your classmates might be different, e.g, liking sports, going new places, meeting new people, etc.

The Tallest Shortest Longest Greenest Brownest Animal in the Jungle!,
by Keith Faulkner
(NY: Dutton Children's Books, 2002). Gr. K-2

Summary: The animals find the ways they are each unique. When the snake claims all the titles, it doesn't matter, because they are all friends.

1. There are lots of ways to look at what we are like. (For each quality, list a continuum or a category division on the board.) Line up according to:

    a. Short / Shortest

    b. Tall / Tallest

    c. No jewelry / Jewelry

    d. Light hair / Dark hair

    e. Brown eyes / Green eyes / Blue eyes

2. Give an example of other ways we are different. Give an example of other ways we are alike.

3. At the end, was the elephant right when he said he was the biggest?

My Name is Yoon, by Helen Recorvits
(NY: Farrar, Straus and Giroux 2003) Gr. 1-3

Summary: Even though she knows her name in English means Shining Wisdom, Yoon misses her Korean home and will not write her name at school. Instead, she writes other names, CAT, BIRD, and CUPCAKE – until she makes a friend.

1. Why did Yoon want to write other words instead of her own name?

2. What changed in Yoon's life and helped her feel more comfortable writing her own name?

3. How can we help others in this class feel comfortable using their own names?

Handout: Different Names

Find someone who…

1. has a pet.   _____

2. is the oldest child in
   their family.   _____

3. is wearing the same kind
   of shoes as you.   _____

4. has a brother or sister who
   goes to this school.   _____

5. likes to sing.   _____

6. saw the movie you saw last.   _____

7. likes your favorite ice cream.   _____

Creating a Positive Classroom Environment

 Emotional Literacy

CASEL SEL COMPETENCIES

SO   Social Awareness

RS   Relationship Skills

Gathering: Mirrors

Tell students they are going to play a mirroring game. Have a volunteer come up to help you demonstrate the game. Ask the volunteer to stand facing you and ask her to copy all your movements, just as if she were a mirror. Tell students the goal is to work together so that someone just coming in the room would not be able to tell who was initiating the movements. Point out that the person initiating will need to move slowly in order to be successful. Divide students into pairs, facing one another. (See Teaching Tools for suggestions about pairing students.) Have pairs choose one person to be A and one to be B. Person B reflects all the movements initiated by Person A, including facial expressions. After a short time, call "change" so that the positions are reversed. Ask: **Was it difficult to mirror someone? What did it feel like? Did you feel you worked together well enough so that an outsider would not know which one of you was the mirror?**

Agenda Check

Working well together as a class will be important to everyone. The gathering started us off with a game that let us practice working together (Gathering). **Today's lesson will help us think about how our behavior affects each other** (Feelings and Behavior of Others). **We will do an activity that will help us discuss what kind of behavior we all want to have in our classroom so that each of us can feel good about ourselves and be successful as students** (The Caring Being). **Then we will make some agreements about how we want our class to be** (Summary). **Finally, we will end our lesson with a rainstorm game** (Closing).

Activity: Feelings and Behavior of Others

1. Ask students: **What behaviors or actions in classrooms have made you or someone you know feel angry, sad, or hurt?**

2. Give students time to think, and then ask them to write and/or draw symbols and pictures that represent those behaviors.

3. Ask for a few volunteers to share their ideas, drawings, or writings without naming individual people.

Workshop Agenda

- Gathering: Mirrors
- Agenda Check
- Activity: Feelings and Behavior of Others
- Activity: The Caring Being
- Summary
- Closing: Rainstorm

Materials

- Workshop agenda, write on chart paper and posted
- Paper and drawing/writing material for each student
- A large sheet or sheets of paper (big enough for the outline of a child)

Learning Outcomes

- Students will be able to identify and describe positive and negative classroom behavior.
- Students will be able to identify and create a set of classroom guidelines for behavior.

Connections to Standards

Behavioral Studies

- Understands that rules let individuals know what to expect and can reduce disputes

Language Arts

Listening and Speaking

- Able to make contributions in class and group discussions

Writing

- Uses descriptive words to convey basic ideas

Working with Others

- Contributes to the development of a supportive climate in groups

4. Ask: **What behaviors in classrooms have made you or someone you know feel good?** Allow students to write and/or draw symbols and pictures that represent those behaviors.

5. Ask for a few volunteers to share.

Activity: The Caring Being

Choose one version of this activity. Version A is a whole-class version. Version B is a cooperative group project.

Version A

1. Have a volunteer lie down on a large sheet of paper.

2. Ask a few students to trace the outline of her body. This outline becomes the Caring Being. You can also create the outline before the lesson so that the Caring Being is ready to use.

3. Gather everyone around the Caring Being or have the Caring Being attached to a wall or board at the front of the class. Ask students to think about what actions, ways of treating one another, and attitudes would make their classroom the best possible place to be.

4. Have a brief discussion about each contribution as you use a marker to write these positive things inside the outline of the Caring Being. (Some possible things to include are: sharing, listening, taking turns, giving put-ups.) Feel free to include your own suggestions after the students have had a chance to share.

5. Ask the group to think of some actions, ways of treating one another, or attitudes that they do *not* want as part of your classroom because of their negative consequences (put-downs, name-calling, exclusion, etc.). As the students contribute, briefly discuss and write these words on the outside of the Caring Being. Add your ideas. Have students say what they meant by the words offered. Even if the words were the same as someone else's, the meaning may be slightly (or greatly) different.

6. Hang up your classroom's Caring Being where everyone can see it. If the group wants to, name your Being!

Version B

1. Divide students into cooperative groups. (See Teaching Tools for suggestions about grouping strategies.)

2. Give each group a large sheet of paper and some markers.

3. Have each group choose a volunteer to lie down on the large sheet of paper and have other students trace the outline of her body. This outline becomes the group's Caring Being.

4. Ask each group to gather around its Caring Being with the papers they completed in the Feelings and Behaviors of Others activity and share them with their group.

5. Ask students to think about what actions, ways of treating one another, and attitudes would make their classroom the best possible place to be. They should find ideas they all agree on and then take a marker and write or draw symbols of these positive things inside the outline of the Caring Being. (Some possible things to include are: sharing, listening, waiting one's turn, giving put-ups.) Circulate among groups to help them with writing.

6. Ask the groups to think of some actions, ways of treating one another, or attitudes that they do *not* want as part of their classroom because of their negative consequences (put-downs, name-calling, exclusion, etc.). Students can briefly discuss ideas and write the words or symbols they agree upon on the outside of their Caring Being.

7. When completed, have each group present and explain its creation. Hang up the groups' Caring Beings where everyone can see them. If the groups want to, they could name their Being!

Summary – Group Agreements

Today we have talked about ways we would like to be treated. Who can think of some agreements we could make as a class that would help create the kind of class we all would like? Record these ideas.

After everyone who wants to has contributed, ask if there are agreements that can be combined because they are similar (many children might say the same thing in different words, so this step is important). Make sure that the students understand you are grouping similar ideas, not changing their words. Draw a circle with the same colored marker around similar items. Feel free to include your own suggestions after the students have had a chance to share.

Once each suggestion has been refined into an agreement, ask students if they can agree to that guideline. Work toward consensus, rather than taking a vote. Read each agreement in its entirety: "We agree not to call each other names...," etc. and have students agree to it by saying *yes*. This part can be made fun by asking students to create a cheer to go along with the YES! of the agreement. For each guideline, students could stand and cheer YES! or do a fun handshake with a partner, etc.

Closing: Rainstorm

A great way to introduce this activity is to say something like: **Today we have worked hard together to create some agreements: now we are going to get to work together to make some noise!**

This is a cooperative game in which students work together to make the sounds of a rainstorm. With students standing in a circle, the teacher moves around the inside of the circle facing the students. When the teacher demonstrates a motion, students copy that motion and continue to make the motion until the teacher comes around again and changes the motion. They then continue with the new motion until another is introduced.

Begin by rubbing your hands together in front of one person in the circle. That person imitates the motion. Then go around the circle, gradually bringing everyone into the motion. The second time around the circle, snap your fingers in front of each student to indicate that she should switch from rubbing hands to snapping fingers. The third time around, make a loud pattering sound by slapping your thighs, indicating, as you go round the circle, for students to join you. Now go round the circle one more time, stomping your feet.

At this point the rainstorm is at its peak. The next time around, substitute feet stomping for thigh slapping. Once you've completed the circle, move to finger snapping and then hand rubbing. On the very last trip around, have students stop and hold their hands together silently.

At the end, the group may want to applaud their successful cooperation that created a rainstorm.

Extensions and Infusion Ideas

Formalizing Class Agreements

Write up the agreements and have them printed on special paper. Have a place for each class member, including you, to sign the document officially. Copies of the official class agreements can be made and sent home with students to show parents what has been accomplished.

Consequences

Revisit the Class Agreements regularly and ask how students think things have been going. Brainstorm with students: What can we do when we, or someone else, forget to adhere to our agreements? List the children's ideas and add any of the following: make the person an apology picture, do something else nice for that person, apologize and tell that person something you like about her, etc. Help students see the difference between consequences that are just punitive and those that might help people learn to do better next time. Remind them that everyone, including you, makes mistakes from time to time. The important thing is for us to have some ideas about how to make things right again. Things that can help us are respectful to everyone involved.

Car Wash

Explain: **The purpose of a car wash is to help cars get clean and sparkling. Just as cars collect dust and dirt from being out in the world, people some can feel "dirtied" by the exposure to all of the negative things they encounter, like the things that we put on the outside of our Caring Being(s). We are all Caring Beings at heart, but sometimes the negative things out in the world cover up our ability to shine. Receiving put-ups can be a way of helping us remember our positive qualities and helping us truly act and feel like caring beings.**

Select one or more students to "go through the car wash." Review what put-ups are and ask students to think of some put-ups for the students who are going to go through the "wash." (Note: *See Grade 1, Lesson 2 for a review or reinforcement of put-ups.*)

Have the students who are going to be the "car wash" form two lines facing each other with enough room for students to walk between. Students proceed slowly through the "car wash" with students on either side giving them a put-up as the "car" briefly pauses in front of them.

For Further Exploration

Educators for Social Responsibility has partnered with another nonprofit organization, Operation Respect, to create an anti-bullying initiative that includes classroom activities as well as a great song, "Don't Laugh At Me," other music, and a video. The curriculum material includes activities to create "Ridicule-Free Zones" and "Constitutions of Caring." To access these free materials, educators can log onto **http://www.operationrespect.org.**

Connecting to Literature

As you read books or stories that portray problems within a group, ask and discuss how things might have been different if the group had created agreements like the class did.

The Brand New Kid, by Katie Couric
(New York: Doubleday, 2000) Gr. P-3

Summary: Lazlo is excluded and sad until Ellie McSnelly reaches out to him and gets to know him.

1. At the picture of Lazlo sitting alone in the cafeteria, ask:
   a. What do you think Lazlo is feeling right now? Have you ever felt like that?
   b. If you were there, what could you do to help Lazlo?
   c. Why would it take courage to help Lazlo?
2. After reading the book, ask: What might have happened if Ellie had not gotten to know Lazlo? Why is Lazlo not the only one who would have lost out?

Chrysanthemum, by Kevin Henkes
(New York: Greenwillow Books,1991) [Video also available.] Gr. P-2

Summary: A classmate makes fun of the heroine's name. Then the popular teacher chooses it for her new baby.

1. After Victoria says, "You're named after a *flower*!", ask: How is Chrysanthemum feeling now? What happened to change Chrysanthemum's feelings about her name?

2. After Victoria says a chrysanthemum "lives in a garden with worms and other dirty things," ask: If you were there, what could you say that would help Chrysanthemum feel better?

3. After reading the book, ask: In the epilogue, how do you think Victoria felt when she forgot her lines and Chrysanthemum giggled?

GRADE 2, LESSON 3
Exploring Feelings

Gathering: How We're Feeling Today

Choose one of the following versions. You can also read *Today I Feel Silly & Other Moods That Make My Day*, by Jamie Lee Curtis (New York: Harper Collins, 1998) before either gathering. See Connecting to Literature.

Version A

1. On the board, write the numbers 1 through 5.

2. Ask students to think about how they are feeling today. Explain that some days we can feel wonderful, other days we can feel pretty bad. Remind them that all feelings are okay, and that we all feel sad or angry sometimes.

3. Tell them that you are going to ask them to choose a number that best indicates how they are feeling. The numbers are like a "joy meter." They should choose a 1 if this is one of their worst days and a 5 if they feel as great today as they've ever felt. Have them identify which number is in the middle (3), and tell them they should choose this number if their feelings are in the middle. The number 2 would mean that they are feeling a little sad or upset and 4 indicates that they're feeling a little happier than average.

4. In a go-round, ask each student to say a number that reflects the way he is feeling. Create a chart similar to the illustration below. You may also want to invite them to share a brief sentence about why they chose that number if they wish to do so.

1	2	3	4	5
X	X	X	X	X
	X	X	X	X
	X	X	X	X
		X		X
		X		X
				X

5. Discuss what came up on the chart. Ask questions appropriate to your class about what they can read mathematically from the chart. For example, **Which feeling number had the most responses? Which had the fewest? Are more people happy or sad today?** Be sure that students know and feel that all answers are "right," whether or not anybody else chose the same number as they did.

Workshop Agenda

- Gathering: How We're Feeling Today
- Agenda Check
- Activity: Feelings Families
- Activity: Creating Feelings Charts
- Activity: Feelings Change Story
- Summary
- Closing: One Word

Materials

- Workshop agenda, written on chart paper and posted
- Chart paper and markers
- Feelings Chart
- Feelings Chart forms for each student
- Talking Object

Learning Outcomes

- Students will identify words that describe different feelings.
- Students will be able to incorporate these words into regular communication.
- Students will be able to identify facial expressions that indicate particular feelings.
- Students will understand how feelings change over time.

Connections to Standards

Health

- Identifies and shares feelings in appropriate ways

Language Arts

Writing

- Uses writing and other methods to describe familiar experiences
- Writes in a variety of forms or genres (picture books, letters, stories, etc.)

Connections to Standards, cont.

Viewing

- Knows that different features (e.g. facial expressions, body language) affect a viewer's perceptions of characters in visual media

(Note: *You may want to repeat this activity a week later to make comparisons and show that moods change.*)

Version B

1. Have students make a circle.

2. Using the Talking Object, have students share how they are feeling today and why.

Agenda Check

Introduce the importance of feelings by saying something like: **We are always feeling something. That's what makes us human. Feelings can make life fun. They can also help us do something that we need to do. How many of you have felt sad when you accidentally hurt someone you care about? Feeling sad that we have hurt someone can help us apologize and make things better. Feeling angry about someone making fun of a friend can help give us the strength and courage to tell the person who is bullying to stop. Conflict can cause lots of feelings and sometimes our feelings cause conflicts. It is important for us to learn to know and to use our feelings wisely.**

We've already talked about how we're feeling today (Gathering). **The first thing we will do in our lesson is think of feelings words and see how some of them are related** (Feelings Families). **Next we'll explore how we communicate our feelings by making a feelings chart** (Creating Feelings Charts). **Then we'll listen to a story to see how feelings can change** (Feelings Change). **We'll summarize what we learned** (Summary) **and end with a fun activity** (Closing).

Activity: Feelings Families

The following activities can also be presented as a complete workshop and done over several time periods.

1. Write the word *Feelings* on the board or chart paper and circle it. Tell students you want them to think of as many different feeling words as possible. As they think of words, attach them in the form of a web.

2. This is a great opportunity to engage a student with problematic behaviors, or one who might monopolize, by asking him to be your assistant and call on students so that you can face the board and focus on constructing the web. You might remind him that you know he will choose quickly and fairly, instead of just calling on friends, for example.

3. As students contribute words, group similar or synonymous feelings to-gether. If students have trouble thinking of some feelings, ask questions such as: How would you feel if there were a huge, loud boom / you got to school and realized you had put on two different kinds of shoes / your dog ran away, etc.

By the end, there will probably be four major families of feelings relating to the four basic emotions of anger, sadness, fear, and happiness. If students have not mentioned one of these basic emotions, try to elicit it through questioning. There might also be other complex emotions that are not directly connected to one of the families.

Your web might look something like this:

Save the chart for use in Lesson 6.

Activity: Creating Feelings Charts

1. **Now we are going to explore how we communicate feelings. One way to communicate feelings is with words, but a major way we communicate is through how we look.** Choose a feeling from the web and portray that feeling with your face. Or bring in pictures of people that show different emotions. Ask students to guess what feeling you are showing or what they see in the picture.

2. Through questions and comments, have students become aware of the facial features that distinguish different feelings. For example, if you chose *sad*, ask them how you were communicating sadness with your face. Have them verbalize that your mouth turned down, that your eyes looked down and were not open wide, but half-closed. Have them describe in words the orientation of your whole face, the tone of your muscles, etc. As you do this with all of the basic emotions, have students compare and contrast the facial expressions they observe.

3. Explain that students will now make their own Feelings Charts. Show them an example. (See example on page 194, or use any of the many commercial varieties available.) Next, show them the blank Feelings Chart forms and tell them they are going to create their own version. Have them write the name of a feeling along with a caricature of a face that demonstrates that emotion.

Time spent on this activity can vary. Students can do a few to check for understanding, then complete more at a later time, or work on more at home with their families.

Activity: Feelings Change Story

1. Tell students you are now going to invite them to help you make up a story to illustrate another important thing about feelings.

2. **We are going to create a story about a person who is just your age.** Choose a name for the character that is not related to anyone in the class— in this example, Clarence. **One day, Clarence was feeling really happy about something that had happened to him. What do you think that could have been?** Take a few suggestions and then continue the story with one of the ideas. After elaborating sufficiently, say: **Then something sad happened to Clarence. What do you think happened?** After a few suggestions, again take an idea and elaborate into the next section of the story. **Then Clarence was feeling happy again. What could have happened?** Again elicit suggestions and elaborate on one of the ideas. **Then something happened that caused Clarence to feel scared. What could that have been?** Repeat this sentence using the word *angry* and end with: **but then Clarence felt happy again. What do you think might happen to end the story with Clarence feeling this way again?**

3. Write each feeling word on the board as you tell the story so that students at the end can recall the sequence. (happy – sad – happy – scared – angry – happy) **What does this story tell us about feelings?** Summarize responses by saying something like: **Things can cause us to feel differently. Sometimes, especially when we are feeling an uncomfortable feeling, we may think that the feeling will last forever. But feelings can always change.**

Summary

What's one of the things we learned today? Facilitate a discussion that includes the fact that we often communicate feelings by the way we look; that there are many different words for feelings that can help us better express how we are feeling; and that one of the realities about feelings is that they do not stay the same. **As we learn more about how to recognize and manage our own feelings, as well as how to "read" the feelings of others, we will be much better at solving conflicts and enjoying life.**

Closing: One Word

This activity can be done as a go-round or popcorn style. If appropriate, you can gently toss a soft ball or Talking Object to different students, one at a time, to invite their responses. Remind students that they always have the right to pass.

For the closing, I want you each to think of one thing that makes you feel happy. Then I want you to think of just *one* word that would best describe that thing. Share an example, such as: **For example, I like going for walks on the beach, so I could say "walks" or "beach." I also like traveling to visit my friends, so I could say "traveling" or "friends," but I think the most important part is being with my friends, so I would say "friends."**

Extensions and Infusion Ideas

Writing

Have students choose two or three (or more) of the emotions they have included in their Feelings Chart. Have them write a story about a time when they experienced that particular sequence of emotions. For a more creative writing assignment, you could randomly choose a certain number of feelings and have students write stories in which a sequence of events and decisions have a protagonist experience these feelings.

This is a great exercise in getting students to think about causality, about what could happen in a story that would then lead to the next feeling. There are many ways for students to share their products when complete.

Teachable Moments

As events that stimulate emotion happen in the classroom or between students, have the participants try to identify and then reflect what feeling they think their classmate(s) might be feeling. Have them identify things that could lead to more pleasurable feelings.

Feelings Collages

For this activity you will need magazines, paste, scissors, and paper.

Each child or group of children chooses a feeling word. They write the word on a piece of drawing paper by cutting the appropriate letters out of magazines and pasting them to the paper.

Have children illustrate the feeling by cutting out and pasting pictures that show faces expressing that feeling. When the collages are finished, have children share them. Repeat the activity if there is time.

Questions for reflection:

- How did you decide which feeling words to illustrate?

- What words were easiest to illustrate?

Connecting to Literature

Today I Feel Silly and Other Moods That Make My Day, by Jamie Lee Curtis (New York: Harper Collins, 1998) Gr. P-2

Summary: A child's emotions range from silliness to anger to excitement, coloring and changing each day.

Have the participants try to identify and then reflect what feeling they think their classmate(s) might be feeling.

1. We all have lots of different moods. Describe one of the moods the child in the story felt, why he felt that way, and what he wanted to do.

2. For each mood listed, describe some of the things you might feel like doing: silly , bad, grumpy, mean, angry, joyful, confused, quiet, excited, cranky, lonely, happy, discouraged, frustrated, sad, heavy, gray, great.

3. At the end we are told, "But moods are just . . . okay!" Why is it okay to have moods that don't feel good?

How are You Peeling?, by Saxon Freymann and Joost Elffers
(New York: Arthur A. Levine Books, 1999) Gr. P-2

Summary: Clever pictures of food are used to show different feelings.

1. Before reading the book, show students the pages and ask them to tell the feelings they think are being depicted in each picture.

2. Read the book and compare the feelings guessed by the students with those given by the authors.

3. After reading the book, ask: Is there a feeling that describes the way you feel right now?

Today was a Terrible Day, by Patricia Reilly Giff
(New York: Puffin Books, 1980) Gr. K-3

Summary: Everything goes wrong at school for Ronald but his teacher, Miss Tyler, writes an understanding note and says the next day will be good because it is her birthday and they will make it a happy day; all ends well.

1. Name some of the things that happened to Ronald Morgan. For each thing that happened, ask: How do you think Ronald probably felt when that happened?

2. For the remaining incidents, ask: How did Ronald feel (and why) when:

   a. Miss Tyler asked why he was under the table?

   b. he was corrected for signing his mother's name on his homework?

   c. Miss Tyler went to the closet when he was eating a sandwich?

   d. he didn't remember how to do the workbook page?

   e. Mrs. Gallop took him to see Miss Tyler after the drinking fountain incident?

   f. he missed the ball in left field?

   g. he had no money for ice cream at lunch?

   h. he made a mistake in reading?

   i. he watered the plants?

3. Do you like it when you receive a note from the teacher? Why?

Alexander and the Terrible, Horrible, No Good, Very Bad Day,
by Judith Viorst and Ray Cruz
(New York: Aladdin, 1987) Gr. K-2

Summary: One thing after another goes wrong for Alexander and he becomes more and more angry.

1. Before reading the book, ask: Did you ever have a day when everything went wrong? Alexander had a day like that.

2. After reading page 5 or 6, ask: What was terrible about Alexander's day? What happened to him? How was he feeling? What did he do?

3. After the muddy and fighting incident, ask: Now what happened? What did Alexander do? Who got in trouble?

4. After reading the book, ask: Mom said that some days are like that. Did you ever have a really bad day?

Handout: Feelings Chart

NAME   DATE

HAPPY

MAD

SAD

SHY

SCARED

SUPRISED

Handout: Feelings Chart

NAME   DATE

GRADE 2, LESSON 4
Empathy

Emotional Literacy

CASEL SEL COMPETENCIES

SM Self-Management

RS Relationship Skills

Gathering: I Feel Sad When…

This gathering can be done as a go-round, or a soft ball or Talking Object could be rolled or tossed across the group from person to person until everyone has had a turn.

Have students make a circle. Introduce the activity by saying something like: **Today we are going to share something we feel sad about. We'll also show others that we have heard what they have said. In a minute, I am going to ask you to finish this sentence, "I feel sad when… ." After you have shared, you will pass the Talking Object to the next person, who will start by saying back what you just said. Then she will complete the same sentence.**

Demonstrate by asking who would like to start, and then having that person toss the object to you after they have completed the sentence. If you are doing a go-round, choose one of the students on either side of you to start and then have them pass the object to you. Remind students that we all feel sad about many different things. They can choose one thing they feel comfortable sharing with the class. Also remind students that they can always pass.

When the first person is ready to start, repeat the prompt, "I feel sad when…", and after she has shared, paraphrase what she said and then complete the sentence yourself.

Agenda Check

Comment on what happened during the gathering, pointing out the differences and the things in common that came up in the responses. Then continue saying something like this:

We have been working a lot on understanding feelings. What is something important you remember from our last lesson? (Discuss) **Today we are going to learn about something that is very important. It is called** *empathy*. **Empathy is being able to understand how another person is feeling, what it is like to "be in their shoes." We have already been practicing an important empathy skill, saying back what the other person has shared** (Gathering). **Next we are going to play a charades game that will give us practice trying to "read" feelings by the way people look and sound** (Feelings Charades). **Often we guess how somebody else is feeling by thinking of how we would feel if we had the same experience. Sometimes this helps, but it can also cause us to make mistakes. We will do another activity to help us see how not to make these mistakes** (Do We All Feel the Same?). **Then we'll review what we learned** (Summary) **and do a closing** (Closing).

Workshop Agenda

- Gathering: I Feel Sad When…
- Agenda Check
- Activity: Feelings Charades
- Activity: Do We All Feel the Same?
- Summary
- Closing: One-Word Feeling

Materials

- Workshop agenda, written on chart paper and posted
- Talking Object or small, soft ball
- Feeling Families Web Chart from Lesson 3
- 3 index cards and a marker for each student

Learning Outcomes

- Students will begin to identify and recognize how other people are feeling.
- Students will understand that people often feel differently about the same experience.

Connections to Standards

Behavioral Studies
- Understands that people are different and alike in many ways

Working with Others
- Displays empathy with others

Activity: Feelings Charades

This activity can be done in a circle format, but also lends itself to a format in which students are facing the same direction. Students can move back to their seats or into a theatre arrangement.

1. Put up the Feelings Families Chart from Lesson 3.

2. Explain that students are going to try to guess how someone is feeling by the way they look and sound, without the person using a feeling word. One student will stand up at the front, choose a feeling from the chart, then turn and show the feeling to the class without using the word. She will show the feeling with her face, body, and voice as she says one sentence. The sentence is: **I'm in Mrs. McGillicutty's class.**

    The class should listen as if the speaker were a favorite cousin talking about her school experience. Remind students that the "cousin" could be very excited to be with the teacher she wanted to have, or disappointed, sad, or angry about not having the teacher she would have liked. She could be surprised, nervous, or even scared, etc. Remind students of the ways actors and actresses demonstrate feelings and encourage expression.

3. Choose a student to start the activity.

4. Have her choose a feeling without saying what it is, turn, face the class, and "act out" the feeling while saying, "I'm in Mrs. McGillicutty's class."

5. Students should raise their hand when they think they know what the feeling is.

6. Have the student acting out the feeling call on students to guess.

7. If you feel your students could handle something a little more advanced, you could ask that they express their guess in the following format:

    *   "Are you feeling _____ about being in Mrs. McGillicutty's class?"

    Variations would be:

    *   "Sounds like you're feeling _____ about being in Mrs. McGillicutty's class."

    *   "Looks like you're feeling _____ about being in Mrs. McGillicutty's class."

    *   "Seems like you're feeling _____ about being in Mrs. McGillicutty's class."

    If you choose to do this you might have a chart ready with these formats.

8. Continue to play while interest is high, or until you have covered at least the major feeling groups.

Activity: Do We All Feel the Same?

This activity can be done in a circle format, but also lends itself to a format in which students are facing the same direction. Students can move back to their seats or into a theatre arrangement.

1. Pass out three index cards and markers to each child.

2. Ask students the following questions and have them write down a feeling word that best describes how they would feel in each situation. Tell them they will have a chance to show their cards later, but should keep them private for now.

   - **"How would you feel if a friend gave you a pet snake for your birthday?"** Ask students to write the word for how they would feel on one of the cards, turn it over, and put a number 1 on the back of that card.

   - **"How would you feel if someone made fun of you because of the way you looked?"** Ask students to write the word for how they would feel on one of the cards and to put a number 2 on the back of that card.

   - **"How would you feel if you were told you were going on a huge roller coaster that only children 12 and older are allowed to ride?"** Ask students to write the word for how they would feel on one of the cards and to put a number 3 on the back of that card.

3. Say: **Now we are going to play a slightly different version of our charades game. I am going to ask two students at a time to come up, and then we will role-play one of the situations we just talked about. The two students will then each use their faces and bodies to tell us how they would feel. Our job will be to guess their feelings and then notice if they are the same or different.**

4. Ask two students to come up to the front with their number 1 cards without showing others the feeling word that is written on it. Tell them you are going to role-play giving them a box with a snake in it and they should each show how they would feel. Encourage them to be physically expressive. After the class has been able to see their feelings, ask if the feelings seem to be the same or different.

5. Have students guess what the feelings are.

6. Repeat with different students if the first students had the same feeling. The goal is to get at least one pair of students who demonstrate different feeling responses.

7. At the end have all students hold up their Number 1 card for the class to see. Verbally acknowledge all the different feelings that were a response to the same situation. Point out similarities and differences.

8. Repeat the process with the Number 2 cards and then the Number 3 cards if there is time and interest.

Summary

What have we learned about feelings today? Facilitate a discussion that acknowledges that people can have different feelings even when they are in the same situation. **Empathy means understanding how another person feels. Sometimes we can think about how we would feel if we were in that particular situation, but we always have to pay attention to the messages a person is sending by the way she looks and acts to really know what it is like for her. It can feel really good to have someone understand your feelings by saying something like, "It looks like you're kind of nervous about being in Mrs. McGillicutty's class." Also, it's always okay to ask someone how he or she is feeling about something if you're not sure.**

Closing: One-Word Feeling

Ask students to say one word that describes how they are feeling right now. This could be done as a go-round, popcorn style, or a ball toss.

Extensions and Infusion Ideas

Looking for Empathy

As students read books and stories, ask them how they think different characters are feeling. Point out examples in stories when characters are being empathetic with each other and when they are not. Ask students to notice when classmates are being empathetic with each other. Help students see the consequences of having empathy for others.

Feelings Relay

For this activity you will need five 3x5 or 5x8 cards for each group. Write a different feeling word on each card.

Divide the group into teams of four or five. Have each group stand at equal distances from you. Explain that one member from each team will come to you and get a Feeling Card, read it and leave it at your feet. The team member will return to the group and act out the feeling on the card for the other team members without talking. When the group has guessed the feeling correctly, the next person goes to get a card. The first group to guess all their cards wins.

Establish the order in which students will act so that each person in the group gets a turn. If time is limited, have the students present alphabetically. When everyone is ready, say *go*.

If a group gets really stuck on a word, or the person acting does not know what the word means, pull that card out and substitute a new one.

Classroom Management

When problems or conflicts occur, ask students to put themselves in the other person's shoes and guess what their feelings and needs are. You could have two pairs of shoe prints (oversized) cut out of construction paper. When two students are upset with each other, have them take out the shoe prints and set them in pairs facing each other. Have the students stand on the prints and take turns telling each other how they are feeling and what they want. Then have them physically trade places, and speak from the other person's point of view. This can be especially effective if repeated after students have been through the next four lessons.

Connecting to Literature

Literature is full of emotion. As you read books together, ask students what feelings the characters in the stories are expressing. Ask students to identify what makes them think a character is experiencing a particular feeling. Frequently, students may come up with different feeling words or even different feelings to describe the same experience. This is a great opportunity to acknowledge the diversity in opinions. It is also a great way to underscore that while it is important to try to understand how other people are feeling, no one but the person experiencing the emotion knows for sure. Sometimes, even the person experiencing the emotion does not know what she is feeling!

The Berenstain Bears and the Trouble with Grownups
by Stan and Jan Berenstain
(New York: Random House, 1992) Gr. K-3

Summary: Brother and Sister play-act the trouble they have with their parents, and their parents reciprocate.

1. The parents and the cubs put themselves into each other's shoes. Name some of the things they learned about each other.

2. Tell about a time when you disagreed with one of your parents or guardians or brothers or sisters. Now, try to put yourself into that person's shoes.

    a. What would you be seeing and hearing and thinking and feeling?

    b. What might you do differently because of seeing the other person's point of view?

    c. If appropriate, role-play the situation to show how it could be done differently.

Trouble in the Barkers' Class, by Tomie De Paola
(New York: G. P. Putnam's Sons, 2003) Gr. P-2

Summary: Carole Anne, the new student, is unpleasant and mean. Then Morgie learns that she is just afraid no one will like her and really wants friends.

1. After Carole Anne is introduced and "she just looked away," ask: How do you think Carole Anne is feeling now?

2. After Billy and Morgie say they wish Carole Anne weren't in their class, ask: How do you think Carole Anne has been feeling? How would you feel if you were Billy? Morgie?

3. After reading the book, ask: How did Morgie help Carole Anne feel safe in sharing her feelings?

4. Does anyone in our class understand how Carole Anne felt during those first days?

Edgar Badger's Butterfly Day, by Monica Kulling
(Greenvale, NY: Mondo Publishing, 1999) Gr. 2-5

Summary: Edgar is sad to see the end of summer.

1. Describe the ways that Edgar's friends feel differently from him.

2. Describe the ways that Edgar's friends were patient with him.

3. What might have happened if Edgar's friends had not tried to understand or help him?

Point of View

Gathering: Two Sides of An Object

Have an object with two different sides available to use but out of the students' sight. (For example, a reversible piece of material that is different on each side, a ball that has two different-colored halves, a stack of paper made up of two different-colored, but same-size papers, an object that is plain on one side and richly decorated on the other.) Tell students you are going to start the lesson with a little game. The object of the game will be to see how well they can describe an object after looking at it quickly. Randomly choose four or six volunteers. Divide the volunteers into two teams in front of the class. Ask them to close their eyes. Make sure the other students know that they should not give anything away as they are watching the game. While the participants' eyes are closed, uncover the object and carefully position it so that each team sees only one of the sides. Tell participants to open their eyes and silently look at the object. After a few seconds, ask them to close their eyes again and then hide the object. Ask them to open their eyes. Give them a brief time to confer privately with the others on their team and then ask each team to give a description of what they saw. Based on their point of view, the descriptions should be very different. Reflect on any dynamics that surface, feelings that the teams may have toward the other team, etc. Point out that they are experiencing a conflict. **When people think they are right, especially if there are others on their side who agree with them, they can often think the other point of view is wrong.** Show them the object from all sides so they can see that actually both teams were right from their point of view.

Agenda Check

Today we are going to be looking at point of view and how important it is to understand another's point of view in solving conflicts. As we saw in the gathering (Gathering), **one thing can appear very different from different positions or points of view. Empathy is all about being able to see things from the other person's point of view. We have been learning that we are all different in many different ways. We all see things from our own position. If we don't realize that another person's point of view can also be "right," we can sometimes get stuck in a fight instead of being able to work together to solve a conflict. Today we are going to explore this concept of point of view with a story** (Wolf Story) **and then look at how this relates to conflicts we might have with others—for example, with a brother or sister** (Examining Point of View). **We'll summarize what we learned** (Summary) **and end by sharing a favorite fairy tale** (Closing).

Workshop Agenda

Gathering: Two Sides of an Object

Agenda Check

Activity: Wolf Story

Activity: Examining Point of View

Summary

Closing: A Favorite Fairy Tale

Materials

- Workshop agenda, written on chart paper and posted
- An object with two distinctly different sides
- A wolf puppet (if possible)
- Two puppets (to dramatize a sibling conflict)

Learning Outcomes

- Students will understand that people do not always share the same point of view.
- Students will recognize the importance of considering different points of view when solving problems or managing conflict.

Connections to Standards

Language Arts

Reading

- Knows main ideas or theme of a story

Working with Others

- Displays empathy with others

Activity: Wolf Story

If your students are unfamiliar with the story of "Little Red Riding Hood," review it before beginning this activity.

Version A: With a Wolf Puppet

1. Have the puppet come out and greet the students. You might tell the students that you know the wolf has been through a pretty bad experience and could use some friends who are good listeners to hear his story. This is a great opportunity to point out how helpful friends can be just by being good listeners to each other, especially when someone is upset or not feeling good about something.

2. Have the wolf tell his story directly to the students.

Version B: Without a Puppet

1. Explain to the students that you are going to tell them a story based on a fairy tale they already know. Ask them to listen carefully, and while they are listening, to think about how the story might be different from the version they are accustomed to hearing.

2. Tell the story of "The Maligned Wolf" in language your class will understand. Be prepared to tell the story without reading it.

The Maligned Wolf

The forest was my home. I lived there and I cared about it. I tried to keep it neat and clean. Then one day, while I was cleaning up some garbage a camper had left behind, I heard footsteps. I leaped behind a tree and saw a little girl coming down the trail carrying a basket. I was suspicious of her right away because she was dressed funny – all in red, and with her head covered up so it seemed like she didn't want people to know who she was. Naturally, I stopped to check her out. I asked who she was, where she was going, where she had come from, and all that. She turned up her nose and told me in a snooty way that she was going to her grandmother's house. As she walked on down the path, she took a candy bar out of her basket and started to eat it, throwing the wrapper on the ground. Imagine that! Bad enough that she had come into my forest without permission and had been rude to me. Now she was littering my home. I decided to teach her a lesson.

I ran ahead to her grandmother's house. When I saw the old woman, I realized that I knew her. Years before, I had helped her get rid of some rats in her house. When I explained what had happened, she agreed to help me teach her granddaughter a lesson. She agreed to hide under the bed until I called her.

When the girl arrived, I invited her into the bedroom. I was in the bed, dressed like her grandmother. The girl came in and the first thing she did was to say something nasty about my big ears.

I've been insulted before, so I made the best of it by suggesting that my big ears would help me to hear her better. Then she made another nasty remark, this time about my bulging eyes. Since I try always to stay cool, I ignored her insult and told her my big eyes help me see better. But her next insult really got to me. She said something about my big teeth. At that point, I lost it. I know I should have been able to handle the situation, but I just couldn't control my anger any longer. I jumped up from the bed and growled at her and said, "My teeth will help me eat you better."

No wolf would ever eat a little girl. I certainly didn't intend to eat her. (She probably would have tasted bad anyway.) All I wanted to do was scare her a bit. But the crazy kid started running around the house screaming. I started chasing her, thinking that if I could catch her I might be able to calm her down.

All of a sudden the door came crashing open and a big lumberjack was standing there with an ax. I knew I was in trouble, so I jumped out the window and got out of there as fast as I could.

And that's not the end of it. The grandmother never did tell my side of the story. Before long the word got around that I was mean and nasty. Now everyone avoids me. Maybe the little girl has lived happily ever after, but I haven't.

3. Discuss these questions:

   - What fairy tale is this? What makes it different from the version of "Little Red Riding Hood" that you are familiar with?

   - What do we think of Little Red Riding Hood in the original story? What do we think about the wolf?

   - In the story of "The Maligned Wolf," why did the wolf decide to teach the girl a lesson? What does he do when he can't control his anger any longer? Do you believe the wolf's story?

4. Explain that in a conflict each of the people involved has his own point of view. For example, according to Little Red Riding Hood, the bad wolf was trying to eat her. According to the wolf's point of view (as expressed in "The Maligned Wolf"), he was merely trying to teach her a lesson. Often we assume that one side (usually our side) has all of the truth and goodness and that the other side is all wrong and bad. But it's not usually that simple. Before deciding who's right and who's wrong, it's important to understand both sides of a conflict.

Activity: Examining Point of View

1. Introduce the activity, saying something like: **Many of the conflicts that people have come about because people see things from different points of view, like Little Red Riding Hood and the Maligned Wolf.**

2. Using two puppets, dramatize a conflict over which TV show to watch. One puppet claims that a particular show is his favorite and he watches it every day. The other puppet argues that the first puppet always picks the shows they watch and that he never gets a turn to pick one.

3. Discuss each puppet's point of view.

4. Ask for volunteers to describe a time when they had a conflict because their point of view was different from another person's. What happened? Who was involved? How were the points of view different?

Summary

What does *point of view* mean? The next time you have a conflict with your mom or dad or someone else, what could you remember about the lesson today that may help you resolve the conflict better?

Closing: A Favorite Fairy Tale

In a go-round, ask students to share what their favorite fairy tale or story is and why.

Extensions and Infusion Ideas

"Red Riding Hood Meets the Maligned Wolf" Skit

Have students act out scenes from the stories of Little Red Riding Hood and the Maligned Wolf that combine the two points of view. For example, Little Red Riding Hood as characterized in the traditional story sets off for grandmother's house and meets the Maligned Wolf. After the scene has been played, ask such questions as: **How do you think Little Red Riding Hood felt when she met the wolf in the forest? Can you think of a time when you had a similar feeling? How do you think the wolf felt?**

Revising Fairy Tales

Have students revise other fairy tales from points of view different from the usual. For example, they could retell Cinderella as told by the stepsisters, Jack and the Beanstalk as told by the giant.

Connecting to Literature

Point out the points of view from which different books and stories are written. Literature is a rich source for the ongoing exploration of point of view. Ask students to examine how other characters might feel or see things differently from the protagonist.

The Pain and the Great One, by Judy Blume
(New York: Dragonfly Books, 1985) Gr. 1-4

Summary: A third-grade girl describes her younger brother and then he describes her.

1. How did the little brother annoy his big sister?

2. How did the big sister annoy her little brother?

3. Name some things they might do differently if they could understand each other's point of view.

4. If you have little brothers or sisters, how do you think they see you?

My Big Brother, by Valorie Fisher
(New York: Atheneum Books for Young Readers, 2002) Gr. P-2

Summary: We see a boy from his baby brother's viewpoint.

1. If you were the little brother in this story, how would you see your big brother?

2. Suppose you were the big brother.

   a. What things would surprise you the most about the way your little brother sees you?

   b. What are some ways you might have misunderstood your little brother's actions?

3. Think about another person in your life. What might they say if they wrote a book about you?

Captain Kangaroo: Do You See What I See?, by Wendy Wax
(New York: Perennial Currents, 1998) Gr. P-1

Summary: A "mooseunderstanding" between a moose and a rabbit. Captain Kangaroo helps them see things from each other's perspective.

1. Why did Moose and Bunny have an argument? What helped them settle it?

2. Have you ever seen things differently from someone else?

Exploring Conflict

CASEL SEL COMPETENCIES

SA   Self-Awareness

RS   Relationship Skills

Gathering: Imagining a Class Field Trip

Tell students to imagine that the class has been given permission and the
funding to go on a field trip to any place they wanted to go. Ask them to think
silently about where they think it would be the most fun to go. Using the
Talking Object, have them share with the group the place they would choose
for the whole class to go.

Agenda Check

Acknowledge the diversity of choices that came up in the gathering. Point
out that if students did not agree on a choice for the trip, this could result in a
conflict. Fortunately, though, this was an imaginary exercise. Explain: **Today
we are going to look at some different types of conflicts. We are going
to look at what the word** *conflict* **means. Then we will look at misunderstandings by playing a game that many of you may have already played at
some time. It is called Telephone** (Conflict and Misunderstandings). **After
that, we'll talk about differences and conflict** (Differences and Conflict).
**Sometimes just having differences creates conflicts. Then we'll summa-
rize what we've learned** (Summary) **and end with a closing** (Closing). **How
does that sound?**

Activity: Conflict and Misunderstandings

1. Start by writing the word *conflict* on the board or on chart paper. Then
    choose one of the following introductions.

Introduction – Version A

A conflict is an argument, a disagreement, fight, or struggle. Lead a small
discussion that points out that conflict is a regular part of daily life. It is the
way we deal with conflict that creates violence or peace. Remind students
that conflicts can occur over who has access to limited resources (the two
puppet siblings both wanting the one last cookie), but that conflict can
also be the result of misunderstandings or just differences. See Grade 1,
Lesson 9 to review more about conflicts.

Introduction – Version B

Draw a circle around the word *conflict*. Ask the students what words or
phrases they think of when they hear the word, and record their responses
as a web. Write their contributions on the board, using lines to connect
each word to the word *conflict* or related words. Continue for a few minutes.

Workshop Agenda

- Gathering: Imagining a Class Field Trip
- Agenda Check
- Activity: Conflict and Misunderstandings
- Activity: Differences and Conflict
- Summary
- Closing: Sharing Win-Win Stories

Materials

- Workshop agenda, written on chart paper and posted
- Talking Object
- Chart paper and marker
- Two puppets (for Version A of the activities)

Learning Outcomes

- Students will be able to define conflict.
- Students will understand how misunderstandings and differences may cause conflicts.

Connections to Standards

Behavioral Studies

- Knows that disagreements are common, even between family and friends

Language Arts

Writing

- Relates stories to personal experiences (e.g. events, characters, conflicts, themes)

Working with Others

- Determines the causes of conflicts
- Identifies an explicit strategy to deal with conflict

Using their responses, help them come to a definition of *conflict* as an argument, disagreement, struggle, or fight.

Some questions to ask:

- What do you notice about the web?

- Can we make any generalizations about it?

- Why are most of our associations negative? Does conflict equal violence?

- What is the difference between conflict and violence?

Point out that conflict and violence are not the same thing; conflicts do not have to lead to violence. Make the point that conflict is a natural and normal part of life; that we all experience conflicts at home, at work, in school, on the street, and that countries also have conflicts with each other.

Make the point that conflict is a natural and normal part of life.

2. Say: **Now we are going to play a game to help us look at one of the things that can cause conflicts.**

3. Have students make a circle.

4. Tell them that you are going to whisper a message to the person next to you that will get relayed around the group. Tell them that the point of the game is to try to get the message communicated clearly one person at a time. If a student does not hear what she is told, she may ask only once for the message to be repeated. Then, she needs to convey whatever she thinks she heard as best she can to the next person. (While most children love this activity, some may get overly anxious if not able to convey the message "correctly." If someone gets very upset, remind her that she can choose to pass. In that case, the last person sending the message repeats it to the next student in the circle.)

5. Whisper a message to a student next to you. (An example might be: At recess, I need the last student to go and tell the office that we will be in room 22 for P.E. today.) After the message has gone individually around the circle, ask the last person who received the message to tell the group what she heard.

6. Tell students the original message and discuss briefly: **At what points along the way did it change? What happened when it changed?** Point out the potential consequences that any distortions or changes in the message could have in creating a conflict for the people involved. What helps getting the right message around?

7. Ask: **What are some examples of misunderstandings in real life that can cause conflicts?** Elicit a discussion from the examples that students share. Point out how easily misunderstandings can take place. Highlight the differences in point of view when a misunderstanding occurs.

Activity: Differences and Conflict

Say: **We've just seen how misunderstandings can contribute to conflicts. But sometimes, just differences by themselves can also create conflicts, even when there is no misunderstanding.** Choose one version of the activity.

Version A

1. Have the puppets act out a scenario of friends who want to play together but want to play different games. Stop at a point at which the disagreement is beginning to heat up.

2. Have students discuss what is happening.

3. Review the possible ways conflict can be resolved: win-lose, lose-lose, and win-win. Have the class help the puppets through the ABCD Problem Solving format to arrive at a win-win solution. (See Grade 1, Lesson 9 to review the ABCD Problem Solving format.)

Version B

1. Ask the class if they have ever had a conflict with a friend about what game to play.

2. Use these examples to review win-win solutions and problem solving steps. (See Grade 1, Lesson 11.)

Summary

Ask students to give a definition of *conflict*. Explain: **Conflicts can occur for different reasons. Conflict can develop when there is not enough of something that everybody needs or wants. What is one example of that kind of conflict?** Elicit and discuss contributions. **Conflicts also can start either because of a misunderstanding or just a difference in what two people want. What is an example of a misunderstanding? How can differences cause conflicts?**

No matter how conflicts start, we can always choose the way we want to respond. Conflict happens all the time; it does not have to be violent. What are some things that are important to remember in solving conflicts so that both sides can get to a win-win solution?

Closing: Sharing Win-Win Stories

Invite a few students to share stories of conflicts they resolved successfully in a win-win fashion.

Extensions and Infusion Ideas

Recalling Personal Conflicts

(Note: *In this part of the lesson, you will be describing a real conflict in your life. It is important to choose a story that is meaningful, but one that also is appropriate to share with your students. Choose a conflict that you feel comfortable that they know about and one that clearly models the* where, who, what, end, *and* feel *that you are going to ask them to use in their stories.*)

Think of a conflict you have had recently with another person. Share this story with students, including concrete details of where the conflict happened, who was involved, what happened, how it ended, and how you felt about it in the end. Ask students if they can tell if the conflict was based on a misunderstanding, on a difference, or on a limited resource.

Then ask students to raise their hands if they can remember a conflict they have had. Call on a few to describe their conflicts. You might tell students to use the words *friend* or *classmate* instead of another student's name so that people do not feel uncomfortable about being identified in someone else's story.

Divide the class into pairs. Ask students to take turns telling their partners about a conflict they have had, including who was involved, how it started, how it ended, and how they felt when it ended. Write the words *where, who, what, end,* and *feel* on the board as a reminder of what the story is to include. Limit the time devoted to each story to two or three minutes.

Writing

Have students write about their personal stories of conflicts. Ask them to include who was involved, how it started, how it ended, and how they felt when it ended. Write the words *where, who, what, end,* and *feel* on the board as a reminder of what the story is to include.

Connecting to Literature

Why Mosquitoes Buzz in People's Ears, by Verna Aardema.
(New York: Dial Books for Young Readers, 1976) [Video also available.] Gr. K-3

Summary: The iguana puts sticks in his ears so he can no longer hear mosquito's stories. This begins a chain reaction of misunderstandings.

1. Describe the ways some misunderstandings made this conflict worse.

2. How was an accident part of the conflict?

3. Did the solution to the conflict make everyone happy? Explain.

Nobody Likes Me!, by Raoul Krischanitz
(New York: North-South Books, 1999) Gr. K-3

Summary: Buddy, a new dog in the neighborhood, assumes nobody likes him, until he checks out his assumptions and finds out the other animals were afraid of him.

1. After Buddy walks away from the sheep, ask:

    a. Do you think the mouse, the cats, the rabbits, and the sheep really dislike Buddy?

    b. Suppose you were one of those animals. What might you be thinking about Buddy?

    c. What are some strong words that Buddy might use to say that he would like to play?

2. After reading the book, ask: What did Buddy find out when he asked the other animals why they didn't play with him?

3. Tell what this story teaches about making friends.

4. What has helped you make friends with others?

Too Close Friends, by Shen Roddie
(New York: Dial Books for Young, 1997) Gr. P-2

Summary: Pig and Hippo get along better when the hedge is high enough for privacy and they go to visit each other.

1. What caused the conflict between Pig and Hippo?

2. How did they end the conflict they were having?

3. How did they help prevent future conflicts?

4. What do you and your friends do to prevent conflicts?

The Hating Book, by Charlotte Zolotow
(New York: Harper Collins, 1969) Gr. K-2

Summary: The story of two friends who get into a feud as the result of a misunderstanding.

1. How did the conflict get started? What happened?

2. What was the misunderstanding? Why was her friend acting mean to her?

3. The little girl did not want to ask her friend, "Why?" What was bothering her?

4. What happened when she finally did?

GRADE 2, LESSON 7
Communication

Gathering: Cooper Says

This is a variation of "Simon Says." Give students a series of directions that they are to follow only when preceded by the words "Cooper Says." The difference between the two games is that everyone remains in the game whether or not they follow the instructions accurately. The name "Cooper" derives from the word *cooperation*.

Ask everyone to face you and listen closely to your directions, following only those that are preceded by "Cooper Says." (Examples: Cooper says, Smile; Cooper says, Touch your hair, Jump.)

Agenda Check

What do you have to do to play the game we just played in the gathering? Today we are going to look at what is needed to communicate well. We'll look at what communication is (What Is Communication?), **what's involved in being a good listener** (Good Listening), **and how to help people understand what you want them to know** (Sending Clear Messages). **Then we will summarize what we learned** (Summary) **and end with a closing** (Closing).

Activity: What Is Communication?

1. Choose two students to come to the front of the class and toss the ball back and forth to each other. Ask the class to observe carefully for a few seconds.

2. Ask the two students to freeze for a minute and then ask the class: **What did _____ and _____ have to do to keep the ball going back and forth successfully?**

3. Facilitate a discussion and ask questions that get at these basic concepts:

   - This game requires two skills: catching and throwing.

   - Mistakes can happen while catching or throwing that can cause problems.

   - The farther away you are from each other, the harder the game is. At some point, it will become impossible.

   - It is important to pay attention if you want to keep the ball going back and forth smoothly.

   - If someone throws the ball too hard or too fast, the other person will probably have trouble catching it.

Workshop Agenda
- Gathering: Cooper Says
- Agenda Check
- Activity: What Is Communication?
- Activity: Good Listening
- Activity: Sending Clear Messages
- Summary
- Closing: Listening or Speaking?

Materials
- Workshop agenda, written on chart paper and posted
- Ball to toss back and forth
- Chart paper and markers
- Paper and pencils for students

Learning Outcomes
- Students will understand communication as a process of sending and receiving messages.
- Students will be able to identify and demonstrate behaviors that are important for effective communication.

Connections to Standards
Language Arts

Listening and Speaking
- Asks and responds to questions
- Follows rules of conversation (e.g., focuses attention on speaker)
- Gives and responds to oral directions

Working with Others
- Engages in Active Listening
- Uses nonverbal communication such as eye contact, body positions, and voice tone effectively
- Communicates clearly during conversation

- This game can be fun when it goes smoothly, but people can get upset when it doesn't.

4. Summarize by saying something like: **Communication is a lot like throwing a ball back and forth. Communication takes place when one person uses words or body language to let another person know what he is thinking or feeling. The other person listens in order to receive or understand the communication. It's a kind of tossing and catching, just like the game we played, only instead of a ball, we use words or body language.**

Activity: Good Listening

To review good listening, see Grade 1, Lesson 1.

1. Introduce the activity by saying: **What do people need to do to understand clearly what people are telling them? We are going to make a chart of the things we need to do to be really good listeners. But first, I want you to think about what parts of your body you use when you're listening. Think of somebody who is catching the ball that you are throwing to them. Do they just use their hands to catch it? What else do they use?**

2. Draw out responses that acknowledge that one needs to use his eyes, his brain, and his whole body as well as his hands in order to catch a ball. Similarly, listening requires more than just ears.

3. Ask: **What should go on our Good Listening chart?** Use the recent responses and experiences to generate a chart that includes what people are doing with their eyes, minds, and bodies to demonstrate good listening.

   The completed chart might look something like this:

   Good Listening

   - Eyes on speaker.
   - Bodies still.
   - Think about the topic.
   - No interrupting.
   - Smile, nod head.
   - Show feeling expression.

4. Save the chart for use in Lesson 8.

Activity: Sending Clear Messages

Before the lesson, create a model drawing based on the graphic.

1. Introduce the activity by saying: **Now we are going to do an activity to help us see what is important on the other side of communication, what we need to do to send messages clearly.**

2. Distribute paper and pencils or crayons.

3. Explain that you are going to give students directions for making a drawing. They will have to listen very carefully because you want them to draw the picture from your verbal directions as best they can. This will be one-way communication. You won't look to see how they are doing and they cannot ask questions.

4. Have students make a drawing giving only the following directions:

    • **Draw a circle in the middle of your paper. Above the circle, make a dot.**

    • **Below the circle, make an X.**

    • **Draw a box around the whole thing.**

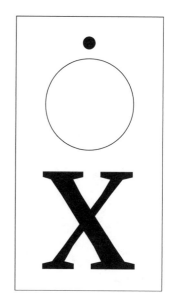

5. Discuss: **What was it like to do that? Were there any problems? What were they?** Tell the students about your end of the communication process. What did not looking at their drawings or answering questions feel like for you?

6. Ask the students to take a second piece of paper to do the drawing again. This time they will be able to ask as many questions as they want. Repeat the directions above, adding any detail or elaboration you feel is needed for the drawing and answer students' questions.

7. Show your drawing. Ask students to compare their drawings with yours. Discuss: **Was your first or second drawing closer to the original? What made the difference? Which way took more time?**

8. Summarize the things that go into making communication clear. Communication works best if the person speaking is clear about what he is saying and can check for understanding. It's a two-way process; with the speaker making sure the listener understands.

Summary

Who can give me a good definition of *communication?* Make the point that communication is a process of sending and receiving information – feelings and thoughts. If their definitions are not very broad, ask questions designed to expand their thinking. Examples might be, "Do dogs communicate? How?" **What is important to remember about listening? What do we need to remember about sending clear messages?**

Closing: Listening or Speaking?

What part of communication is easiest for you, speaking or listening? Students can answer in a go-round or popcorn style. Acknowledge contributions and end by observing that we can all become better at communication by sharpening our communication skills.

Extensions and Infusion Ideas

Impulse

Join the group in forming a circle holding hands. There should be a comfortable amount of space between each person, so that they are neither squeezed nor stretched.

Explain that you are going to create a wave impulse that will travel through the group.

Start by visibly, but lightly squeezing the hand of one of your neighbors. That person should then pass the impulse to his neighbor, and so on until it comes back to you.

Experiment with sending the impulse in the other direction, and then in both directions at the same time. If those variations work, introduce a stopwatch. Establish a time and then try to better it. Try timing it with all eyes closed except the leader's.

Discuss:

- Did we move the wave impulse throughout the group smoothly?
- When did it work best?
- When did it not work?
- What did you learn about communication from this exercise?

Bumper Cars

Designate a large rectangular space that is large enough so that everyone is able to walk around each other. Be certain that your group is ready to play safely and make it clear that intentional crashing is not acceptable behavior.

Set the scene by saying something like: **Many of you would probably like to drive a car. Now is your big chance. But since we are making this special opportunity available to you, you will need to be very careful with your car. Your car trusts you to drive carefully and not crash it into any other cars. You have a very expensive, sporty car. Be careful!**

Organize students with a partner. In each pair, one person is the car and one person is the driver. The car will keep his eyes closed while the driver drives it around.

The driver's goal is to drive around during an allotted time period (two minutes) without any crashes. The driver will tell the car to move forward by placing both hands on his partner's shoulders. To make the car stop, the driver will remove his hands. To turn right, he will lightly tap his partner's right shoulder. To turn left, he will lightly tap his partner's left shoulder. The driver and car may not talk (of course, cars do not talk!).

Once the time period is up, have partners switch roles.

Bring the class back together in a circle. Ask each person to complete the sentence, "I liked being the (car or driver) best because... ."

Go around the group, getting their responses. **Did anyone find it difficult to be the car? Why? Did your driver do anything that made you feel safe? Unsafe? If you were a car, did you trust your driver? Why? Did anyone who was a car keep his eyes open? What was it like for those of you who were drivers? What did your car do that made it easy to drive? Difficult?**

Can You Guess?

Ask students: **Who thinks they are good at figuring out directions?** Choose two volunteers and have them leave the room. Tell students: **While they are gone, the rest of us will think of a simple direction for the volunteers to follow when they return. We will not be able to talk to the volunteers when they return, however. The class can communicate only by clapping – loud clapping when the volunteers are close to following the direction and no clapping if they are not close at all. Give a standing ovation when they've got it!**

The directions for the volunteers must be simple. Help guide the group to agree on a simple, appropriate direction. For example, the volunteers could be directed to come into the room and pick up a piece of paper. Set a time limit for selecting the direction.

When the volunteers return to the room, explain the rules to them. The volunteers may need some help getting started. The best way to figure out what the direction is is to start doing things around the room. Encourage the volunteers to stay active. If they seem stumped, give them a hint.

Try several rounds.

Afterward, talk about the different rounds. **What made some volunteers more successful at finding the solution than others?** Work with the group to identify those things that made communication easier. Conclude by talking about the relationship between the volunteers and the group. Tell the children that communication cannot rely on one person. It is a relationship between two people or groups.

Connecting to Literature

Did You Hear about Jake?, by Louise Vitellaro Tidd
(Brookfield, CT: The Millbrook Press, 1999) Gr. K-2

Summary: A message gets garbled because of noisy conditions.

1. Why did the message get so mixed up?

2. What could have been helpful in getting the message straight?

Armadillo Tattletale, by Helen Ketteman
(New York: Scholastic, 2000) Gr. K-3

Summary: Armadillo had long ears and would overhear other animals and repeat what they had said, garbling it.

1. What is important when we communicate with others? Tell how Armadillo caused problems by telling things inaccurately.

2. Suppose you and a friend were having a good game of catch, and someone came along, took the ball, and threw it to someone else.

    a. How would you feel?

    b. Explain how this is similar to the time in the story when two animals were talking and Armadillo met up with them.

3. In what ways did Armadillo's talking seem like tattling?

GRADE 2, LESSON 8
Active Listening

Gathering: Pantomime

Ask students to think of something they like to do. Tell them you will act out something you enjoy doing without using any words. Ask students to raise their hand quietly when they think they know what it is. Pantomime the activity you enjoy doing. Call on students to guess what the activity is until you get a correct response. Have that student come up and pantomime an activity she likes to do. Continue for a while, stopping at your discretion or when interest wanes. If a student who answers correctly does not want to pantomime, you could have her choose another student to take her place.

Agenda Check

Was what we just did communication? Briefly discuss responses. **In the last lesson, we learned that communication consists of sending information and receiving it. Today we are going to practice two important listening skills. Good listening is not like resting; we have to work actively at doing a good job. Sometimes we call this kind of listening Active Listening. One thing that active listeners do well is paraphrase, or say back, what the speaker said. Have you ever seen famous people being interviewed on TV? Today some of you are going to be interviewed and then we will practice paraphrasing the things we learned during the interviews** (Paraphrasing Interviews). **Another thing that active listeners do is to ask clarifying questions. Clarifying questions help the speaker say more about what she is talking about so that we can understand her better. We will also practice this** (Clarifying Questions). **At the end, we will review what we did** (Summary) **and then do a closing** (Closing).

Activity: Paraphrasing Interviews

1. Choose a volunteer to come to the front of the class to be interviewed.

2. Ask the audience to use all their good listening skills because after the interview you are going to see how much they can remember and ask them to paraphrase it back.

3. Welcome the student onto the show. Using the "microphone," ask questions and then point the "microphone" toward your "guest." Some possible questions are:

   • What kind of things do you like to do?

   • Tell me about your family.

Workshop Agenda
- Gathering: Pantomime
- Agenda Check
- Activity: Paraphrasing Interviews
- Activity: Clarifying Questions
- Summary
- Closing: Something New

Materials
- Workshop agenda, written on chart paper and posted
- Good Listening Chart from Lesson 7
- Prop to use as a microphone

Learning Outcomes
- Students will be able to demonstrate paraphrasing skills.
- Students will be able to ask clarifying questions to increase understanding.

Connections to Standards
Behavioral Studies
- Understands that practice helps us improve and also how often and hard we try to learn

Working with Others
- Demonstrates respect for others in the group
- Engages in Active Listening

- Do you have pets?
- What's your favorite ____ (color, food, book, movie, etc.)?
- If you could go anywhere in the world, where would you go?
- What kind of work do you think you might like to do when you're older?

4. Once you have asked a general question and the student has responded, try to ask clarifying questions. For example, if you asked about pets and the student replied, "I have a dog," you could ask, "What's your dog's name?", "What kind of dog is it?", "Have you had him a long time?" etc.

5. Have the student stay in front of the audience and ask students to raise their hand if they can paraphrase one thing they learned about the interviewee. Have students share their paraphrase directly with the student. Rather than saying, "She has a dog named Rover," have the student look at the interviewee and say, "You have a dog named Rover." If a student remembers something inaccurately, the interviewee usually corrects it instinctively, saying something like, "His name is Rascal." This is a good opportunity to point out one of the benefits of paraphrasing.

6. You or the interviewee can call on students. Continue until they have recalled everything or can't remember any more information. At the end of the interview, thank the student for appearing. (Applause is nice.)

7. Repeat with another volunteer, if time permits.

Activity: Clarifying Questions

1. Tell students that for the next interview, you are going to have the audience think of, and ask, clarifying questions.

2. Begin the interview as with the previous ones, but once the interviewee has responded with something that could be elaborated upon, ask members of the audience to raise their hand if they can think of a good question related to what the speaker just said. Remind them that clarifying questions do not change the subject; they just ask the speaker for more information about what has already been said. With each category or subject you introduce, have the other students ask all the clarifying questions. When the questions have stopped, or interest has waned, open up a new subject with a different question.

3. If time is available and interest is still high, you could do one more interview.

Summary

Today we have practiced two very important active listening skills. What does it mean to paraphrase? What is good about paraphrasing? (People feel listened to when the person they are talking to repeats what they have said and they have a chance to correct any misunderstandings.) **How did it feel to be interviewed?**

How did it feel when students asked clarifying questions? When someone asks us for more information about something we have just talked about, it can feel like people are really interested in us and that feels good. Where do you think you can practice these active listening skills?

Closing: Something New

How many of you learned something new about someone in our class? What's something you learned? Have a few students share, popcorn style.

Extensions and Infusion Ideas

Continued Interviews

Continue with student interviews until all students have been interviewed.

Adult Interviews

Invite an adult such as the principal, or other community leader that your students would know or be interested in, to come to your class for an interview. Help the students brainstorm questions ahead of time. Plan and rehearse the interview process. Then brainstorm and practice what kind of clarifying questions might be appropriate as follow-ups to likely responses to major interview questions.

Active Listening Role-Plays

Have students brainstorm a list of common conflicts. Choose one of the conflicts from the list and have volunteer students role-play the scenario. Stop the role-play; discuss what is happening in the conflict and how the characters are feeling. Ask students: **Are they being good listeners? What could they do differently?**

When conflicts occur, encourage the participants to paraphrase what the other person has said or is feeling.

After a short discussion, have the role-players continue, using the audience's suggestions to help resolve the conflict. Point out and encourage paraphrasing. Have the players complete the role-play, continuing to incorporate the suggestions from the class. The goal is to show how good listening can make a difference when solving problems. Encourage students to talk from their own perspective. Suggest that they begin their sentences with the word *I*.

Ask: **How did the conflict change once the actors started listening to each other? What did they do to be better listeners? Did you hear any clarifying questions? What difference did it make when the characters paraphrased or started with the word** *I*?

Teachable Moments

There are many opportunities in the school day when we can help students practice better listening skills. When conflicts occur, encourage the participants to paraphrase what the other person has said or is feeling. When a student has asked an inappropriate, off-topic question, gently point out that the question was not a clarifying question.

Describe what it feels like for you to be interrupted with an off-topic question, and help the student identify a more appropriate time for her question to be asked.

Connecting to Literature

How Jackrabbit Got His Very Long Ears, by Heather Irbinskas
(Flagstaff, AZ: Northland Publishing, 1994) Gr. K-3

Summary: The Great Spirit makes creatures to live in the desert and then assigns Jackrabbit to acquaint the creatures with their new homes. Because he doesn't listen carefully, Jackrabbit gives incorrect information to Tortoise, Bobcat, and Roadrunner, harming their self-esteem. The Great Spirit kindly affirms the other creatures and gives Jackrabbit ears that will help him in the future.

1. Why didn't Jackrabbit listen well to the Great Spirit?

2. What wrong messages did Jackrabbit give the other animals, and what should he have told each?

3. What happened as a result of Jackrabbit's wrong messages?

4. Can you think of some things that might happen if someone gives you a message and you do not hear it correctly.

The Big Bad Rumor, by Jonathan Meres
(New York: Orchard Books, 2000) Gr. K-3

Summary: The goose says a big bad wolf is coming and the message gets garbled throughout. At the end there is a sad little wolf – and his dad.

1. Why do you think the animals had such a hard time listening?

2. What happens when we don't listen? Give an example if you can.

3. How could the animals have made sure they heard the message correctly before passing it on?

Using Words to Be Strong

Caring and Effective
Communication

CASEL SEL COMPETENCY

RS   Relationship Skills

Gathering: When I Get Angry

Have students sit or stand in a circle. Ask students to think about times when they get angry. **How do you let other people know you are mad? I am going to ask you to finish this sentence, "When I get angry, I usually... ."** Model by finishing the sentence yourself and then pass the Talking Object to the next student. As students share, accept each student's response without comment and then move on to the next one. (Note: *It is best to maintain a calm manner if violent or attention-getting responses come up.*)

Agenda Check

Today we're going to talk about some strong ways to deal with angry feelings. We've been working on learning better communication skills. In the last lesson, we focused on listening skills, how to "catch" the messages others are sending more accurately. Today we are going to be focusing on how to better "send" messages. This is especially important in conflicts or at other times when we might have strong feelings. Sometimes when we are really angry or upset we feel like being mean. What we really want to be is strong, but it takes knowledge and practice to be really strong. Today we are going to look at a tool to help us be strong (I-messages) **and then we'll practice constructing I-messages** (Constructing I-messages). **At the end, we'll review what we've learned** (Summary) **and do a closing** (Closing).

Activity: I-Messages

The following activities build on the foundation laid in Grade 1, Lessons 8 and 10.

1. Introduce the activity by saying: **Remember that in communication, when we send a message it's like we are throwing a ball to another person. The way we throw it is important in getting the other person to catch it. If you got really mad at someone, you might feel like throwing the ball *at* him instead of *to* him and if you were just throwing the ball to hit him, chances are he's not going to catch it. We call those kinds of messages "you-messages." Instead of communicating our feelings and needs, you-messages just attack, criticize or blame. Instead of being strong, they are "mean." I-messages tell the other person what *I* am feeling, thinking, and wanting. It is like throwing the ball directly to someone so that they can catch it.**

Workshop Agenda

- Gathering: When I Get Angry
- Agenda Check
- Activity: I-messages
- Activity: Constructing I-messages
- Summary
- Closing: Strong People

Materials

- Workshop agenda, written on chart paper and posted
- Talking Object
- Two puppets
- I-message formula, written on chart paper.
- Copies of worksheet for each pair of students

Learning Outcomes

- Students will be able to articulate feelings.
- Students will be able to construct an "I-message."

Connections to Standards

Behavioral Studies

- Understands that practice helps us improve

Working with Others

- Does not blame others for problems
- Identifies an explicit strategy to deal with conflict
- Expresses emotions appropriately in personal dialogues

When the speaker uses an I-message, he can say in a strong way that he is angry without attacking, blaming, or putting down the other person.

If we want to open up communication and solve conflicts creatively, we're usually better off using I-messages. Suppose someone borrowed your ball and didn't bring it back. What might a you-message be? (Example: Where's my ball, you stupid jerk? You shouldn't be allowed to borrow anything.) **Here is an example of an I-message: I feel angry when you borrow my ball and don't bring it back, because then I don't have it when I want it. I'd like you to bring it back to me now.**

These puppets are going to help us explore the effects of you-messages and I-messages.

2. Introduce the puppets and play out a scene full of you-messages, either the one below or one you have made up.

The scripts provided can be used as is, or as an example for one you create yourself.

PUPPET ONE: You're a lousy friend. You didn't even invite me to your birthday party. I have you over to my house all the time, and you couldn't even invite me to one stupid party. I bet it was a stinking party anyway. You don't know how to have fun. Nobody would want to go to your party.

PUPPET TWO: Why don't you shut up! Who cares what you think anyway? It was a wonderful party, but you wouldn't have known how to behave right. You always make trouble. You would have ruined it if I'd invited you.

3. Ask: **How do you think Puppet One felt about Puppet Two in this skit? How do you think Puppet Two felt about Puppet One? Do you think there is a good chance they will go on being friends? Why? Why not?**

4. Replay the scene, this time using I-messages.

PUPPET ONE: I felt really hurt and angry when I learned that you had a birthday party and didn't invite me because I thought we were good friends. It just doesn't seem to me like something a good friend would do. When Pam and Keisha told me they were invited and you didn't invite me, I just felt like, okay, that's that. I guess we're not friends any more.

PUPPET TWO: I'm sorry I couldn't invite you to my party. I wanted to but my mother said I could only invite two friends because all my cousins were coming. I wanted to talk about it before the party, but I didn't know how to tell you. I'd really like to go on being friends.

5. Ask: **How do you think Puppet One felt about Puppet Two this time? How do you think Puppet Two felt about Puppet One? Do you think there is a good chance they will go on being friends? Why? Why not?**

6. Compare the two skits: **What were some of the comments Puppet One made in the first skit? What was the tone of voice like in the first skit? What were some of the comments made in the second skit? What was the tone of voice like in the second skit? Which comments would be more likely to break up the relationship?**

7. Summarize the effects of you-messages and how they differ from I-messages: **When you send a you-message, the listener feels judged or blamed. You seem to be saying he is a bad person. The listener does not think about changing his behavior, but thinks instead about defending himself. This makes anger grow instead of shrink. With an I-message, the speaker expresses his own wants, needs, or concerns to the listener. When the listener hears an I-message, he learns that he has done something the speaker didn't like. The listener may feel bad about it, but that's quite different from feeling accused of being a terrible or incapable person. I-messages are a clear and nonthreatening way of telling people what you want and how you feel.**

Activity: Constructing I-Messages

1. Display the chart with the formula for I-messages you have previously prepared.

2. Say: **There are four potential parts to an I-message. Here's an example of an I-message.** Point out the different parts, filling in with an example, such as:

> I feel *angry*
>
> when *I see students looking around the room*
>
> because *it makes me feel that what I'm saying is not important*
>
> and what I would like is *for you all to show me respectful listening by looking at me while I'm speaking.*

In the first part we only use feelings words. What are some examples of feelings words?

In the next part we only describe; it is "just the facts." We only talk about things we ourselves can experience. For example, if I said, "I feel angry when *I see bad listeners*," that is an opinion that would be based on the fact I saw students looking around the room. But that doesn't necessarily mean you are "bad listeners."

The *because* part is a place for us to explain why we feel the way we do. As we learned in Lesson 6, people can feel differently about the same thing. This also lets the listener know we have a reason for our feelings and what we want.

The last part explains what it is we want the other person to do so that there aren't any misunderstandings.

3. Ask students to make a list of potential conflicts at school or at home in which it would be helpful to use an I-message. (Examples: someone monopolizing equipment, someone getting pushed or tripped, a sibling feeling that he doesn't have equal say in what TV shows to watch, etc.) Post the list or write it on the board.

4. Divide the class into pairs. Give each pair a worksheet. Have each pair choose a situation from the list. Give the pairs five minutes to use the form to design an I-message to apply to the situation. Have one of them write down their sentence on the worksheet form.

5. Ask for volunteers to read the I-message they constructed. Help the class give positive, constructive feedback about the I-message.

6. Discuss: **Was it a feeling word? Did they use just facts in describing the "when?" Did they explain why they felt the way they did? Was their request possible?**

Summary

Today we have talked about how to send strong messages by using I-messages. What are the four parts of an I-message? Have students repeat "I feel, when, because, and I would like" several times until it is somewhat memorized. **Why would we want to use I-messages instead of you-messages?** Lead a discussion that includes the probability that I-messages are going to be more effective, that they protect each person's self-esteem, and that they keep the speaker from going up the anger thermometer (See Grade 1, Lesson 12.) **All of these things allow conflicts to be resolved creatively in a win-win manner. We will explore win-win problem solving in our next lesson.**

Closing: Strong People

Who is someone you know who knows how to be strong without being mean? Help students think of people in their families, among their friends, in their classroom, or at school who model nonviolent strength.

Extensions and Infusion Ideas

Body Language Can Send I-Messages

(Note: *Be sensitive to the variety and styles of body language in your class. For example, some postures and voice tones are culturally influenced and some may be influenced by a disability. The point is not to belittle anyone, but to help students become aware that our tone of voice and our body language send powerful messages. If we are aware of the effects of our body language, we can make sure it matches our strong, calm words.*)

Put the following words on the board: *weak, strong,* and *mean.* Say: **We have talked a lot about how we communicate feelings not only with words, but also with the tone of our voice and our body language.**

For I-messages to be really strong, we need to use the format we learned, but we also need to send strong messages with our voices and our bodies.

Pick an example of an I-message, either one you make up or one from those that students have generated. Be sure the words are a good example of an I-message. Tell the students to listen as you deliver the I-message and then tell you if your body language was weak, strong, or mean. First deliver the I-message in a very weak tone of voice, with your head down and your body caved in. Ask students which category it fits in (weak). Next say the same I-message, but make your face look very angry, tighten your whole body, and sort of yell the words. Acknowledge that even though the words are strong, if they are delivered in that tone of voice they will feel like a you-message. Discuss strong body language. Then deliver the same I-message with your body tall and relaxed, in a clear, strong voice that is still congruent with the emotion, but is respectful, calm and in control. Have one or two volunteers try out an I-message using strong body language.

I-Message Role-Plays

Have students work in pairs to create short role-play skits (similar to the puppet skits) around different conflict situations. Have them present a you-message version as well as an I-message one. Have pairs perform their skits for the class. Discuss the effects of the two kinds of communication on the characters and the potential resolution of their conflict.

Positive I-Messages

I-messages can also be used when people want to tell someone that they appreciate something the person has done or said. For example, "I feel happy when you come to my house after school because I have fun playing with you and I would like for you to come again tomorrow." Divide students into pairs and ask them to help each other craft an appropriate I-message for someone they would like to show appreciation to.

Teachable Moments

Your students will need more than one or two workshops to become comfortable using I-messages in real situations. The more practice you can give them the better. Call attention to I-messages and you-messages that come up in real conflicts in your classroom and use them as teachable moments. With practice, I-messages become easier and easier to use. They are especially helpful for people who are afraid to ask for what they want. They can prevent a conflict from building up to a boiling point because both parties failed to talk over the problem when it was small and simple. When you see potential areas of conflict beginning, invite students to try I-messages to prevent the issues from escalating.

Journal Writing

Students can write in their journals (or create a special journal) about times when they have used I-messages and what happened when they did.

I-messages can prevent a conflict from building up to a boiling point because both parties failed to talk over the problem when it was small and simple.

Connecting to Literature

Have students look for examples of you-messages and I-messages in stories and books that they read.

Marvin and the Mean Words, by Suzy Kline
(New York: G. P. Putnam's Sons, 1997) Gr. 2-5

Summary: Second-grader Marvin misunderstands his teacher and thinks she hates him. The experience teaches him empathy with those he had previously teased.

1. At the end of Chapter 2, ask: Why was Marvin mean to Mary?

2. After reading the book, ask: Why did Marvin stop teasing Mary about her stuttering?

3. How was Marvin's life harder when he thought his teacher had said mean words about him? What I-message could Marvin have given to his teacher when he was first upset?

Snail Started It!, by Katja Reider
(New York: North-South Books, 1997) Gr. K-3

Summary: Snail's unkind words to pig set off a chain reaction that continues until unkind words reach snail, whose apology sets off a healing chain reaction.

1. Why were the animals mean to one another?

2. What happened to stop the stream of mean comments?

3. What I-messages would have changed this story? Go back through the story and think of an I-message each character could have said.

Handout: I-Message Worksheet

I feel _____

when _____

_____

because _____

_____

and I would like _____

_____.

Win-Win Problem Solving

Conflict Management and
Decision Making

CASEL SEL COMPETENCIES

DM   Responsible Decision Making
RS   Relationship Skills

Gathering: New and Good

Stand or sit in a circle. Ask students to share something that happened in the last day or two that they felt good about. This can be something they saw, something they did, something nice someone said to them, something they ate – anything that made them feel good. Start by sharing something new and good in your life and then pass the Talking Object to the next person.

Agenda Check

We have been working on developing all kinds of skills that help us deal with conflicts when they occur. Today we are going to look at how conflicts can end and how to use our skills to get to the kind of solutions that we really want to happen. What does it mean to win? How do people feel when they win? What does it mean to lose? How does that feel?

Winning and losing in sports and games is very different from winning and losing in conflicts. Most of our conflicts are with people we really care about, like our family, our friends, and people we work with.

Today we are going to look at the different ways conflict can end (Conflict Outcomes), **then we'll look at how we can use some of the communication skills we have been working on to get to a win-win solution** (Creating Win-Win Solutions). **At the end, we'll reflect on what we learned** (Summary) **and do a closing** (Closing).

Activity: Conflict Outcomes

This role-play should be set up ahead of time. It can be done with two puppets, two adults, or two students.

1. Give the puppets, or the people role-playing the scenario, made-up names. Have them role-play the following sibling situation.

Role-Play Scenario

The older sibling, who is in junior high school, has just settled into studying for an important test that is coming up tomorrow. The younger sibling, an elementary student, comes home from school, turns on the stereo and starts dancing. The younger sibling has just finished a whole week of testing at her school and she hasn't even been able to play outside for the last couple of days because of rain. The older sibling gets up and orders the younger one to turn off the stereo. She responds by saying, "You're not the boss of me," and turns the stereo up.

Workshop Agenda

- Gathering: New and Good
- Agenda Check
- Activity: Conflict Outcomes
- Activity: Creating Win-Win Solutions
- Summary
- Closing: People We Want to Have Win-Win Situations With

Materials

- Workshop agenda, written on chart paper and posted
- Chart showing the four possible outcomes to a conflict
- Talking Object

Learning Outcomes

- Students will be able to identify win-lose, lose-lose, and win-win solutions to a conflict.
- Students will be able to create win-win solutions to solve a problem.

Connections to Standards

Behavioral Studies

- Understands that some ways of dealing with disagreements work better than others, and people not directly involved in an argument may be helpful in solving it

Language Arts
Reading

- Makes simple inferences regarding the order of events and possible outcomes

Self-Regulation

- Understands personal wants versus personal needs

Working with Others

- Resolves conflicts of interest
- Determines the causes of conflicts
- Identifies an explicit strategy to deal with conflict

2. Ask the class to describe what's going on.

3. Make a chart on the board like the first one below, writing the two names of the siblings and the word *wants*.

4. Ask: **What does the older sibling want right now? What does the younger one want to do?** Fill in the chart as students answer. (The older one wants the music to be turned off, the younger one wants it on. You want students to see that at this level, they both cannot get their wants met.)

5. Write the word *needs* in the next column and ask students: **What does the oldest need? What does the youngest need?** As students answer, fill in that part of the chart. (The older needs quiet so she can study and do well on the test. The younger one needs to let off some steam, to relax, to do something fun.)

	Wants	Needs
Older Sibling	Music off	Quiet to study so can do well on test
Younger Sibling	Music on	To relax, have fun

6. Ask: **If the older won, what would she get? How would she feel? If the younger won, what would she get? How would she feel?**

   Show students the following chart you have prepared of ways the conflict could come out.

	Younger sibling gets what she needs	Younger sibling doesn't get what she needs
Older sibling gets what she needs	win–win	win–lose
Older sibling doesn't get what she needs	lose–win	lose–lose

Activity: Creating Win-Win Solutions

1. Divide the class into groups of four or five and ask each group to think of a lose-lose, win-lose, and several win-win solutions for the role-play scenario in the previous activity.

2. After groups have thought of different possibilities, refer to the chart and ask for an example of the oldest winning and the younger sibling losing. Ask what could happen that would end in the younger one winning and the older sibling losing. **What could happen so that they would both lose, and neither would get what they need?** Finally, ask students for examples of win-win solutions. Try to elicit as many different ideas as possible.

3. If possible, have students role-play the different win-win solutions. The group that contributed a particular idea could choose two people to role-play that idea either as a straight role-play or with the puppets. Point out active listening and I-messages as you hear them.

Summary

Today we have looked at how conflicts can end. Sometimes conflicts end with only one person getting her needs met. We call this a win-lose solution. Most of the time when this happens it really turns into a lose-lose ending because most of the conflicts we have are with people we care about. It doesn't really feel very good if you get what you need, but your friend or family member ends up losing. Fortunately, if we work hard enough, we can often find a win-win solution so both people can get what they need. How do you think this makes people feel?

Closing: People We Want to Have Win-Win Solutions With

Today, for the closing, I'm going to ask you to think about different people you sometimes have conflicts with. Who is someone you can think of that you would always want to work out a win-win solution with? You can have students share their answers in a go-round or a quick popcorn style check-in. Remind students not to use names of friends.

Extensions and Infusion Ideas

"The Zax," by Dr. Seuss

Read students the Dr. Seuss story "The Zax," from *The Sneetches and Other Stories* (New York: Random House, 1961). Stop before reading the last page. Have students identify the wants and needs of each Zax. They each want the other one to move out of their way. Each needs to go only north or only south. They each think that having the other Zax move is the only way they can get their needs met, but there are other ways. Encourage students to think of true win-win solutions that don't require either of the Zaxes to give up their needs.

Frequently, students will suggest that both Zaxes agree to move a little to one side or the other. Point out that this is a compromise that does result in a peaceful solution, and that it is fair, but that it is not really a win-win solution. Both Zaxes have lost as well as won.

Have students pair up with a partner and brainstorm a win-win solution. When they have some ideas, invite pairs that would like to, to demonstrate their solution. You can play the narrator as they begin to reenact the beginning of the story.

The pair should then act out what the two Zaxes would say to each other that would allow them to arrive at the suggested win-win solution. Demonstrating the process of communication that is involved in achieving win-win solutions is an essential part of the exercise.

The two most common win-win solutions that students come up with are 1) having one Zax jump or leap over the other one, and 2) having one Zax crawl under the other Zax's legs.

Rewriting Fairy Tales

Have students take a classic fairy tale and try to think of a way that the characters could come up with a different ending that met everyone's needs. For example, in *Jack and the Beanstock*, how might Jack and the Giant both end up being happy?

Teachable Moments

As conflicts occur in the classroom, ask students to think of win-win possibilities for solutions. Although not all conflicts may be resolvable with a win-win solution, all conflicts can be approached with a win-win attitude. Let students know this is the attitude you expect, and the attitude that will promote a positive classroom atmosphere.

Classroom Management

Make sure your approach to discipline issues models a win-win attitude. Situations in which students are directly involved in a conflict with you or with the needs of the group can present powerful learning opportunities. Dealing with situations challenges us to use all our skills and encourages our own growth as teachers. It is at the heart of what discipline is really all about.

Connecting to Literature

In the books you are reading, have students notice how characters resolve conflicts and how they feel if they win or lose. Have students brainstorm win-win solutions for stories that end in win-lose or lose-lose situations.

The Terrible Thing that Happened at Our House, by Marge Blaine
(New York: Four Winds Press, 1975) Gr. 1-3

Summary: When the mother returns to teaching, things are miserable at home. The daughter finally gets heard and the family finds a solution.

1. What happened in the family when the mother went back to teaching?

2. How did the family solve each of the problems so that everyone was happy?

3. Could the kind of meeting the family had be helpful in our classroom? What things would we need to do to make it work well?

Although not all conflicts may be resolvable with a win-win solution, all conflicts can be approached with a win-win attitude.

Cecil's Garden, by Holly Keller
(New York: Greenwillow Books, 2002) Gr. P-2

Summary: When Cecil, Jake, and Posey cannot agree which vegetables to plant, the garden is empty until Cecil comes up with a solution.

1. Describe the conflict about the garden. How did Cecil settle it? Explain why this was a win-win solution.

2. Explain how their conflicts affected the mice and the moles.

3. Can you think of a possible win-win solution for the mice? For the moles?

4. Have you ever been involved in working on a project with someone in which you couldn't agree on how to work it out? What helped you solve the conflict?

Escalation

 Conflict Management and
Decision Making

CASEL SEL COMPETENCIES

SA Self-Awareness

SM Self-Management

Gathering: When I Get Upset

When you get upset about something, what pushes your anger up to a higher level? As our gathering today, I am going to ask you to complete this sentence, "When I get upset, one thing that makes it worse is... ." Explain that students may say what they do that makes things worse, or what someone else may say or do that makes things worse. Model by completing the sentence yourself. Repeat the prompt and have students complete the sentence in a go-round or popcorn style.

Agenda Check

One of the things we need to do in order to resolve problems and create win-win solutions is to stay calm enough to be able to think clearly. When conflict gets worse, we say it "escalates." What does an escalator do? (Briefly discuss what an escalator is. The important point is that escalators go up, or down, one step at a time.) Conflict usually begins with something very small. It might start when someone says or does something that upsets you. Then you might say something mean. That upsets the other person even more so they may say or do something mean back. Now you're both more upset. At this point, your own anger thermometer could be close to the top, which is not a good position to be in to think of a peaceful solution.

In our gathering, we talked about things that can make a conflict worse. Today we're going to do a role-play to see how escalation works (Conflict Skit). Then we'll make a chart of the different steps up the escalator and the feelings that go with them (Conflict Escalators). At the end, we will talk about what we learned (Summary) and do a closing (Closing).

Activity: Conflict Skit

1. Choose two students and give them copies of the Backpack Conflict script ahead of time (page 242). Have students choose names that are unrelated to anyone in the class. If time permits, you may want to coach them before their performance.

2. Have the two student volunteers act out the Backpack Conflict. Ask the audience to see if the conflict gets "hotter" and to notice the things that push the conflict up toward the top of the escalator.

3. At the end of the role-play, ask students if the conflict seemed to go right to the top all at once or if it seemed to go up step-by-step.

Workshop Agenda

- Gathering: When I Get Upset
- Agenda Check
- Activity: Conflict Skit
- Activity: Conflict Escalators
- Summary
- Closing: What Helps You Cool Off

Materials

- Workshop agenda, written on chart paper and posted
- Copies of Backpack Conflict for each group of 2–3 students
- Copies of Escalator worksheet for each group of 2-3 students
- Talking Object

Learning Outcomes

- Students will be able to identify factors that escalate conflict.
- Students will be able to analyze conflict and label the behaviors that contribute to conflict escalation.
- Students will be able to name the feelings associated with the behaviors that escalate conflict.

Connections to Standards

Language Arts

Reading

- Identifies setting, main characters, events, sequence, and problems in stories

Working with Others

- Determines the causes of conflicts

4. Discuss: **What were some of the things that escalated the conflict? How could you tell the conflict was getting hotter?**

Activity: Conflict Escalators

1. Divide students into groups of two or three and give each group a copy of the Backpack Conflict script along with an Escalator Worksheet (page 243).

2. Have students identify each step in the script that escalated the conflict and write it on the worksheet on the ascending steps of the escalator.

3. Under each step, have the groups select the feeling from the anger thermometer that they think best matches what the characters in the script were feeling.

4. Discuss how the conflict escalated: **What was the first thing that happened in this conflict? What did you place at the top of your escalator? What things did the characters do that made this conflict worse?**

Summary

A conflict can feel like taking a ride on an escalator – once it starts, you're on your way to the top. Fortunately, understanding things that make conflict escalate can help you control where the conflict is going. You noticed that we put the feelings the characters were having underneath the steps of the escalator. Feelings are like the motor underneath an escalator; they drive the escalator. The higher one goes, the harder it is to come down because the feelings have intensified. Sometimes our feelings carry us away from clear thinking. Then we do things we are sorry for later. This is why it's helpful to recognize escalation, so we can choose to stop and stay cool. This allows us to work toward strong, win-win solutions to conflicts.

Closing: What Helps You Cool Off

We started the lesson today sharing things that push our anger up the escalator. For the closing, I am going to ask you to think about what kinds of things help you de-escalate, or come down the escalator when you are starting to get mad. Have students form a circle, either standing or sitting. Begin by sharing one thing that helps you calm down. Then pass the Talking Object to the next student. Students can either share things they like others to do or things they can do themselves. Examples of things they'd like from others might be, "when people apologize to me," or "when they really listen to what I am saying." Examples of things they can do themselves might be, "saying to myself that I am not going to get hot" or "walking away and thinking of a favorite song."

Extensions and Infusion Ideas

Identifying Conflict Escalation

When students experience conflicts with each other, unless they are already at the top of the escalator, you could ask them to plot the events that happened and the feelings involved. As an exercise in self-reflection, this can further the calming required for problem solving. It can also help students begin to take responsibility for their choices and the consequences of their choices. If a student is too upset about something that just occurred, however, he may need other things to cool him down before this can be attempted successfully.

Connecting to Literature

Children's literature is full of books in which a conflict escalates to a climactic point and then is resolved in some fashion. Have students identify conflicts in stories and then use the conflict escalator handout to plot the step-by-step development of the action and the corresponding feelings that the characters experience.

Little Bear and the Big Fight, by Jutta Langreuter and Vera Sobat (Brookfield, CT: The Millbrook Press, 1998) Gr. P-2

Summary: When Little Bear's best friend Brandon won't share the pink clay, Little Bear gets so angry he bites Brandon's ear. After losing his best friend, Little Bear takes some time to decide to say, "Sorry."

1. After the other bear cubs looked away from Little Bear, ask: How is Little Bear feeling? What should he do?

2. After reading the book, ask: Little Bear and Brandon got on the Conflict Escalator. Describe what happens on each step of the Conflict Escalator as they move up. What stopped the bears from continuing to go up the escalator?

3. What were the steps as the bears came down the escalator?

4. Point out various steps and ask students what suggestions they would give to Little Bear and Brandon to help them get off the Conflict Escalator.

Why Are You Fighting, Davy?, by Brigitte Weninger (New York: North-South Books, 1999) Gr. P-2

Summary: Eddie builds a dam and Davy builds a boat. They have a fight and then resolve it.

1. Davy and Eddie got on the Conflict Escalator. Tell what happens on each step of the Conflict Escalator as they move up.

2. What were the steps as Davy and Eddie came down the escalator?

3. Point out various steps and ask students what suggestions they would give to Davy and Eddie to help them get off the Conflict Escalator.

Handout: Backpack Conflict

NAME   DATE

STUDENT #1: (*trips over Students #2's backpack*) "Oww!"

STUDENT #2: (*smiles or laughs at Student #1*)

STUDENT #1: Is this your stupid backpack?

STUDENT #2: You're the dummy who tripped over it.
Don't be such a baby!

STUDENT #1: (*kicks Student #2's backpack*)

STUDENT #2: Hey! (*stands up and pushes Student #1*)

NAME

DATE

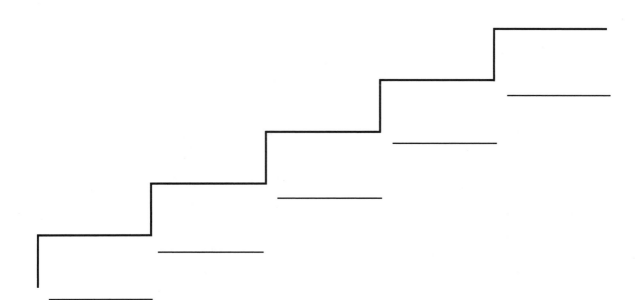

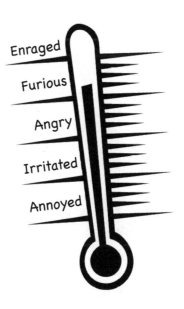

De-Escalating Problem Solving

Conflict Management and Decision Making

CASEL SEL COMPETENCIES

SM   Self-Management

RS   Relationship Skills

Gathering: "There Is Always Something You Can Do"

Teach the first verse of the song, "There Is Always Something You Can Do" from *Linking Up!*, by Sarah Pirtle. See music and lyrics on page 150.

Agenda Check

Just as the song says, there is always something you can do. There are usually lots of different things you can do. We've been learning many skills that can help us act in strong ways when we are in a conflict. Today we are going to review and list some of the important things we have been learning (Conflict Tool Box). **Then we will practice using different skills by doing some role-plays** (Practice Role-Plays). **At the end we will summarize what we did together** (Summary) **and do a closing** (Closing).

Activity: Conflict Tool Box

1. Create a two-column chart on chart paper titled *Conflict Tool Box*. Label one column *Tools for Me* and the other *Tools to Use with Others*.

2. Ask: **What are some examples of tools? Hammers are useful tools. When would you use a hammer? What tool would you use to tighten a screw? Would a hammer work? Just as we need a variety of tools to build or repair something, we need a variety of skills to handle conflict well. That's why we will call this chart our Conflict Tool Box. We want to list on it all the different tools that can help us solve conflicts in strong ways. Under *Tools for Me* we are going to list things that we can do to keep cool and thinking our best. On the other side, *Tools to Use with Others*, we want to list all the skills we've been working on that can help us get to win-win solutions.**

3. Ask: **Let's review some of the things that can help us stay calm.** Elicit and discuss responses as you begin to fill in the first column. If things come up that belong in the other column, put them there, discuss briefly, and return to personal cooling-down techniques. By asking probing questions or through suggestions, try to include the following tools:

Materials

- Workshop agenda, written on chart paper and posted
- Conflict Tool Box Chart
- Chart paper and markers

Learning Outcomes

- Students will be able to identify ways to "cool off" and respond to conflicts constructively.
- Students will demonstrate responding to conflict positively.

Connections to Standards

Behavioral Studies

- Understands that practice helps us improve and also how often and hard we try to learn

Language Arts

Reading

- Relates new information to prior knowledge and experience

Listening and Speaking

- Makes contributions in class and group discussions

Self-Regulation

- Determines explicit behaviors that are used and should be adopted to obtain wants and/or needs
- Uses postive techniques to offset the negative effects of mistakes

Take a deep breath; Count to 10 (25 or 50); Walk away; Think about a favorite relaxing place; Use self-talk such as "I can stay calm," "This isn't worth getting upset about," "Stop, don't get hot," etc.

4. Discuss: **Now that we have thought of things that can keep us cool, what are some of the skills we have been learning this year that we might need in solving a conflict with others in a strong way?** Elicit and discuss responses as you begin to fill in the second column. Ask questions that help students remember things that have been covered earlier in the year and even things that were introduced last year. Things to include on this list might be: use put-ups (not put-downs); think about point of view (we all see things differently); empathy (the ability to guess the other person's feelings); active listening, paraphrasing; I-messages; ABCD problem solving; win-win attitude; compromising; saying "sorry," etc.

Activity: Practice Role-Plays

1. Introduce the activity by saying: **Now we are going to think of some conflicts that we can use in our role-playing.**

2. Ask students to think about different kinds of conflict that happen at school, at home, or even in the community.

3. Make a list on chart paper. The list might include such things as a disagreement about what game to play at recess, an argument over the ownership of an item, someone "cutting" in line, siblings fighting over what TV show to watch, a parent and child arguing about homework, etc.

4. Tell students that you are going to pair them with a partner. (See Teaching Tools for suggestions about pairing students.) You will give them about five minutes (or an appropriate time frame) to work with their partner to decide on a conflict and plan a role-play. The goal is to show characters using as many of the tools from the tool box as needed to solve their problem in a strong way.

5. Ask for volunteers to role-play their scenario in front of the class. Ask the students watching to look for the tools that are being used. At the end of the role-play, have students identify the tools that were used and describe the effect they had on the conflict.

Summary

Today we have reviewed and practiced a lot of important skills. We need to have different things we can do when conflicts occur so that we can resolve them in peaceful ways. We need to have a lot of tools in our Tool Box.

Closing: One Tool

Have students make a circle. This closing can be done as a go-round or popcorn style. **As you think of all the skills or tools that we have talked about today, what one thing do you think would be most important for you to remember to use in order to be really strong in solving conflicts?**

Extensions and Infusion Ideas

More Role-Plays

Have more students demonstrate their scenarios and process each one with the class.

Bulletin Board

Design a Tool Box bulletin board with a large box containing tool cut-outs that are labeled with particular conflict resolution skills.

Individual Tool Boxes

Have students draw a picture of a tool box and write on their paper the names of different tools that they feel they know how to use. On another piece of paper, have them write the tools that they need to practice using or learn more about. These could be taken home and shared with their families.

Connecting to Literature

As students read books where there are conflict situations, have them identify the different tools characters in the stories used. If it looks as if a character is getting into difficulties, ask students to name a tool they think might help the character solve a problem more positively.

The Day I Saw My Father Cry, by Bill Cosby
(New York: Scholastic, 2000) Gr. 1-4

Summary: Alan Mills taught Little Bill and his brother Bobby to say, "Merry Christmas!" to de-escalate fights. When Alan died, Bill's dad cried.

1. How does saying, "Merry Christmas!" help the people in conflict?

2. What are some of the conflicts in the story?

    a. How did the conflict start?

    b. How did they solve it?

    c. Were both happy with the solution?

3. What did Little Bill learn from his father about feeling sad?

4. What did you learn that might help you solve conflicts?

Meanest Thing to Say, by Bill Cosby
(New York: Scholastic, 1997) Gr. K-3

Summary: Michael Reilly cannot get Little Bill to join him in saying mean things. Bill and his friends say, "So?" and later invite Michael to play with them.

1. Why do you think Michael wanted to say mean things?

2. Tell about a time when you might say, "So?"

3. What tools from your Conflict Tool Box could have helped Little Bill?

Enemy Pie, by Derek Munson
(San Francisco: Chronicle Books, 2000) Gr. K-3

Summary: Jeremy Ross moves next door to the narrator's best friend, and becomes an enemy. Dad shows the narrator how to make a pie that turns an enemy into a friend.

1. After Jeremy opens the door and he looks confused, ask: What do you think Jeremy is thinking? Feeling?

2. After reading the book, ask: How does enemy pie really work?

3. If we had an enemy, how could we turn her into a friend?

Fairness and Discrimination

Gathering: Wake Up in the Jungle

Have students stand in a circle. Ask each person to think of an animal noise. At first, they pretend to be the animal asleep. Then they wake up and start making the animal noises, softly at first, but then louder and louder until they are yelling very loudly.

Agenda Check

We've been learning a lot about feelings and conflicts. One of the things that can cause conflicts, and intense feelings as well, is a situation in which people are treated unfairly. What does it mean to be fair? Facilitate a brief discussion. **Today we are going to talk about times when things are not fair** (It Isn't Fair!). **We have also been learning how we can be strong and solve problems. Today you are going to get an opportunity to think about what you would do about things that are not fair if you were in charge** (If I Were In Charge). **Each of you can do something – even a small thing – that can make the world a better place. As you get older, there are more and more opportunities to take action and make more things fair. Today you're going to draw a picture of one of the ideas you come up with to make things better. After that, we'll look back at what we learned** (Summary) **and then do a closing** (Closing).

Activity: It Isn't Fair!

(Note: *It is helpful if students have previously been exposed to the concepts of prejudice and discrimination. To review these concepts, see Grade 1, Lesson 13 and Grade 1, Lesson 14.*)

1. Ask the children to describe things they think are unfair: for example, "It isn't fair when Jane talks to me, and I'm the one who gets in trouble for talking."

2. Write the list on chart paper. Try to make the examples as specific and personal as possible.

3. At some point, students may cite an example of prejudice or discrimination: for example, "It isn't fair when people make fun of you because of your clothes." "It isn't fair when people won't let you play a game because you're a girl."

Workshop Agenda
- Gathering: Wake Up in the Jungle
- Agenda Check
- Activity: It Isn't Fair!
- Activity: If I Were In Charge...
- Summary
- Closing: Sharing Pictures

Materials
- Workshop agenda, written on chart paper and posted
- Chart paper and markers
- Paper and art materials

Learning Outcomes
- Students will be able to define discrimination and name examples of injustice.
- Students will be able to identify remedies for things that are unfair, including prejudice and discrimination.

Connections to Standards
Language Arts
Reading
- Understands level-appropriate sight words and vocabulary

Self-Regulation
- Sets and manages goals

If you haven't reviewed Grade 1, Lessons 13 and 14, you may need to help students define the word *prejudice*. Help students extend their list by asking such questions as: **Can you think of an example of prejudice you've seen on TV? In a story we've read? Can you think of an example of prejudice against someone because of his or her ethnic group? Have people been treated unfairly just because they were a boy or a girl? Because they were young? Old? Disabled? Poor? Because of their religion? Because their family was different?**

4. Explain the difference between prejudice and discrimination. Prejudice is an opinion or attitude formed without knowledge. Discrimination is acting unfairly on the basis of those negative opinions, stereotypes, and attitudes. Acts of discrimination are not fair; they are examples of injustice.

Discrimination is acting unfairly on the basis of those negative opinions, stereotypes, and attitudes.

Activity: If I Were In Charge

1. In this activity, students will take the list of things that they just created and brainstorm a list of things that could be done to make them more equitable. **When things are unfair, some people may benefit, but others are hurt.** Refer to the list of things that students just created and ask: **If you were in charge, what would you do to make these things fair?**

2. Take each of the examples on the list of unfair things and ask students to brainstorm remedies for the injustices. List them on chart paper. Help them go beyond the obvious, reality-based, and superficial solutions to more detailed and imaginative ones. Remember that the goal is not for the students actually to cure the social ills, but rather to become aware of them as problems that need solutions and to think freely and imaginatively about what they would like to do.

3. Say: **Now I am going to ask you to think of one of these unfair things on the list and something you would like to do about it if you could. You are going to draw a picture that represents what you would do if you were in charge.** Give directions about materials, where students will work, and how much time they will have.

Summary

When time is up, ask students to focus on you, if you proceed with Closing Version A, or to form a circle if you choose Closing Version B. **Is life always fair? How do people feel when they are treated unfairly? Many times unfair treatment is the result of prejudice, of not getting to know people or giving them a chance. When people are treated unfairly just because they belong to some group or look a certain way, we call that discrimination. What is an example of discrimination? If you got to tell your family about our lesson today, how would you define discrimination? For our closing, we are going to share ways we might change things if we were in charge.**

Closing: Sharing Pictures

Version A

Have students find a partner and give them a few minutes to tell their partner about their picture. Ask a few volunteers to share with the class.

Version B

Have the class make a circle, putting their pictures face-down in front of them. Explain that each student will have an opportunity to share his picture if he would like. Remind students about respectful listening. Explain: **It would be very unfair if someone got less attention, for example, just because he was one of the last people to share.** Review and remind students what they can count on from others when it is their turn to share. Then choose one person to start. He should hold up his picture so everyone can see it while he briefly describes what it is. Remind students that they should only touch their pictures when it is their turn to share.

Extensions and Infusion Ideas

"If I Were In Charge" Bulletin Board or Book

Create a bulletin board of students' work as a colorful reminder of working toward equality. Their work could also be laminated and made into a class book.

Finding Examples of Inequity

When examples of things that are not fair occur at school or in the community, invite students to think of things that could be done "if they were in charge." You might add to the chart already created.

Connecting to Literature

Have students look for and identify examples of discrimination when they occur in written material. Help them suggest things that the characters could do to make things more fair.

Courtney's Birthday Party, by Loretta Long
(East Orange, New York: Just Us Books, 1998) Gr. K-3

Summary: Courtney cannot invite her best friend Diana to her party because Diana is black. Finally, the parents understand the girls' friendship.

1. What does it mean to be prejudiced? Did Courtney's mother, Mrs. Crowley, dislike Diana's mother, Mrs. Davis, or was she prejudiced? Explain.

2. Explain how Diana's not getting an invitation was an act of discrimination.

3. Why did the two mothers think that when their daughters were older they would understand Diana's not getting an invitation?

4. Some day, if you have children, how will you help them include children of all races?

GRADE 2, LESSON 14
Stopping Prejudice

Gathering: Qualities Needed for Helping

Arrange students in pairs. (See Teaching Tools for information about pairing.) Ask them to tell their partners about a time they have helped others or would have liked to help others who were being excluded or treated unfairly. Give them two or three minutes; let them know when half the time is up so they can switch.

Ask for volunteers to share with the group a time when they helped someone. **What qualities do we need to have so that we can help others?** (For example, courage, kindness, and empathy.) Make a list of the qualities on chart paper.

Agenda Check

In the last lesson, we looked at ways things can be unfair and what we might do about them if we were in charge. Today, we are going to talk about something very unfair that happens, unfortunately, far too often. We are going to get an opportunity to look at ways students at our school are prejudiced and treat people unfairly and what we can begin to do about it (Stopping Prejudice). **We will also think and talk about what kinds of qualities we need in order to be strong in standing up against prejudice and discrimination** (Realizing Our Power). **Then we'll summarize what we've covered** (Summary) **and sing a song for the closing** (Closing).

Activity: Stopping Prejudice

1. Introduce the puppets by saying: **Today these puppets are going to help us think about what to do when kids are being mean or are treating each other unfairly because of prejudices.**

2. Ask: **Do you see or hear teasing, either in class or on the playground or in the lunchroom? Are some people left out of games or conversations because of some difference? What kinds of mean things do you see or hear kids in this school do or say that show discrimination? What kinds of differences are used as excuses for being unfair to others?**

3. Choose either one of the incidents described by the students or a situation based on your own knowledge and use the puppets to dramatize it. Modify the incident, if necessary, so that no one in the class is put on the spot.

    Example: Puppet 1 (Jason) is teasing Puppet 2 (Abby) about wearing glasses. Present the role-play. Show Jason teasing Abby, who is clearly upset. Freeze the action before Abby makes any clear response.

Workshop Agenda

- Gathering: Qualities Needed for Helping
- Agenda Check
- Activity: Stopping Prejudice
- Activity: Realizing Our Power
- Summary
- Closing: Song, "There is Always Something You Can Do"

Materials

- Workshop agenda, written on chart paper and posted
- Chart paper and markers
- Two puppets

Learning Outcomes

- Students will be able to identify a time when they have helped others who were in an unfair situation.
- Students will be able to identify qualities needed to prevent or resist prejudice and discrimination.
- Students will be able to identify actions that can interrupt biased behavior.

Connections to Standards

Language Arts

Reading

- Relates stories to personal experiences (e.g. events, characters, conflicts, themes)

Self-Regulation

- Identifies basic values

Working with Others

- Identifies an explicit strategy to deal with conflict

Language Arts

Reading

- Relates stories to personal experiences (e.g. events, characters, conflicts, themes)

4. To provide students with a thinking process they can use to address incidents of prejudice or discrimination, ask the following questions:

    - What's happening here? (Encourage students to describe it as objectively and clearly as possible.)

    - How are the puppets feeling?

    - How are you feeling, watching this?

    - Has anything like this ever happened to you?

    - What kind of difference is being used as an excuse for the teasing?

    - Do you have any questions for Jason or Abby? (You can have the puppets respond to these questions, having them speak as a spunky child might.)

    - What suggestions do you have for Abby?

    - If you were a third person who noticed this happening, what could you do?

    - Does this kind of thing ever happen in our class?

    - What do we do about it? Do you think we should do anything different?

5. Review some of the ways the students thought that Abby could stop Jason or that a third party could help. Summarize: **It is important to let people who are making prejudiced statements or discriminating against others know that this is not acceptable. If we begin to do this, we can make our classroom and our world a nicer place to live. This is not always easy. It can help to realize our power.**

Activity: Realizing Our Power

1. Remind the class of the story of *The Wizard of Oz*. The Straw Man went to the Land of Oz in search of brains, the Lion in search of courage, and the Tin Man in search of a heart. As they helped Dorothy along on their journey, they discovered they already possessed those qualities: they had only to use them.

2. Say: **Remember, in the gathering you got to tell a partner about a time when you helped someone. Who would like to share a time when you helped, or would have liked to help, others who were being discriminated against?** Facilitate a sharing of stories.

3. Bring out the list created during the gathering. **Are there any other qualities you can think of that a person might need in order to work for what's fair for everyone?** List any additional qualities on the list. Ask each student to think about which of those qualities they would like to have more of in order to make a real difference in the world. This quality would be something that could help them prevent or resist prejudice and discrimination. Model the activity first. For example, "I sometimes don't recognize prejudice. It goes by me, and I don't notice it because I'm so used

to it. I would like enough knowledge about all kinds of prejudices to help me be more aware of prejudices when they happen." Go around the group and ask each student to describe the quality they have selected.

4. Say: **Just like the characters from *The Wizard of Oz*, you may already have the qualities that you would like to have. You just have to discover them. How would your life be different if you realized you had that quality and used it? How might the lives of other people be different?**

5. Have students partner up and then take turns talking about what they might do with the quality that they have selected.

6. Give students two or three minutes, letting them know when half the time is up so they can switch. When they are finished, ask for a few volunteers to share their ideas. Use active listening to draw them out.

Summary

All of us get a lot of misinformation about other people, and we develop prejudices about them. Because prejudiced behavior is learned, we can unlearn it by really getting to know each other. Then we can start to create a world where there is less prejudice and discrimination, a world that is more fair. To start this work, it is important for us to take a look at why we need to help others, ways in which we can help others, and the qualities and skills we will need to be effective.

What do you think is the most important thing for you to remember about today's lesson that will help you be stronger in helping others?

Closing: "There Is Always Something You Can Do"

Sing the first verse of the song, "There Is Always Something You Can Do." from *Linking Up!*, by Sarah Pirtle. See lyrics on page 150.

Extensions and Infusion Ideas

Chicken Sunday

For this activity, you will need a copy of the book, *Chicken Sunday*, by Patricia Polacco (New York: Philomel Books, 1992). *Chicken Sunday* is a wonderfully warm book that explores many different themes and issues at one time. Modeled on her own childhood relationships, the book is a story about interracial and interfaith relations, about prejudice and misunderstanding, about caring and working together, about courage and honesty, and about problem solving. It is also a great illustration of how feelings can change and what people can do when someone is upset with them about something that they did not do.

As you read the book, frequently ask students how the characters are feeling. When you get to the egg-throwing scene, ask students why they think the big kids were targeting Mr. Kodinski for acts of violence. Try to elicit a small discussion about prejudice and bias, if possible. Then ask: **Why did Mr. Kodinski think Patricia, Winston, and Stewart threw the eggs? How is he feeling? How are the children feeling?**

After finishing the book, ask: **How did the children's feelings about Mr. Kodinski change? What helped him change his feelings about them? Have you ever been upset about something you think a family member or friend did and then have those feelings change when they apologized or you found out more information?** Lead a short discussion about good ways to handle misunderstandings. Ask students if they have ever heard of making a "peace offering." Brainstorm ways of going about changing someone's feelings when they are upset with you.

Teachable Moments

Be observant, and acknowledge those times when students have stood up for others.

Look for opportunities for students to practice interrupting prejudice. Unless there is a need for adult intervention, coach students to intervene in situations in which you or they see prejudice or an unfair situation. Be observant, and acknowledge those times when students have stood up for others.

Connecting to Literature

As you read books and stories, look for examples of characters who stand up against prejudice. Help students identify the qualities and skills the characters possess that allow them to be effective. Ask students how they demonstrate these same qualities and skills. The goal is to help students identify with heroes and heroines in concrete ways and relate their actions to behavior that they themselves can model in specific ways.

Horace and Morris but mostly Dolores, by James Howe
(New York: Atheneum Books for Young Readers, 1999) Gr. P-2

Summary: Boys' and Girls' Clubs exclude each other until some decide to break the rules.

1. Why did Horace and Morris leave Dolores?

2. Why did Dolores join the Cheese Puffs?

3. Were these clubs a form of discrimination? Explain.

4. How did Dolores work against prejudice?

5. Dolores decided that things did not always have to be the way they had become. Is there something you would like to change? Tell how you might begin making the change.

The Other Side, by Jacqueline Woodson
(New York: G. P. Putnam's Sons, 2001) Gr. P-2

Summary: Clover, who is black, and Annie, who is white, sit on the fence that divides them.

1. After reading "... somewhere near the fence," ask: Write two endings for this story, one happy and the other sad.

2. After reading "... I just made believe I didn't care," ask: What do you think will happen now?

3. After reading the book, note that Clover still got to be friends with Sandra. We say that children are our future. If you could do one thing to make the world a better place, what would it be?

GRADE 2, LESSON 15
Dealing with Bullying Behavior

Caring and Effective Communication

CASEL SEL COMPETENCY

RS   Relationship Skills

Gathering: Counting to Five

The challenge in this game is to have people in the class call out the numbers from one to five without having two people talking at once. Introduce the game by explaining the following rules:

- Anyone can call out a number, starting with one.

- The numbers have to be in order.

- Each person can only say one number.

- If two people say the same number at the same time, the class has to start over.

Check to see if everybody understands the rules. Tell the class that if they hear two people talking at once, they will need to start over. Tell them that you will help out by monitoring, and will raise your hand to signal that you heard two people. The game will start over. Set a timer for three minutes. If the group doesn't master the task by that time, they will just become frustrated.

Discuss: **What made this hard? What would make it easier?**

Agenda Check

We have just learned that it's not always easy to work together to accomplish something. We also learned that sometimes it's essential to work together to get something done. It takes all of us working together to build a world that is safe and respectful. Bullying is a big problem. Today we are going to be looking at this problem and what we can do about it (Bullies and What to Do about Them). **Then we'll practice ways we can be strong in standing up to bullies** (The Bullying Buster Machine). **At the end, we will look back over what we did together** (Summary) **and do a closing** (Closing).

Materials

- Workshop agenda, written and posted on chart paper
- Chart paper and markers
- Talking Object

Learning Outcomes

- Students will be able to identify behaviors that constitute bullying.
- Students will be able to articulate a variety of constructive responses to bullying.
- Students will be able to demonstrate confronting bullying with assertive language.

Connections to Standards

Behavioral Studies

- Understands that some ways of dealing with disagreements work better than others, and that people not involved in an argument may be helpful in solving it

Self-Regulation

- Weighs risks in making decisions and solving problems
- Selects an appropriate course of action in an emergency
- Identifies emergency and safety procedures before undertaking hazardous practices

Connections to Standards, cont.

- Persists in the face of difficulty

Working with Others

- Helps the group establish goals
- Identifies an explicit strategy to deal with conflict
- Determines the seriousness of conflicts
- Does not react to a speaker's inflammatory delivery

Activity: Bullies and What to Do about Them

(Note: *This lesson involves using I-messages. If students have not had a lot of practice with this skill, it would be helpful to review and practice it before doing this lesson. See Grade 2, Lesson 9.*)

1. Introduce the activity by saying: **All of us have been mean or unkind to someone at some time. Bullies are people who have gotten stuck in using mean ways of acting toward others to get something that they need or want or to make themselves feel better. Underneath the bullying behavior they are all people, just like you and me. What types of behavior constitute bullying?** (Explain that someone is being bullied when he is repeatedly called names, made fun of, picked on, hit, kicked, shoved, pushed, pinched, threatened, or excluded from a group.) **How many of you have ever seen or heard about someone being bullied?**

2. Have students turn to a partner and tell each other about what they saw or heard. Tell students not to use people's names or anything that would identify individuals.

3. Ask for a few volunteers to share.

4. Ask: **Did anyone in this class ever do anything to help when someone was bullied? Or did any of you stand up for yourself when you were being bullied or treated badly?** (If someone did, have him share what he did.)

5. Explain that we are going to turn our attention to what we can do when we see someone being treated unkindly. Brainstorm with students a list of things they can do when they see or experience bullying. Record ideas on chart paper in two columns: ideas that mean confronting the bully and ideas that do not. Add to the children's ideas with suggestions from the following list:

    - Refuse to join in. (doesn't involve confrontation)

    - Report bullying you know about or see to an adult. (doesn't involve confrontation)

    - Invite the person being hurt to join your group. (might involve confrontation)

    - Then ask the person who was bullied if it's okay to have the bully join your group if the bully apologizes. (does involve confrontation)

    - Speak out, using an I-message. Say, "I don't like it when you treat him like that." (does involve confrontation)

    - Say: "I want you to stop calling him that name." "I'm going to tell an adult right now." (does involve confrontation)

    - Be a friend to the person who has been bullied by showing him you care about him: put an arm around him; give him a put-up, etc. (doesn't involve confrontation)

    - Distract the bully with a joke or something else so he stops the behavior. (does involve confrontation).

5. Tell students that there is one important rule: if students see someone being hurt physically, or see an interaction that might escalate into physical violence, they should *not* confront the bully. Rather, they should quickly go and get help from an adult. Discuss with students signs that might indicate such a physical threat.

Activity: The Bullying Buster Machine

1. Introduce the activity by saying: **It takes practice and courage to act strong without being mean when someone is bullying or treating you or another child unkindly.** Tell the students you would like them to pretend they are a Bullying Buster machine.

2. Form the machine. Have children break into two lines facing one another, about three feet apart. They should imagine that their right arm is a switch. You will walk down the aisle between the students, pretending to be a bully. When a student thinks of a way to stop the bullying behavior, he should raise his switch by bending his elbow and sticking his right hand out in front. When you touch an arm, the Bullying Buster machine switches on. Once a child is "switched on," that child should give out a strong (but not mean) verbal message to the bully.

3. Walk along the aisle between the students. Recite a scenario from the ones listed below, or act it out if you are comfortable doing that. Switch on a student who has his hand out with a touch on the arm or hand to get a strong Bullying Buster response. Practice with several students before moving on to another scenario. Some possible situations:

   • Someone calls you a mean name. (Possible Bullying Buster machine response: "I feel hurt and angry when you call me that name. Please don't do that.")

   • Someone tells you to do something you don't want to do.

   • Someone is calling someone else a bad name.

   • Someone is making fun of someone because he is blind.

   • Someone tells you that you can't play in the game.

   • Someone demands that you give him your afternoon snack.

   • Someone is teasing a friend of yours.

4. Without being critical of student responses, help them differentiate among strong, mean, or weak responses. This can be done by having a general discussion about which of the responses were strongest and why. You might also ask if students heard any responses that might be interpreted as weak or mean.

Summary

Today we have talked about bullying behavior and what we can do about it. Sometimes people who are being bullied can stand up in a strong way. Many times, because of the feelings involved, this can be difficult. That's why it is important that all of us know how, and that all of us are willing to stand up for others when they are being bullied. Bullying can only be stopped if we all work together. What are some of the ways we can stand up against bullying? (Facilitate a discussion that summarizes the chart made earlier, adding items if appropriate.)

Closing: One Commitment

Have students form a circle either standing or sitting. **For the closing I'm going to ask you to think of one thing you can do to make our classroom and our school a "Bully-Free Zone."** Holding the Talking Object, model by sharing one thing you can commit to doing. Then pass the object around the group. Let students know that it is all right to say something that has already been said by someone else.

Extensions and Infusion Ideas

Pledges

Ask students individually to write a pledge to be a Bullying Buster. What promises are they willing to make to the rest of the class today? What promises are they willing to make to the rest of the school today? They can begin their pledge with, "I promise to... ."

Have them illustrate their pledge with a picture.

Here are several suggested activities using completed pledges:

- Do a go-round in which each child reads his pledge.

- Make a Bullying Prevention bulletin board with student pledges.

- Gather the pledges together in a Bullying Buster book to keep in your classroom.

- Have students incorporate their pledges into a notebook or other personal item they usually carry with them.

Geography

On bulletin board paper, have students draw one huge map of your school and its school grounds. Have students create the Caring School. This activity is modeled on the Caring Being activity in Lesson 2. Brainstorm a list of places where they would most like to feel safe (the playground, the bus, the cafeteria, the library, the classroom, etc.). Have them write in the words and ideas that they would like to see characterized in each place. Use this map as a launching point for discussion about what other classes and people they could involve to insure that all children feel safe, wherever they may be.

Connecting to Literature

Point out bullying as it occurs in stories and books. Have students discuss the different options the characters could employ to stand up to the behavior in strong ways.

Baseball Ballerina Strikes Out!, by Kathryn Cristaldi
(New York: Random House, 2000) Gr 1-3

Summary: The dancer is the star player until some boys scare her into losing her confidence. The coach helps her get it back.

1. After Baseball Ballerina tells Mr. Lee about the bullying problem, ask: Is Baseball Ballerina tattling or reporting? Give a reason for your answer.

2. After reading the book, ask: Was Mr. Lee mean or strong with the Colby twins? Explain your answer.

3. Usually adults do not have gorilla outfits handy. Can you think of another ending to the story that has Mr. Lee helping Baseball Ballerina without a gorilla suit?

4. If Baseball Ballerina and Mary Ann had been scared that the Colby twins might hurt them, what could they have done?

Who's Afraid of the Big Bad Bully?, by Teddy Slater
(New York: Scholastic, 1995)

Summary: Bertha terrorizes Max and the other children until she threatens Max's dog, Fang. Then Max and his friends hold their own. At the end, Bertha is just another kid.

1. Explain why Bertha had so much power in the beginning.

2. In Chapter 4, Bertha said, "GIVE ME THAT DOG!":

   a. What did Max do?

   b. Why was that response wiser than attacking Bertha?

3. Why did Max's refusal change the way the other children responded to Bertha?

4. Explain why the children could be called Bullying Busters.

5. If Bertha had been mean, what could Max have done differently?

GRADE 2, LESSON 16
Peace Pledges

Cultural Competence and
Social Responsibility

CASEL SEL COMPETENCY

SA Self-Awareness

SO Social Awareness

RD Responcible Decision Making

Gathering: Peace Is…

Have students form a circle. Using the Talking Object, have students complete this sentence, "Peace is…" The rest of the class should focus on active, respectful listening. To expand students' ideas of peace, give an example or two from your own life, such as: **I feel really peaceful when it's a summer day and I'm playing in the sand at the beach. So I would say, 'Peace is playing in the sand.' Or, I feel peaceful when I get a nice hug from a child I love. So I would say, 'Peace is getting a good hug.'**

Agenda Check

All year, we have been working hard to develop the skills we need to be strong and kind and to make our class and the world a better place. Today, we're going to think about some specific things we can choose to do that will create more peace in our world. First, we'll focus on some current conflicts and how they could be resolved peacefully (Images of Peace and Conflict). **Then, we will talk about what a pledge is and design our own pledges for peace** (Making a Peace Pledge). **We'll end our lesson, as usual, with a summary** (Summary) **and a closing** (Closing).

Activity: Images of Peace and Conflict

Note: To review *what a peacemaker is and what things peacemakers do*, see Grade 1, Lesson 16.

1. Review the concepts of peace students discussed in the Gathering.

2. Ask a few volunteers to describe a conflict that is going on in their life right now. Ask them not to use names.

3. Ask students to think of conflicts they have heard about going on in their neighborhood, in the world, or on television. Ask them to imagine that they are looking at that conflict. **What is happening? What are people saying? What are they seeing?** Ask a few volunteers to share their images with the group.

4. Ask students: **What makes a solution peaceful?** Now ask them to imagine a situation that is a peaceful solution to the conflict they were just thinking about. **How did the solution come about? Who helped find the solution? What does the situation look like now?** (Stress that the solution does not have to be realistic.)

Workshop Agenda

- Gathering: Peace Is…
- Agenda Check
- Activity: Images of Peace and Conflict
- Activity: Making a Peace Pledge
- Summary
- Closing: One Gift

Materials

- Workshop agenda, written on the board or on chart paper
- Talking Object
- Crayons or markers
- A blank Peace Pledge for each student
- Scratch paper

Learning Outcomes

- Students will design Peace Pledges.

Connections to Standards

Working with Others

- Identifies an explicit strategy for dealing with conflict

Self-Regulation

- Sets and manages goals

Activity: Making a Peace Pledge

1. Ask students what the word *pledge* or *promise* means. After eliciting the definitions, ask them what makes a pledge or promise work. Ask: **When do pledges and promises not work?** Summarize the discussion by saying that a pledge is a promise. Explain: **A pledge works if we are willing and able to do what we have promised.**

2. Brainstorm some actions and behaviors that might make school or home more peaceful. Make a list or create a web.

3. Elicit specific examples from students' ideas and add them to the list or web. For example, if a student has said, "I can help my mother," ask, "What are some of the ways we can help our parents?" Stress that the more specific we are, the more doable our pledge will be.

4. Ask students to pledge to do one thing to create a little bit of peace in school or at home. They can choose something from the list or think of something else.

5. On scratch paper, have students draft their pledges. Remind them that their pledge should describe in a concrete way what they can do to create peace.

6. When students feel satisfied with their draft, hand out the blank Peace Pledge (page 269) for them to use to create a final pledge complete with illustrations.

Summary

Have students gather in a circle. **Today we looked at what each of us can do to make our world more peaceful. What do you think will be different if you keep your promise? What will be hard about keeping that pledge? Can you imagine what the world would be like if everyone made a pledge to be more peaceful?** If students would like to, they can share their pledge with the class.

Closing: One Gift

Using the Talking Object, ask each student to answer: **If you could give one gift to the world, what would it be?**

Extensions and Infusion Ideas

Writing

After a week or two, have students write about the outcomes of their peace pledges.

Bulletin Boards

Arrange student pledges in a prominent place in the classroom. Some schools devise campus-wide ways of displaying pledges from multiple classes.

Art

Have students draw symbolic pictures of their pledges on square pieces of paper or cloth. Sew or glue them together to form a Peace Quilt. Hang it in the classroom or in a common area of the campus.

Books about Peace

There are many resources that can help expand students' awareness of peace. The following books are a few suggestions that you may find useful.

Make Someone Smile and 40 More Ways to Be a Peaceful Person, by Judy Lalli (Minneapolis: Free Spirit Publishing Inc., 1996)

This read-aloud book shows children modeling the skills of peacemaking and conflict resolution. Simple words complement black-and-white photographs.

Peace on the Playground: Nonviolent Ways of Problem-Solving, by Eileen Lucas (New York: Franklin Watts, 1991)

This short chapter book explores peace and peacemaking in detail by introducing related vocabulary, presenting famous peacemakers, and suggesting concrete ways students can create peace on the playground, and contribute to peace in the world.

The Kid's Guide to Service Projects, by Barbara A. Lewis (Minneapolis: Free Spirit Publishing Inc., 1995)

With over 500 service ideas for young people who want to make a difference, this book provides project sranging from simple (running an errand for a friend) to complex ones (working to change a state law).

Peace Begins with You, by Katherine Scholes (Boston: Little, Brown and Company, 1990)

This small, poetic book explains clearly and simply how and why peace has a place in all of our lives. Beginning at a personal level, it looks at how different people's needs and wants can become a source of conflict, and then explores ways in which conflicts can be resolved. It then looks at national and international issues, and suggests that the best way to protect peace is to ensure that everyone is treated fairly.

Connecting to Literature

The Bully Blockers Club, by Teresa Bateman (Morton Grove, IL: Albert Whitman, 2004) Gr. K-3

Summary: After Lotty Raccoon tries several ways of dealing with Grant Grizzly's bullying, she successfully enlists the aid of her classmates.

1. How might the story have ended if Lotty had gone to her teacher before trying the Club?

2. In which ending do you think Lotty would be stronger? Why?

Teammates, by Peter Golenbock
(New York: Harcourt Brace Jovanovich, 1990) Gr. K-3

Summary: A story about how Jackie Robinson, the first African-American major league baseball player, was discriminated against.

1. Name two ways that Pee Wee Reese showed that he was a peacemaker.

2. How did Jackie Robinson show that he was a peacemaker?

Handout: Peace Pledge

NAME   DATE

Draw a picture of your pledge:

Write your pledge:

_____

_____

_____

_____

_____

APPENDIX A
RCCP Research

There have been a number of research studies and evaluations of the *Resolving Conflict Creatively Program* (RCCP). Here are highlights from the findings of those studies.

National Center for Children in Poverty (NCCP)

ESR/Metropolitan Area sponsored an intensive two-year research study of RCCP in participating schools in New York City during the 1994-95 and 1995-96 school years. It was supported with funding from the federal Centers for Disease Control and Prevention and the WT Grant Foundation. The research assessed the impact of RCCP on 5,000 children in 15 New York City elementary schools. The study, directed by J. Lawrence Aber, was conducted by the National Center for Children in Poverty (NCCP) at the Mailman School of Public Health of Columbia University.

Overall, the study found that children receiving substantial RCCP instruction from their classroom teachers developed more positively than their peers. They saw their social world in a less hostile way, saw violence as an unacceptable option, and chose nonviolent ways to resolve conflict. They also scored higher on standardized tests in reading and math. More specifically, NCCP's evaluation found that RCCP had a significant positive impact when teachers taught a high number of lessons from the RCCP curriculum (on average, 25 lessons over the school year). Researchers compared groups of children on their rate of change in the targeted outcomes over the course of the first year of the evaluation. Independent of their participation, it is important to note that children's aggressive thoughts and behaviors increase over time. However, children receiving a high number of lessons demonstrated the following:

- Significantly slower growth rate in self-reported hostile attributions
- Significantly slower growth rate in aggressive fantasies
- Significantly slower growth rate in aggressive problem-solving strategies
- Significantly slower growth rate in teacher-reported aggressive behavior

In addition, children in the high lessons group (compared to those receiving a low number of lessons or no lessons) received increased ratings from their teachers on:

- Positive social behaviors and emotional control
- Greater improvement on standardized academic achievement

Results also indicate that RCCP benefits all children regardless of gender, grade, or risk-status. According to analyses, each year that a student participates in RCCP has an additive effect on slowing rates of many of the risk factors for aggression and violence.

Metis Associates, WestEd, and the Northwest Regional Educational Laboratory

Metis Associates of New York City carried out evaluations of RCCP implementation in Anchorage, AK; Atlanta, GA; Newark, NJ; and New York City. WestEd, based in San Francisco, conducted an evaluation of RCCP in Phoenix, AZ, and the Northwest Regional Educational Laboratory located in Portland, OR did an evaluation of RCCP in Lincoln County, OR.

Among the findings, when teachers implement RCCP, students:

- Feel better about themselves

- Indicate increased awareness of feelings and verbalization of feelings

- Show more caring behavior toward other students

- Exhibit more acceptance of differences

- Develop improved listening, communication, and anger management skills

- Understand and use effective conflict resolution strategies

- Feel an increased sense of empowerment

- Have better relations with their teachers and other students

Moreover, the majority of teachers who implement RCCP in their classrooms indicate they notice changes in their own attitudes and behaviors. Teachers say as a result of participation in RCCP they listen better to children and have more positive attitudes toward conflict and the possibilities of resolving conflicts in mutually satisfying ways. Most note positive classroom climate changes. Teachers also describe the creation of a common language throughout the school for understanding and managing conflict, the development of a sense of community among staff members, and the growth of skills that support them in forging positive relationships with students.

Data collected across a number of professionally conducted studies shows that RCCP also has the following impact in schools:

- Improved rates of attendance

- Reduced drop out rates

- Decreased levels of disciplinary referrals and rates of suspension

- Less violence in the classroom

- Reduction in the number of reported violent incidences among students on campus

In addition, parents report an increase in their own communication and problem-solving skills.

Resolving Conflict Creatively Program Model

The Resolving Conflict Creatively Program is a well-evaluated, K-8 program in character education and social and emotional learning. It is the nation's largest and longest running school program with a special focus on conflict resolution and intergroup relations. RCCP has served over 400 schools across the country and is characterized by a comprehensive, multi-year strategy for preventing violence and creating caring and peaceable communities of learning that improve school success for all children.

The RCCP model includes:

Needs and resource assessment

District and school leaders, with ESR staff, identify local needs and assess resources currently available to address them. This assessment guides the development of RCCP program and provides baseline data so the effectiveness of RCCP in your school can be measured.

Professional development for teachers

Teachers participate in 18 to 24 hours of interactive training that builds student skills. This training prepares staff to build community and implement classroom practices that support the social, emotional, and academic development of children. Teachers receive either an elementary or middle school curriculum manual. Consistent delivery of the RCCP curricula is shown to help students learn and develop the skills necessary to be socially, emotionally, and academically successful.

On-site classroom support

ESR staff developers model or co-lead activities with children, observe and provide feedback, and meet with teachers to provide individual coaching.

Leadership training for administrators

Administrators explore how their leadership can contribute to a positive school culture and enhance the effective implementation of the program.

Parent workshops

Peace in the Family workshops help parents and caregivers develop skills for dealing with conflict and prejudice at home.

Support staff workshop

A workshop for support personnel includes an introduction to the skills and concepts of conflict resolution and intergroup relations.

Advanced training workshops

Experienced RCCP classroom teachers participate in professional development workshops tailored specifically to needs identified by the teachers. Some workshops have included more in-depth exploration of topics from the introductory workshop, integrating life skills instruction into the core curriculum, and exploring conflict through literature or social studies.

Peer mediation and other student leadership programs

ESR staff train carefully selected students to serve as peer mediators. RCCP provides peer mediation coaches with an orientation to the intricacies of establishing effective and sustainable peer mediation through an on-site workshop and follow-up visits.

District capacity

ESR works with the district to identify school- and district-based trainer and mentor candidates. The candidates attend trainer-of-trainers and trainer-of-mentors workshops. Following initial program implementation, district-based staff and ESR staff co-facilitate training and on-site support.

APPENDIX C
RCCP as a Violence Prevention Program

Violence among youth is an issue that has come to the forefront of the American agenda. In the United States today, young people are routinely exposed to violence, particularly youth residing in urban areas (Garbarino, Dubrow, Kostelny, & Pardo, 1998; Lorion, 1998; Schwab-Stone, Chen, Greenberger, Silver, Lichtman, & Voyce, 1999). In fact, research indicates that children and youth are disproportionately involved in intentional interpersonal violence as victims and as perpetrators, resulting in a significant public health issue (Hamburg, 1998; Hammond & Young, 1993).

Importantly, schools are not safe havens from aggression and violence. On the contrary, researchers have found that physical fighting, weapons carrying, and other violent behaviors are prevalent in America's schools (Loeber & Stoughthamer-Loeber, 1998; Lorion, 1998; Schwab-Stone et al., 1999). According to the National Center for Education Statistics, in 2001, students between the ages of 12 and 18 were the victims of approximately 764,000 violent crimes at school, including 161,000 serious violent crimes (e.g., robbery, rape, and aggravated assault) (National Center for Education Statistics, 2003). In addition, studies suggest that incidents of bullying are extremely prevalent in school settings, with victims often suffering devastating social and emotional impacts, as well as academic difficulties associated with high rates of school absenteeism (Harris & Petrie, 2003; Kaufman, Chen, Choy, Peter, Ruddy, Miller, Fleury, Chandler, Plany, & Rand, 2001; Nansel, Overpeck, Pilla, Ruan, Simons-Morton, & Scheidt, 2001; National Center for Education Statistics, 2003; Pelligrini & Bartini, 2000). Given such knowledge, while violence in schools has declined overall since the early 1990s, the prevention of school violence continues to be a concern in communities across the nation.

There is evidence to suggest that middle school students may be at particularly high risk of experiencing violence within the school setting. In 2001, students ages 12-14 were significantly more likely to be victims of crime at school, including theft, violent crimes, and serious violent crimes, than students ages 15-18 (National Center for Education Statistics, 2003). Such findings are not surprising, since the middle school years are a time of social and emotional risk, when youth are struggling to learn to appropriately identify and manage their emotions in the face of significant developmental change (Jackson & Davis, 2000).

---

[1] Written by Chirs Graham-Rawling of Metis Associates, Inc

In order to address the problem of violence in the nation's middle schools, researchers, educators and other professionals have increasingly emphasized the need for interventions designed to prevent or mitigate behavioral and psychological risk factors associated with violent behavior. Specifically, studies show that poor anger management, inadequate problem-solving skills, and poor impulse control are closely linked with antisocial and violent behavior (Baranowski, Perry, & Parcel, 1997; Page, Becker-Kitchin, Solovan, Golec, & Helbert, 1992; Pepler & Slaby, 1994; University of North Florida, 2001). Programs which seek to address these risk factors are the best equipped for preventing acts of violence and fostering a positive school climate (Crawford & Bodine, 1996; Special Education and Rehabilitative Services, 2000; University of North Florida, 2001; Wilde, 1995).

In addition to reducing risk factors for violence, research suggests that successful violence prevention programs are those with the ability to foster social and emotional literacy and related protective factors. For instance, available literature indicates that it is important for intervention programs to help students develop the capacity for caring and effective communication, including observation and perspective-taking abilities and strong "sending" and "receiving" skills (Elias, Zins, Weisberg, Frey, Greenberg, Haynes, Kessler, Schwab-Stone, & Shriver, 1997). Effective programs are also those that help children acquire skills associated with cultural competence and alliance building, including the ability to counter acts of bullying, harassment, discrimination, and prejudice (Bayles, Tomeda, Kim, Hopper, Munoz, & Mahendra, 2001). Conflict management, problem-solving, and decision-making skills are important strengths developed within effective violence prevention programs, as well, according to the literature, including the development of a repertoire of negotiation and mediation strategies (Elias et al., 1997; DuRant, Treiber, Getts, McCloud, Linder, & Woods, 1999; Jones & Compton, 2003; Jones & Sanford, 2003).

References

Baranowski, T., Perry, C.L., & Parcel, G.S. (1997). How individuals, environments, and health behavior interact: Social cognitive theory. In K. Glanz, F.M. Lewis, and B.K. Rimer (Eds.), *Health behavior and health education: Theory, research, and practice* (2nd edition). San Francisco, CA: Jossey-Bass.

Bayles, K., Tomoeda, C., Kim, E., Hopper, T., Munoz, M.L., & Mahendra, N. (2001). *Cultivating cultural competence in the workplace, classroom, and clinic.* Presentation to the American Speech-Language Hearing Association Convention.

Crawford, D., & Bodine, R. (1996). *Conflict resolution: A guide to implementing programs in schools, youth-serving organizations, and community and juvenile justice situations.* Washington, DC: Office of Juvenile Justice and Delinquency Prevention, Department of Justice.

DuRant, R.H., Treiber, F., Getts, A., McCloud, K., Linder, C.W., & Woods, E.R. (1996). Comparison of two violence prevention curricula for middle school adolescents. *Journal of Adolescent Health, 19* (2), 111-117.

Elias, M.J., Zins, J.E., Weisberg, R.P., Frey, K.S., Greenberg, M.T., Haynes, N.M., Kessler, R. Schwab-Stone, M.E., & Shriver, P (1997). *Promoting social and emotional learning: Guidelines for educators.* Alexandria, VA: ASCD.

Garbarino, J., Dubrow, N., Kostelny, K., & Pardo, C. (1998). *Children in danger: Coping with the consequences of community violence.* San Francisco, CA: Jossey-Bass.

Hamburg, M.A. (1998). Youth violence is a public health concern. In D.S. Elliott, B. Hamburg, & K.R. Williams (Eds.), *Violence in American Schools: A new perspective* (pp. 94-126). New York, NY: Cambridge University Press.

Harris, S., & Petrie, G. (2003). A study of bullying in the middle school. *National Association of Secondary School Principals, 86 (633),* 42-53.

Jackson, A.W., & Davis, G.A. (2000). *Turning points 2000: Educating adolescents in the 21st Century.* New York, NY: Teachers College Press.

Jones, T.S., & Compton, R.O. (Eds.). (2003). *Kids working it out: Stories and strategies for making peace in our schools.* San Francisco, CA: Jossey-Bass.

Jones, T.S., & Sanford, R. (2003). Building the container: Curriculum infusion and classroom climate. *Conflict Resolution Quarterly,* 21 (1), 115-130.

Kaufman, P., Chen, X., Choy, S., Peter, K., Ruddy, S., Miller, A., Fleury, J., Chandler, K., Plany, M., & Rand, M. (2001). *Indicators of school crime and safety: 2001.* (Report No. NCES 2002-113/NCJ-190075). Washington, DC: U.S. Departments of Education and Justice.

Loeber, R., & Farrington, D.P. (Eds.). (1998). *Serious and violent juvenile offenders: Risk factors and successful interventions.* Thousand Oaks, CA: Sage Publications.

Lorion, R.P. (1998). Exposure to urban violence: Contamination of the school environment. In D.S. Elliott, B. Hamburg, & K.R. Williams (Eds.), *Violence in American Schools: A new perspective* (pp. 94-126). New York, NY: Cambridge University Press.

Nansel, T, Overpeck, M., Pilla, R., Ruan, W, Simons-Morton, B., & Scheidt, P. (2001). Bullying behaviors among U.S. youth: Prevalence and association with psychosocial adjustment. *Journal of the American Medical Association, 285 (16),* 2094-2100.

National Center for Education Statistics. (2003). *Indicators of School Crime and Safety.* National Center for Education Statistics, Bureau of Justice Statistics, Department of Justice.

Page, R.M., Becker-Kitchin, S., Solovan, D., Golec, T.L., & Helbert, D.L. (1992). Interpersonal violence: A priority issue for health education. *Journal of Health Education, 23 (5),* 286-292.

Pelligrini, A.D., & Bartini, M. (2000). A longitudinal study of bullying, victimization, and peer affiliation during the transition from primary school to middle school. *American Educational Research Journal, 37 (3),* 699-725.

Pepler, D., & Slaby, R.G. (1994). Theoretical and developmental perspectives on youth and violence. In L.D. Eron, J.H. Gentry, and P. Schlegel (Eds.), *Reason to hope: A psychosocial perspective on violence and youth.* Washington, DC: American Psychological Association, 27-58.

Schwab-Stone, M., Chen, C., Greenberger, E., Silver, D., Lichtman, J., & Voyce, C. (1999). No Safe Haven II: The effects of violence exposure on urban youth. *Journal of the American Academy of Child and Adolescent Psychiatry, 38, 359-367.*

Special Education and Rehabilitative Services. (2000). *Early warning, timely response: A guide to safer schools.* Washington, DC: U.S. Department of Education.

University of North Florida. (2001). Anger management and schools. *SDDF Notes, 4 (4),* Safe, Disciplined, and Drug-Free Schools Project, Florida Institute of Education.

Wilde, J. (1995). Anger *management in schools: Alternatives to student violence.* Lanham, MD: Scarecrow Press.

APPENDIX D

Lesson Correlation for Countering Bullying and Harassment

The following topics and lessons can be used to address issues of bullying and harassment.

Topic	Kindergarten	Grade 1	Grade 2
Developing empathy	1,2,4,7,9,14,15	2,5,6,15	2,3,4
Expressing Feelings	5,6,7,8,9,10,12,16	5,6,7,8,10,12	2,3,4,9,11,15,16
Speaking Assertively	6,8,10,15	7,10,15	9,12,14,15
Active Listening	3,8,11	1,4,6,8,13	4,7,8
Appreciating Differences	1,2,3,4,5,13,14	1,3,4,13,14	5,6,813,14
Creating Community	1,2,3,4,5,6,7,9, 10,11,12	1,2,3,4,6,9,11, 13,14,15	1,2,3,4,5,6,7,8, 10,11,12

APPENDIX E

Lesson Correlation for Character Education

The following traits and lessons can be used to promote postive character education.

Character Trait	Kindergarten	Grade 1	Grade 2
Respect and responsibility for oneself and others	1,2,3,4,5,6,7,8,9,10, 11,12,13,14,15	1,2,3,4,5,8,911,12, 13,14,15	1,2,3,4,5,6,7,8,9,10, 11,13,14,15
Cultural competence	1,2,3,9,16	3,4,5,13,16	2,4,5,8,9,13,14,16
Fairness and Social Justice	4,5,7,9,10,11,12,13, 14,15,16	2,3,4,5,6,8, 10,3,14,16	2,3,4,5,6,8,10,13,14, 16
Cooperativeness	4,5,8,9,10,11,14	2,4,8,9,11	8,9,12,16
Perseverance	5,10,12	15	8,9,12,
Empathy	7,9,10,11,14,15	2,3,4,5,7,8,	2,3,4,8,14
Self-Management	4,6,7,8,11,12,13,14, 15,16	5,6,7,8,9,10,11,12, 15,16	2,3,4,6,7,9,11,12, 15,16
Relationship skills	1,2,3,5,6,7,8,9,11, 12,13,14,15	1,2,3,4,5,6,7,8,9,10, 11,13,14,15	1,2,3,4,5,6,7,8,9,10, 11,12,13,14,15
Civic virtue and citizenship	1,2,3,4,5,7,9,10,12, 13,14,15,16	2,3,4,5,8,9,11,13, 14,15,16	1,2,4,5,6,8,9,11,12, 13,14

Lesson Correlation for Risk Behavior Prevention

The following lessons can be used to address risk behavior prevention.

Risk Factor	Protective Factor/Asset	Kindergarten	Grade 1	Grade 2
Poor anger management skills	Emotional literacy	6,7,8,9,12, 13,15	2,5,6,7,8,10, 12,16	2,3,4,5,6,7,9, 10,11,15
Inadequate problem solving skills	Problem solving and decision making skills	5,10,13,14, 15	9,10,11,12,15	5,6,8,9,10,11, 12,13,14,15,16
Poor impulse control	Social literacy	2,3,4,5,6,7, 8,9,10,11,12,13	3,4,5,6,7,10, 12,13,14,15	4,5,6,7,8,9,10, 12,13,14,15,16
Poor school performance	Academic competence	1,2,3,4,5,10, 11	2,3,8,15	1,2,3,8,10,12, 13,14,15
Lack of connectedness with school	Feeling connected to school	1,2,3,4,5,10, 11	1,2,3,4,8,11, 13,14,15	1,2,3,4,6,7,8, 9,10,13,14,15

APPENDIX G

What Does a Connected and Respected Classroom Look Like?

A Checklist of Outcomes

Basic Foundations of a Connected and Respected Classroom

- ❑ At the beginning of the school year, agreements among the class are made about how to work, live, and learn together.
- ❑ Conflict resolution strategies are used to resolve student-student, student-teacher, and teacher-class conflicts.
- ❑ Feelings are expressed, acknowledged, accepted, and dealt with.
- ❑ There is more active listening between teachers and students, and students with each other.
- ❑ Class meetings/discussions occur on a regular basis and are used to talk about community and learning issues.
- ❑ Conflict resolution strategies are infused throughout the day or class.
- ❑ Put-downs by both teachers and students are addressed; there is a classroom goal to reduce put-downs by both teachers and students.
- ❑ Stereotyping or racial/ethnic/gender put-downs are addressed and there is a classroom goal to reduce them.
- ❑ There are opportunities for the students to get to know each other (gathering and community building activities), especially as the year begins.
- ❑ There is a clear process for dealing with controversial issues (interpersonal and societal).
- ❑ Teachers clearly identify for the students the academic and social goals for lessons and activities.
- ❑ Positive reinforcement instead of negative reinforcement is used; there is a classroom goal for reducing negative reinforcement.
- ❑ On a regular basis, teachers find ways to get feedback from their students about how it's going for them.
- ❑ Parent involvement is welcome.

Ways to Enrich and Deepen the Connected and Respected Classroom

- ❑ Students have input into what they are learning and the ways (pedagogy) in which they learn those things.
- ❑ Students are allowed and/or encouraged to modify classroom agreements.
- ❑ Teacher and students are sensitive to each other's feelings.
- ❑ Teachers devote a certain amount of time to just listening to the students without interruption.
- ❑ Active listening occurs consistently throughout the day.
- ❑ Conflict resolution concepts are infused into other subject areas.
- ❑ There are no put-downs used by teachers and students.
- ❑ Teachers ensure that their curriculum, approach, examples, and resources represent a variety of race, class, ethnic, and gender perspectives.
- ❑ Many classroom activities involve collaboration and/or group work.
- ❑ Students feel comfortable bringing up controversial issues in the classroom.
- ❑ Students identify academic and social goals for themselves.
- ❑ No negative reinforcement is used, and there is an abundance of positive reinforcement and affirmation.
- ❑ Teachers use a variety of assessment strategies (experienced-based, individual, group, teacher assessment, performance-based).
- ❑ The giving and receiving of feedback is an integral aspect of the classroom culture.
- ❑ Parent involvement is strong and identifiable (they are welcome in the classroom with notice, present during important class activities and/or trips, and give feedback about the classroom).

Teacher Self-Assessment

Integrating Connected and Respected Skills

The following pages list the skills and concepts taught in Connected and Respected correlated to ESR themes. To help you monitor the teaching and learning of these skills, complete this form three times a year – early in the school year, mid-year, and at the end of the year. For each skill/concept check that you have taught or infused the skill, check that you have modeled the skill and assess whether your students use the skill or need more work.

Making Connections

	DIRECT INSTRUCTION		MODELING		ASSESSMENT OF STUDENTS	
	I've taught this skill by teaching a lesson	I've taught this skill through curriculum infusion	I model this skill/ concept with my students	I model this skill in my adult relationships	I've seen __ % of students use this skill	I believe __ % of students need more work on this skill
know the names of everyone in the class and use them	☐	☐	☐	☐	%	%
recognize how people are similar and different from one another	☐	☐	☐	☐	%	%
identify different groups people belong to	☐	☐	☐	☐	%	%
generate a list of class agreements	☐	☐	☐	☐	%	%
recognize self as valued part of classroom community	☐	☐	☐	☐	%	%
know something about each person in the class	☐	☐	☐	☐	%	%
identify positive and negative classroom behavior	☐	☐	☐	☐	%	%
contribute to a group project	☐	☐	☐	☐	%	%
share thoughts in pairs or small groups	☐	☐	☐	☐	%	%
makes decisions jointly or small groups	☐	☐	☐	☐	%	%

Reflection/Comments

Emotional Literacy

	DIRECT INSTRUCTION		MODELING		ASSESSMENT OF STUDENTS	
	I've taught this skill by teaching a lesson	I've taught this skill through curriculum infusion	I model this skill/concept with my students	I model this skill in my adult relationships	I've seen __% of students use this skill	I believe __% of students need more work on this skill
distinguish between assertive and aggressive behavior	☐	☐	☐	☐	%	%
distinguish between constructive and destructive responses to anger	☐	☐	☐	☐	%	%
identify anger triggers	☐	☐	☐	☐	%	%
increase feelings vocabulary	☐	☐	☐	☐	%	%
recognize and name feelings	☐	☐	☐	☐	%	%
recognize and name feelings of others	☐	☐	☐	☐	%	%
recognize feelings are communicated verbally and non-verbally	☐	☐	☐	☐	%	%
recognize physical sensations of anger	☐	☐	☐	☐	%	%
recognize the similarities and differences in how people show feelings	☐	☐	☐	☐	%	%
use appropriate vocabulary when angry	☐	☐	☐	☐	%	%
use I-messages	☐	☐	☐	☐	%	%
value emotion: feelings are natural, human and important	☐	☐	☐	☐	%	%

Reflection/Comments

Caring and Effective Communication

	DIRECT INSTRUCTION		MODELING		ASSESSMENT OF STUDENTS	
	I've taught this skill by teaching a lesson	I've taught this skill through curriculum infusion	I model this skill/concept with my students	I model this skill in my adult relationships	I've seen ___% of students use this skill	I believe ___% of students need more work on this skill
cooperate as a group to reach a common goal	☐	☐	☐	☐	%	%
identify personal strengths and skills	☐	☐	☐	☐	%	%
identify and demonstrate active listening skills	☐	☐	☐	☐	%	%
paraphrase while listening	☐	☐	☐	☐	%	%
distinguish between aggressive and assertive communication	☐	☐	☐	☐	%	%
identify advantages of assertive communication	☐	☐	☐	☐	%	%
create a set of classroom guidelines	☐	☐	☐	☐	%	%
understand and respect different points of view	☐	☐	☐	☐	%	%
understand communication is a two-way street	☐	☐	☐	☐	%	%
identify and demonstrate behaviors for effective communication	☐	☐	☐	☐	%	%
use clarifying questions	☐	☐	☐	☐	%	%
use I-messages	☐	☐	☐	☐	%	%
identify and demonstrate constructive ways to confront/intervene in a bullying situation	☐	☐	☐	☐	%	%
identify behavior that constitutes bullying	☐	☐	☐	☐	%	%

Reflection/Comments

Cultural Competence and Social Responsibility

	DIRECT INSTRUCTION		MODELING		ASSESSMENT OF STUDENTS	
	I've taught this skill by teaching a lesson	I've taught this skill through curriculum infusion	I model this skill/ concept with my students	I model this skill in my adult relationships	I've seen __ % of students use this skill	I believe __ % of students need more work on this skill
come up with ways to counteract discrimination and injustice	☐	☐	☐	☐	%	%
define discrimination and how it affects people	☐	☐	☐	☐	%	%
define peace and understand its meaning varies	☐	☐	☐	☐	%	%
define prejudice and how it affects people	☐	☐	☐	☐	%	%
define stereotype and understand how it affects people	☐	☐	☐	☐	%	%
identify qualities needed to prevent/resist discrimination and prejudice	☐	☐	☐	☐	%	%
identify ways in which people are similar and different from each other	☐	☐	☐	☐	%	%
practice interrupting biased behavior	☐	☐	☐	☐	%	%
recognize the multiple groups a person can belong to	☐	☐	☐	☐	%	%
understand it is ok to disagree with others' opinions	☐	☐	☐	☐	%	%

Reflection/Comments

288

Conflict Management and Decision Making

	DIRECT INSTRUCTION		MODELING		ASSESSMENT OF STUDENTS	
	I've taught this skill by teaching a lesson	I've taught this skill through curriculum infusion	I model this skill/concept with my students	I model this skill in my adult relationships	I've seen ___ % of students use this skill	I believe ___ % of students need more work on this skill
• identify conflict as a disagreement, argument or fight	☐	☐	☐	☐	%	%
• propose multiple solutions to a conflict	☐	☐	☐	☐	%	%
• understand, identify and strive for win-win solutions	☐	☐	☐	☐	%	%
• identify steps to solving a problem	☐	☐	☐	☐	%	%
• identify different points of view in problem solving	☐	☐	☐	☐	%	%
• attitude towards conflict: it is a natural part of being human	☐	☐	☐	☐	%	%
• understands feelings and actions escalate during a conflict	☐	☐	☐	☐	%	%
• can de-escalate conflict situation and conflict emotions with good communication skills	☐	☐	☐	☐	%	%

Reflection/Comments

289

Teacher Self-Assessment

Integrating SEL Competencies

The following page lists the skills and concepts taught in Connected and Respected as aligned with the CASEL competencies. To help monitor the teaching and learning of these competencies, complete this form three times a year—early in the school year, mid-year, and at the end of the year. For each concept check how you have taught, infused or modeled it.

SEL Competencies	DIRECT INSTRUCTION		MODELING		ASSESSMENT OF STUDENTS	
	I've taught this competency by teaching a lesson	I've taught this competency through curriculum infusion	I model this competency with my students	I model this competency in my adult relationships	I've seen __ % of students use this competency	I believe __ % of students need more work on this competency
Self Awareness						
• *identifying emotions:* identifying and labeling one's feelings	☐	☐	☐	☐	%	%
• *recognizing emotions:* identifying and cultivating one's strengths and positive qualities	☐	☐	☐	☐	%	%
Social Awareness						
• *perspective-taking:* identifying and understanding the thoughts and feelings of others	☐	☐	☐	☐	%	%
• *appreciating diversity:* understanding that individual and group differences complement each other and make the world more interesting	☐	☐	☐	☐	%	%
Self-Management						
• *managing emotions:* monitoring and regulating feelings so they aid rather than impede the handling of situations	☐	☐	☐	☐	%	%
• *goal setting:* establishing and working toward the achievement of short- and long-term pro-social goals	☐	☐	☐	☐	%	%

SEL Competencies	DIRECT INSTRUCTION		MODELING		ASSESSMENT OF STUDENTS	
	I've taught this competency by teaching a lesson	I've taught this competency through curriculum infusion	I model this competency with my students	I model this competency in my adult relationships	I've seen __ % of students use this competency	I believe __ % of students need more work on this competency
Responsible Decision Making						
• *analyzing situations:* accurately perceiving situations in which a decision is to be made and assessing factors that might influence one's response	☐	☐	☐	☐	%	%
• *personal responsibility:* recognizing and understanding one's obligation to engage in ethical, safe, and legal behaviors	☐	☐	☐	☐	%	%
• *respecting others:* believing that others deserve to be treated with kindness and compassion, and feeling motivated to contribute to the common good	☐	☐	☐	☐	%	%
• *problem solving:* generating, implementing, and evaluating positive and informed solutions to problems	☐	☐	☐	☐	%	%

SEL Competencies	DIRECT INSTRUCTION		MODELING		ASSESSMENT OF STUDENTS	
	I've taught this competency by teaching a lesson	I've taught this competency through curriculum infusion	I model this competency with my students	I model this competency in my adult relationships	I've seen __ % of students use this competency	I believe __ % of students need more work on this competency
Relationship Skills						
• *communication:* using verbal and non-verbal skills to express oneself and promote positive and effective exchanges with others	☐	☐	☐	☐	%	%
• *building relationships:* establishing and maintaining healthy and rewarding connections with individuals and groups	☐	☐	☐	☐	%	%
• *negotiation:* achieving mutually satisfactory resolutions to conflict by addressing the needs of all concerned	☐	☐	☐	☐	%	%
• *refusal:* Effectively conveying and following through with one's decision not to engage in unwanted, unsafe, unethical, or unlawful conduct	☐	☐	☐	☐	%	%

Reflection/Comments _____

CREDITS

pg 6: "Come Join in the Circle" music and lyrics by Sarah Pirtle. © 1997 Sarah Pirtle. Reprinted with permission. Originally published in *Linking Up!* by Sarah Pirtle. © 1998 Educators for Social Responsibility and Sarah Pirtle.

pg 10: Graph. Originally published in *Teaching Young Children in Violent Times 2nd Edition* by Diane E. Levin. © 2003 Educators for Social Responsibility.

pg 25: Chocolate River adapted from "Cross The River," *Early Childhood Adventures in Peacemaking* by William J. Kreidler and Sandy Tsubokawa Whittal. © 1999 Educators for Social Responsibility.

pg 63: "The Sun and the Wind" Originally published in *Early Childhood Adventures in Peacemaking* by William J. Kreidler and Sandy Tsubokawa Whittal. © 1999 Educators for Social Responsibility.

pg 75-78: Reprinted with permission. © Liza Donnelly. Originally published in *Early Childhood Adventures in Peacemaking* by William J. Kreidler and Sandy Tsubokawa Whittal. © 1999 Educators for Social Responsibility.

pg 74: "Two in a Fight" lyrics by Sarah Pirtle. © 1997 Sarah Pirtle. Reprinted with permission. Originally published in *Linking Up!* by Sarah Pirtle. © 1998 Educators for Social Responsibility and Sarah Pirtle.

pg 84-85: Two Donkeys. Originally published in *Early Childhood Adventures in Peacemaking* by William J. Kreidler and Sandy Tsubokawa Whittal. © 1999 Educators for Social Responsibility.

pg 92: "Speak Up" music and lyrics by Sarah Pirtle. © 1997 Sarah Pirtle. Reprinted with permission. Originally published in *Linking Up!* by Sarah Pirtle. © 1998 Educators for Social Responsibility and Sarah Pirtle.

pg 105: "I Like You" Reprinted with permission from *The Friendly Classroom for a Small Planet*, by Prisciall Prutzman, Lee Stern, M. Leonard Burger, Gretchen Bodenhammer, Dana McMurray. © 1988 New Society Publishers

pg 150: "There is Always Something You Can Do" Reprinted with permission. Originally published in *Linking Up!* by Sarah Pirtle. © 1998 Educators for Social Responsibility and Sarah Pirtle.

pg 157: Cooper Says reprinted with permission from *The Friendly Classroom for a Small Planet* by Priscilla Putzman, Lee Stern, M. Leonard Burger, Gretchen Bodenhammer, Dana McMurray. © 1988 New Society Publishers.

pg 204: Red Riding Hood Meets the Maligned Wolf adapted with permission from *A Curriculum on Conflict Management* by Lief Fearn. © Magic Circle Publishing.

The following lessons and activities were adapted with permission from Educators for Social Responsibility, Metropolitan Area, from the *Resolving Conflict Creatively Program: A Teaching Guide for Grades Kindergarten through Six* by Peggy Ray, Sheila Anderson, Linda Lantieri and Tom Roderick © 1996 Educators for Social Responsibility, Metropolitan Area.

Grade K

pg 7: Alike and Different; pg13: Groups; pg 21: Y-E-S; pg 25: Cooperation; pg 53: Beanbag Partners: pg 56 Frozen Beanbag; Lesson 16 pg 93-94.

Grade 1

pg 98: Good and Poor Listening; pg 99: Stand Up If; pg 103: Put-downs and Put-ups; pg 104: Maria's Story; pg 109: Diversity Puppets; pg 110: Comparing Partners; pg 113: Opinions; pg 114: Corners; Lesson 5: pg 119-121; Lesson 6: pg 123-124; Sharing Stories; pg 127: Things People Do When They're Angry; pg 128: Cooling Off; pg 134: Sharing Circle; pg 139: Lesson 10: pg 143-145; Lesson 11: pg 147- 150: Finding Win-Win Solutions; pg 157: All Boys, All Girls; pg 158: Stretches; pg 162: Dislike vs. Prejudice; Lesson 16: pg 171-173;

Grade 2

pg 175: Name Game; pg 176: Find Someone Who; pg 181: Mirrors; pg 183: Rainstorm; pg 205: Examining Point of View; pg 206: Revising Fairy Tales; pg 212: Recalling Personal Conflicts; pg 216: Sending Clear Messages; pg 233: Conflict Outcomes; pg 253: Stopping Prejudice; pg 261: The Bullying Buster Machine. Lesson 16: pg 265-266

ABOUT THE AUTHORS

KEN BREEDING, PHD

Dr. Ken Breeding has spent his professional life in the fields of psychology and education working to develop and nurture learning communities that promote the development of healthy, whole human beings. He has over 28 years of experience as a teacher, counselor and leader in public schools. He has also taught at the college and university level for almost 16 years.

Hemaintains a small practice in individual and family psychotherapy, but spends most of his time training and consulting with districts in the areas of Social and Emotional Literacy, Conflict Resolution, and Inter-group Relationships.

JANE HARRISON

Jane Harrison has more years of experience than she sometimes likes to admit, and most of those have been in the classroom. It was in the pursuit of materials to improve the learning climate of her own classroom that led her to begin to implement some of the lessons that you'll see in this curriculum. The changes that she saw in the students, in herself, and in her relationship to the students, are what led her to begin her work with Educators for Social Responsibility.

Over the last ten years, she has worked both nationally and internationally with schools, providing training for students, school staffs and parents and has worked with students from pre-kindergarten through high school, in rural, suburban and inner-city settings. She owes a great deal of gratitude to her own children, who gave her the opportunity to continually improve and refine her own conflict resolution skills, and who now provide her with constant love and support.

Educators for Social Responsibility

ESR is a national non-profit organization that was founded in 1982. Our mission is to make teaching social responsibility a core practice in education so that young people develop the convictions and skills to shape a safe, sustainable, democratic, and just world.

ESR is a national leader in educational reform. Our work spans the fields of social and emotional learning, character education, conflict resolution, diversity education, civic engagement, prevention programming, youth development, and secondary school improvement. We offer comprehensive programs, staff development, consultation, and resources for adults who teach children and young people preschool through high school, in settings including K-12 schools, early childhood centers, and afterschool programs.

Our work falls into three broad areas:

- Student Skills and Convictions: ESR works with teachers to help students develop social skills, emotional competencies, and qualities of character that increase interpersonal effectiveness, and reduce intolerance and aggressive, anti-social behavior.

- School and Classroom Climate and Culture: We help schools create safe, caring, respectful, and disciplined learning environments that promote healthy development and academic success for *all* students.

- Response to social crises and world events: ESR helps educators respond effectively to local, national, and international crises related to interpersonal and systemic violence, intolerance, and global conflicts and war.

Visit our website (www.esrnational.org) for more information, to visit our Online Teacher Center, or to sign up for our free monthly e-newsletter.

We can be reached at:

Educators for Social Responsibility
23 Garden Street
Cambridge, MA 02138

617-492-1764
617-864-5164 fax
educators@esrnational.org